THE WARHOL ECONOMY

THE WARHOL ECONOMY

HOW FASHION, ART, AND MUSIC
DRIVE NEW YORK CITY

Elizabeth Currid

PRINCETON UNIVERSITY PRESS
PRINCETON AND OXFORD

Library of Congress Cataloging-in-Publication Data

Currid, Elizabeth, 1978–
The Warhol economy : how fashion, art, and music drive
New York City / Elizabeth Currid.
    p.   cm.
Includes bibliographical references and index.
ISBN-13: 978-0-691-12837-5 (hardcover : alk. paper)
1. Cultural industries—New York (State)—New York. 2. New York (N.Y.)
Social life and customs. 3. Popular culture—Economic aspects—
New York (State)—New York. I. Title.
HD9999.C9473N49   2007
330.9747′1—dc22   2007014019

British Library Cataloging-in-Publication Data is available

This book has been composed in Sabon and Futura Display

Printed on acid-free paper. ∞

press.princeton.edu

Printed in the United States of America

10 9 8 7 6 5 4 3 2 1

For Mom and Dad

THE SOURCE OF ART IS IN THE LIFE OF A PEOPLE.

—ALIFE

Contents

Preface

This book began with fishnet stockings, dozens of them stretched across aggressively thin goddesses coming out of fashion houses—from Donna Karan to Dior to Dolce and Gabbana to Oscar de la Renta—in a glossy September *Vogue*, the fall fashion issue, a several-hundred-page extravaganza. Glancing through this magazine one chilly autumn evening revealed the first inklings of this book. But equally important is the Costume Institute's annual benefit, staying out until 2 a.m. at Bungalow 8, hanging out with punks and hipsters at the Misshapes party, and going to graffiti art exhibitions at Deitch Projects. This book also began with me spending entire portions of my university fellowship on the very shoes and dresses and fishnets that jumped from the pages of *Vogue* and *W* and *Harper's Bazaar*.

I was reading this particular issue of *Vogue* magazine during Fashion Week, the semiannual event for the industry, where the careers of designers are made and broken in thirty minutes on a catwalk under fluorescent lighting. The formal events are only half the story, at best: it's also the week of after-parties and late-night dinners with celebrities, editors, designers, and the rest of the who's who of the creative world (wealthy, famous, wildly eccentric, creative, or all of the above), reported with zest on Gawker.com and in the *New York Post*'s gossip bonanza, Page Six. New York City's Fashion Week and the fall fashion magazines that overflow the newsstands during that time make the city glow with the glamour, carnival, and creativity that drives department stores, luxury boutiques, editorials, magazines and fashion-crazed women for months to come—until, in fact, Spring Fashion Week, when the cycle begins again.

But it's far more meaningful than parties and shopping. To wrap it up in such a way is trite and dismissive of a larger phenomenon. Underneath the glamour and frivolity of art and culture are real social and economic mechanisms, mechanisms that are responsible for thousands of jobs, billions of dollars in revenue, and the very identity of New York City—and the world, for that matter. Within these dynamics are nuance, ambivalences, and contradictions across fashion, art, film, music, design, all the various elements that create New York City and make art and culture work here more than in other places. Even though this book is about New York, more fundamentally it's about how creativity—particularly artistic and cultural creativity—happens and why it happens in some places (New York, London, Los Angeles, Paris) more than others. Art and culture thrive in certain places which are just more conducive to allowing creativity to produce. That's the range of phenomena at the heart of this book.

Fishnets are emblematic of these broader questions and curiosities: Why and how, in an industry so noted for its competitiveness and need to be innovative and creative, could a trend—like the ubiquity of fishnets (or black nail polish, or opaque tights, or skinny jeans)—ever occur in the first place? The same can be said for cultural creativity in general. How do ideas and trends in fashion, music, or art, cultural forms of all sorts, become transmitted across the whole world? How do paradigm shifts in music or sculpture or dress design come to be, and where do they occur? Who gives these new innovations value? How do those whose job it is to assess creativity and transmit cultural ideas (Anna Wintour, Ingrid Sischy, Pitchfork Media) meet those who produce culture (Zac Posen, Quincy Jones, the Talking Heads)? They meet in particular places and their exchange is broadcasted throughout the world in the form of magazines, television, Fashion Week, and record deals. These are the symbiotic and interactive processes by which art, culture, and creativity materialize, and New York has emerged as a central node for where and how these processes occur.

When I was eighteen years old, my parents shipped me off to Carnegie Mellon University, despite the fact that I had already been accepted and planned to attend Vassar College in upstate New York. (They wanted me to go to a "national university" not a "grooming school," as my father put it.) I recall that the only thing that even remotely assuaged my general distress of having to attend a nerdy, technical school in grey, cloudy Pittsburgh, Pennsylvania, was the fact that Andy Warhol had gone there too and so it just couldn't be that bad. (It turns out I that loved Carnegie Mellon within a week of my arrival.) In retrospect, it seems befitting that my initial footsteps into the intellectual world began with Warhol, the very man who encapsulates so much of the social and economic dynamics of New York's artistic and cultural world that I am writing about ten years later.

Frank O'Hara once wrote, "I can't even enjoy a blade of grass unless I know there's a subway handy, or a record store or some other sign that people do not totally regret life."[1] And it's true—this density, diversity, vibrancy, and quirkiness are what define New York and reinforce the lure of the city for countless other artists. This book is the story of how culture creates and recreates itself and the evolution (and revolution) of cultural moments occurring at once in New York and around the world. But *The Warhol Economy* is also about the importance of art and culture in our daily lives, our modern urban economies, the artwork that leaves us awestruck, the music we download to our iPod, the shoes that we (or, well, some of us) spend our university fellowships on. Most importantly, it's about the people who create these worlds.

Acknowledgments

This book is only possible because a lot of people who didn't have to, were way too busy, far too important, and way cooler than I am really went to bat for me and believed in my research. I owe them so much, it's impossible to repay. Actually, it's kind of amazing they still remain my friends/therapist/family/colleagues/editor . . . the list goes on.

I'm not sure about the order of these things, but here goes. There are two people who really made this book a reality: My editor at Princeton University Press, Tim Sullivan, and my longstanding mentor and true comrade, Richard Florida. Thank you, Richard, for taking me under your wing some eight years ago, when I was twenty-one years old, and constantly pushing me to have the chutzpah to make things happen for myself—and when I didn't, you guided me along. You believed in me years before I ever believed in myself. Tim, thank you for actually responding to my chutzpah and devoting your time, energy, and ideas into this book well before even the first page was written. You invested in this project after reading the first draft of the first chapter of my dissertation, before I had even earned a Ph.D. Your patience, creativity, and editing transformed an esoteric thesis into an accessible and relevant book. Hands down, I couldn't ask for a better editor in all the world.

As this research originally stems from my doctoral thesis, I thank my dissertation committee at Columbia University—the brilliant scholars who grilled me, challenged me, stressed me out on an almost daily basis, and ultimately awarded me my degree: Harvey Molotch, Terry Clark, David Stark, Lance Freeman, Richard Florida, and Susan Fainstein. In particular, Susan, the chair of my committee, improved my thesis line by line (literally) turning my ramblings into coherent sentences, my musings into solid theory, and my data into real empirical proof, and in the process also became a wonderful friend. Thank you all for transforming my trite observations about art and culture into real scholarly work.

I also must thank Kevin Stolarick and James Connolly, who have both worked tirelessly on the data collection and analysis. How many tedious emails and Excel charts I have sent their way at all hours of the day and night, how many times I have asked Kevin to extract yet one more data set or James to redo the maps "just this last time, I promise." I drove you crazy and yet you delivered spectacular work without complaint every time. The same can be said for my research assistant, Yoon-Kyung Oh, who worked steadfastly on last-minute copy edits, giving up her weekend to make sure I made my deadline.

On that note, thanks to copyeditor Karen Verde, production editor Terri O'Prey, and all the editors, illustrators, and designers at Princeton University Press and the anonymous reviewers who were able to turn some 250 manuscript pages into a real book. I don't know how you do it, but your work is amazing.

Many of the images in this book of the people and places that shape and make creative New York have been captured by my friends Frederick McSwain and Melissa Webster. Thanks to both of them for trudging throughout the city with me, block after block, hour after hour, to capture the many different angles of New York City. Frederick has been instrumental not only in photographing the city, but also in patiently editing and fine tuning most of the pictures in this book from fuzzy digital camera shots into beautiful images.

And then there are my best friends, dedicated to the cause, whom I dragged to endless gallery openings, parties, and events and who provided their eyes, support, material, and ideas that are woven throughout the book: Marisa Christian, Melissa Webster, Brooke Cutler, Eric Lovecchio, Marissa King, and my sister and brother, Sarah and Evan Currid. Thanks for endlessly thinking about titles and cool people to interview. Thanks for reading a million versions of the same intro paragraph. Thanks for staying out until 4 a.m.

Several people deserve thanks just for being there. Dalton Conley, for offering advice, assuaging my meltdowns, and being a dear friend. Bob Herbert, for listening to ideas, providing a critical eye on titles and writing, and endlessly supporting me and my work. Rob Walker, for taking time from his insane schedule to read my manuscript and offer the most insightful of suggestions for revision, along with generally being a terrific source of information about things both intellectual and cool, much of which is reflected in the material in this book. Jerold Kayden, for his longstanding intellectual support, friendship, and belief in my ideas and research. Former New York City Mayor David Dinkins, for cutting me slack as the most absent-minded, dissertation-obsessed teacher's assistant and, despite my lapses, sending important interview subjects my way, and bringing me a red velvet cake when I got my Ph.D., to boot. Lisa Chamberlain, for being a tremendous advocate of my research in her own writings on urban life. Stephen Blackwell, for providing emergency pro bono editing and endless music contacts. David Sloane, Dowell Myers, and the rest of my colleagues at the University of Southern California who have supported and believed in my research and have provided me the time and resources to continue it in Los Angeles.

Qualitative research depends on real people giving up their time to talk about the social and economic phenomena that define their lives. Without willing participants, social scientists would truly be at an impasse, unable to articulate the world with the same insight. This book is a product of the countless artists, musicians, fashion designers, curators, editors, and so forth who have given me forty-five minutes or three hours of their time to talk about their creative worlds, invite me to their gallery openings, and show me their work. Without them, not one page of this book could have been written. I can only hope that this end product is both an accurate reflection of New York's cultural economy and a useful tool in improving the lives and economies of creative people.

Among the dozens of creative people I interviewed for this book, some particularly stand out for their exceptional belief and investment in my research. Lazaro Hernandez of the fashion house Proenza Schouler was the first designer to give me the time of day. In the harried weeks before Fashion Week, he still took the time to sit down and talk to a fledgling doctoral student for much longer than his assistant had penciled in. Diane von Furstenberg and her director of public relations, Alexis Rodriguez, have been endlessly supportive, providing me images for the book, sending me invitations to fashion shows, and responding to follow-up interview questions, and all with grace and accommodation. Jeffrey Deitch, for his brilliant intellectual contributions and for always keeping his gallery doors open for me to document the New York art scene with the access a researcher only dreams of. Lady Pink for her artistic contributions to the book, as reflected in the book's end papers, which she designed. Lee Quinones has been a terrific source of knowledge and contacts and in the process became a fabulous buddy. Ryan McGinness has spent many hours with me, brainstorming titles and book jacket designs, providing countless contacts to interview, and inviting me to many of the events and parties discussed in this book, his support transcends any professional or research obligation.

I don't know where one thanks their parents, but there's no way this book would have been written without their emotional and shoe budget support. And that's that.

All of us, I suppose, have that person who has handed us a new kaleidoscope through which to view the world. For me, there are two: Richard Florida and Jane Jacobs. Richard taught me to love cities. Jacobs taught me how they work. Jacobs, who died in April 2006, understood the organic nature of urban life better than anyone. She defied her generation's intellectual views on cities and challenged urban planners, sociologists, and economists to think about how cities really work. Her efforts have pioneered a new path of urban development—one that appreciates that diversity drives innovation; messiness of functions, not orderliness, creates vitality; and the social interactions across a wide range of people and places are what ultimately make a great city. These central tenets are what New York City's creativity and this book are all about.

THE WARHOL ECONOMY

Chapter 1

ART, CULTURE, AND NEW YORK CITY

In 1977, a graffiti duo with the name of SAMO (standing for Same Old Shit) began bombarding New York subways and slums. It was the height of graffiti's hold on the city, with thousands of kids running through subway tunnels deep into the night, away from cops and into subway yards where they spent hours painting masterpieces and signature tags on the sides of the subway cars so that, come morning, the trains would barrel through the city displaying their names and artwork like advertisements to anyone waiting on the platform. Thousands of kids wrote graffiti through their teenage years, only to put aside their artistic leanings by the time they reached their twenties, remaining unknown and invisible to anyone who didn't ride the New York subway system during the 1970s and '80s.

But SAMO was different. Still living in the gritty East Village, working and DJ-ing at downtown clubs, by 1981, one-half of the duo, Jean-Michel Basquiat, had attained recognition in the art world as the "Radiant Child" in *ArtForum* magazine. By the early eighties, Basquiat was being shown alongside Julian Schnabel, David Salle, Francesco Clemente, and Keith Haring. Between 1982 and 1985, Basquiat dated a then little-known musician named Madonna, began working with Andy Warhol, was shown by the starmaker gallery owner Mary Boone (his paintings sold for over $20,000), and landed on the cover of the *New York Times Magazine*. In 1988, he died of a heroin overdose. He was twenty-seven years old. Basquiat's paintings are still worth thousands and thousands of dollars, and he is still considered one of the pivotal figures in New York's postmodern, Neo-expressionist art world. Basquiat's life, from his early days as an anonymous graffiti writer to the gritty East Village art and nightlife scene he thrived in, to meeting Mary Boone and Andy Warhol (who radically changed and catapulted his career) is emblematic of the central reason that New York City remains one of the global centers of creativity. In New York, such things happen, and in New York, creativity and creative people are able to succeed.[1]

Basquiat's life, while tragically short, is illustrative of the mythology of artistic creativity. Fashion, art, and music are fun. They are, after all, the industries that drive celebrity and create those ephemeral and elusive qualities of glamour, sexy, and cool. And how they attain these qualities is often impossible, if not downright arbitrary, to predict. Putting value on Mark Rothko's painting or Manolo Blahnik's latest sky-high stiletto is not easy. It's not clear what makes Marc Jacobs' Kurt-Cobain-meets-hot-librarian sweatshirts and dresses so appealing, but that doesn't stop thousands of women around the world from purchasing them in bulk. And people like Marc Jacobs as a person too (people who've never actually even met him). They read about his clothes in Anna Wintour's editorials in *Vogue*, they follow his social life in gossip magazines and columns. The same can be said of any number of creative people, from Quincy Jones to Jay-Z to Diane von Furstenberg—or, more broadly, "cultural producers"—those who create and produce the art and culture consumed by both mass and niche markets.

But this is not just a book devoted to talking about how fashion, art, and music are interesting and fun. For that, you can read *SPIN* or *Vogue* or *ARTnews*. Instead, *The Warhol Economy* is about how and why fashion, art, and music are important to New York City. Despite the random and seemingly arbitrary processes that lead to the success of a music single or a new designer, a pattern emerges: a preponderance of creativity on the global market—and successful creativity at that—comes out of New York City. Why is that?

On a basic level, it's clear that art and culture happen in particular places—New York, Paris, London, Los Angeles, Milan. Parties and clubs and high-profile restaurants are often cited in tandem with the celebrities that frequent them. Entertainment—whether Fashion Week or the MTV Music Awards show—generates lots of money and, if we think a little more, probably lots of jobs. But much of our understanding of art and culture is taken for granted at best, superficial and inconsequential at worst.

Worst because we view the role of art and culture as insignificant and not as a meaningful part of an urban, regional, or national economy. We take it as more fun and less business. And so, although policymakers and urban economists are versed in the mechanics of urban economies or how we think cities work, the role of art and culture is left out of this basic paradigm of city growth and vitality, why some cities are more or less successful than others, and what components are necessary to generate great, vibrant places where people want to live.

Most students of New York see it as a center of finance and investment and understand the city's economy as evolving from industrial production to the FIRE industries (finance, insurance, and real estate) that form its foundation today. And yet, for the better part of the twentieth century and well before, New York City has been considered the world's authority on art and culture. Beginning with its position as the central port on the Atlantic Ocean, New York has been able to export and import culture to and from all parts of the globe. By the middle of the twentieth century, New York was the great home of the bohemian scene, beat writers, and abstract expressionists and later, to new wave and folk music, hip-hop DJs, and Bryant Park's Fashion Week. As Ingrid Sischy, editor-in-chief of *Interview* magazine, remarked, "Before Andy [Warhol] died, when Andy led *Interview* you'd run into people who would say, 'I came to New York because of *Interview*. I read it when I was in college, lonely and alienated and it made me feel not alone. I wanted to come there and be a part of that world'." High-brow, low-brow, high culture, and street culture, New York City's creative scene has always been the global center of artistic and cultural production.

Well, it's New York. But what underneath that cliché propels the greatest urban economy in the world? New York's cultural economy has sustained itself—despite increasing rents, cutthroat competition, the pushing out of creative people to the far corners of Queens and Philadelphia. Within its geographical boundaries are the social and economic mechanisms that allow New York to retain its dominance over other places. As the Nobel Prize–winning economist Robert Lucas pointed out, great cities draw people despite all of the drawbacks of living in a densely packed, noisy, expensive metropolis, because of human beings' desire to be around each other. It is the inherent social nature of people—and of creativity—that makes city life so important to art and culture.

Central is the assumption that cultural economies operate differently from other industries. What we traditionally think of as the lure of New York City for business is different for those who produce art and culture. The central tenets of successful urban economies (the density of suppliers, the closeness of a labor market) are indeed important to fashion, art, and music, but they manifest themselves in a different way. For finance, law, manufacturing, and other traditional industries, these systems and mechanisms are pretty straightforward and, for the most part, operate within a formal, rigid structure. Economists often talk of the agglomeration of labor pools, firms, suppliers, and resources as producing an ensuing social environment where those involved in these different sectors engage each other in informal ways (they hang out in the same bars, live in the same neighborhoods, and so on). But this informal social life that economists often hail as a successful by-product (what they call a positive spillover or externality) of an economic cluster is actually the central force, the raison d'être, for art and culture. The cultural economy is most efficient in the informal social realm and social dynamics underlie the economic system of cultural production. Creativity would not exist as successfully or efficiently without its social world—the social is not the by-product—it is the decisive mechanism by which cultural products and cultural producers are generated, evaluated and sent to the market (more on this in chapters 4 and 5).

The cultural economy operates far from the boardrooms and skyscrapers that pack Manhattan's geography. The evaluation of culture occurs in the tents in Bryant Park during Fashion Week, the galleries in Chelsea, the nightlife of the Lower East Side, or the clandestine nooks in SoHo, Chelsea, or the Meatpacking District that house nightclubs, lounges, and restaurants with bouncers who could be mistaken for Secret Service agents. In these haunts—often exclusive—the cultural economy works most efficiently. Culture is about taste, not performance, and so, unlike a dishwasher or a computer or even a car, there is no method or even means to evaluate how well it performs. We do not make decisions about pieces of art or music to listen to or (for many women) dresses to wear, based on how well they work. We buy these things because we like them . . . for some reason. And that reason is, very often, because it has

been given value by experts—someone or some people or some or-ganization or gallery or newspaper—that has the credibility to crown a dress, a painting, or a new music single with the approval and the cachet that make it worth wearing, buying, or listening to. These people are the gatekeepers, the tastemakers, the "connec-tors," to use Malcom Gladwell's term. They tell us what is worth having, what has taste, in a seemingly arbitrary, symbolic, and sta-tus-driven economy.

Tastemakers and gatekeepers spend a lot of time in the social realm—they (and the creative people who also thrive in the so-cial life of New York) give meaning to a world that many people think of as frivolous, superficial, or filled with beautiful people who

have nothing to say. It is the social life of creativity—from industry
parties to 2 a.m. nights at Passerby or the Double Seven—that is
the central nexus between culture and commerce. It is in this realm
that creative people get jobs, meet with editors and curators who
write reviews and organize exhibitions and shows. Designers like
Dior's Hedi Slimane or the late Stephen Sprouse plug into the
nightlife scene to become inspired for their next collection; simultaneously business deals across creative industries are made while just
hanging out late into the night. When *Vanity Fair* asked Slimane
who the most stylish woman in the world is, he replied, "Some
unknown girl on the dance floor."[2] It is this seemingly informal
social world that drives and sustains the cultural economy, and it

is why New York has been able to maintain its creative edge decade upon decade.

The very idea of a cultural economy deserves further explanation. When we think of art and culture, we often think of film or fashion or art or design but often as separate entities. And while they do cultivate their own following, discipline, and norms, they are also part of a far more encompassing and symbiotic whole than we generally consider them. These separate industries operate within a fluid economy that allows creative industries to collaborate with one another, review each other's products, and offer jobs that cross-fertilize and share skill sets, whether it is an artist who becomes a creative director for a fashion house or a graffiti artist who works for an advertising agency. That there is real importance in the music that designer John Varvatos listens to or what the singer Beyonce wears when she goes out indicates the degree to which those who work in the cultural economy are simultaneously producers and gatekeepers. That the Metropolitan Museum of Art holds the Costume Institute benefit, the annual gala devoted to fashion design, and that Nike hires graffiti artists to design sneakers is evidence of the interdependent nature that artistic and cultural industries have with one another, and their need to be around each other and engaging each other in the same places. And therein lies the significance of New York's informal social life in cultivating the fluidity of creativity and the symbiotic relationships that fashion, art, music, graphic design, and their related industries have with one another. This type of cross-fertilization is partly responsible for how New York maintains its edge across a wide field of cultural industries. Chapter 6 looks at the various ways that such types of relationships form and produce new types of creativity.

Geography plays an important role, too: all of this occurs in the same limited geography, the island of Manhattan and parts of Brooklyn, Queens, and the Bronx. The parties, the nightlife, the gatekeepers, the artists, and fashion designers and musicians and museums, rock venues, and so on are all sharing the same twenty-five square miles or so. (As are the hoops to jump through, the editors and curators to please, the high-powered jobs, the magazines, music labels, and museums that matter to the global

economy.) New York City, due to this dense concentration, is a global tastemaker that dictates the direction of fashion, art, music, and design across the world. So if a creative producer is successful in navigating the networks of New York's cultural economy, she has, in the process, undoubtedly established herself with the rest of the world.

The mechanisms I've discussed so far, and the role of the social, make New York so important to the cultural economy. Part of the cultural economy's success in New York has to do with the city's built environment. The close proximity of galleries in Chelsea, nightlife in the Lower East Side, Meatpacking District, and SoHo, and the artistic community that lives in the West Village, Nolita, and Chelsea create a cultural clustering, both within the neighborhood and in the broader "downtown scene"—after all, most of these neighborhoods are just walking distance from one another. Because the social is so important to their careers, creativity, and access to the gatekeepers that review and valorize their work, the ability of artists, designers, and musicians to share the same dense geographic space with gatekeepers in the cultural industries (record labels, fashion houses, museums) makes possible New York's cultural and artistic economy. The old warehouses left over from industry have made possible the spacious lofts where many designers and artists have studios, galleries, and the like. The "walkability" of New York's streets and neighborhoods makes run-ins possible between those offering artistic skill sets and those needing them (record labels, advertising firms, etc.). (Contrast this to Los Angeles, a city literally driven by the automobile. These random, street-level interactions would be impossible—laughable, even—in L.A.) New York's tight-knit nightlife scene, which directs the fashion, music, and art industries toward the hippest, trendiest place to hang out, means that economic functions are almost always happening in social contexts. Put another way, the city's unique geography and built environment allow for this "perpetual creativity." Our current understanding of cities and of cultural economies only scratches the surface. By its very nature, creativity is capricious, at times ephemeral, making its value and significance hard to grasp. And yet it also exhibits tendencies and characteristics that, when formalized (as done in this book), give us a deeper understanding of creativity and lessons for how to cultivate and sustain it. What we have to remember is that the seeming randomness of nightlife, of lucky breaks, of exhibitions that make an artist's career, of the monumental Fashion Week shows that define a designer's impact exhibit patterns and dynamics in how they became successful (or conversely didn't). The idea that creative people blindly arrive in New York City just because they were told to, or that cultural industries locate here because that is the historical tendency, completely overlooks the systematic understanding that creative people and firms have about how their economy operates and why they need to be in New York City as opposed to somewhere else—and how they contribute to the fundamental character of the city's economic success. Creative people don't just come to New York because of its bohemian mythology. They know creativity happens in New York City and they know why. Social science, as the sociologist Howard Becker once wrote, gives us a greater awareness of things we already know.[3] And this book may strike some—namely, those who actually work in cultural fields—as obvious: the significance of social networks, the importance of nightlife, the fluidity across fashion, art, music, and design. The fact that so much of it happens in New York.

Herein lies the second challenge, and that is to understand culture vis-à-vis how we already understand cities and the functions and mechanisms by which they sustain themselves. As these first pages bring forth, we see that art and culture while exhibiting some of the same tendencies as other industries are also quite different due to their taste-driven nature, and as such, when thinking about how to regulate, cultivate, or optimize, they must be dealt with differently as well.

Of course, the naysayers would challenge that art and culture don't even matter to urban economies, except for their tourism lure or culture's importance as an amenity to attract firms and skilled labor pools from other industries. But these arguments demean the real impact of the cultural economy. Despite the common perception that finance is New York's great distinction, with regard to sheer concentration, the city's greatest stronghold and advantage are in artistic and cultural occupations. As chapter 3 discusses, detailed Census and industry data over the last 250 years show that as early as 1940 and 1950, art and culture combined to form the third largest employer within highly skilled occupations behind only management. These creative industries now employ almost as many people as finance and medicine. New York ranks number one over all major metropolitan regions in art and culture, even outranking Los Angeles within particular film and media occupations. Art and culture are essential in providing not just jobs and revenue but also New York's competitive advantage against other metropolitan and global cities. And they also form a several-billion-dollar industry, the magnitude of which is much harder to grasp than finance or law or manufacturing due to its hybrid nature of not just producing creative products but also providing revenue for tourism and skills for advertising, public relations, and so forth. If we tack on nightlife—a $9.2 billion industry—the impact of the cultural economy rivals and even outperforms that of most other sectors.

In that sense, understanding how art and culture work also gives us a lens through which to see how the biggest city economy in the world operates. And understanding the dynamics by which creativity operates in New York City teaches us more broadly about the ways in which art and culture happen in the world at large and how to cultivate them. New York may be one of the most successful global cities, but the patterns exhibited within its geography are not entirely unique—they are indicative of basic dynamics that occur in urban economies, and particularly with regard to how creativity manifests itself, a topic to be considered in chapter 7. And thus, this book is not about just New York City, it is about how cities work and how creativity occurs within them.

At the same time, the idea of regulating or creating policy regarding art and culture seems foreign and somewhat counterintuitive. Creativity is supposed to be spontaneous and uninhibited, its world is uncensored, and those who achieve success do so by hard work and luck but not through tax breaks and business incentives. When we think of real creative moments, it is the bustling East Village art movement of the early 1980s, where everyone lived in dirt cheap apartments, and galleries and nightlife were fused into one. Or we think of the early days of the West Village, when Bob Dylan played in small venues and people threw money on the floor of the Village Vanguard to pay the jazz musicians who played there. So the idea of policymaking or multimillion-dollar tax incentives to optimize the cultural economy seems misplaced and quite possibly harmful to the organic synergies that emerge out of the density of a creative community. Policymaking is for the floundering manufacturing industry or to lure JPMorgan Chase to set up shop; it is not to keep people like Andy Warhol or Jay-Z or Jean-Michel Basquiat in New York City or to prevent Mary Boone from moving her gallery to New Jersey. The idea that such creative icons would even leave New York doesn't make much sense anyway—they, after all, need New York as much as the city needs them—and it seems unnecessary for the state to get involved in the intimate and intricate relationship that art and culture have with New York City.

Or does it? We have reached a critical juncture in New York City. The very means by which the cultural economy operates—the density of creativity, the interaction of work and social life and the mix of the famous and the not so much, the gatekeepers and the unknowns, the merging of art, film, fashion, and music—is being challenged significantly. The increasing cost prohibition of living in New York, the city's punitive approach toward nightlife, and the exclusivity of nightlife institutions that once kept their doors open to all those who were simply interesting and now charge $300 for

Manhattan skyline from Williamsburg, Brooklyn. Photographer: Frederick McSwain. © Frederick McSwain. Used by permission.

bottle service, are quickly thwarting the artistic and cultural legacy within New York City. Chapter 7 considers some of the economic development policies that could counteract the squelching of the city's cultural economy.

Art and culture thrive in almost bifurcated economies. They are most creative when rents are depressed, gallery space plentiful, and gatekeepers and fledgling artists are able to engage in the same spaces. These conditions lead to what economists call low barriers to entry, which means that the only requirement to participate in the cultural economy is being creative. Because in depressed economies there is no cost-prohibitive factor, huge influxes of talented artists could flood New York, increasing the chances of more creative and interesting work to occur. This most vividly occurred during the East Village art movement of the late 1970s and early 1980s and during the Abstract Expressionism of the 1950s.

The other type of economy in which the creative world thrives is a vibrant and robust one where people—dealers, investment bankers, lawyers, and so forth—have the disposable income to actually purchase artwork at high prices, thus turning the symbolic art form into a very real and highly decided commodity. We have witnessed this type of economy in New York City through the 1980s into the present day.

But what ultimately perpetuates creativity is the influx of a new guard. Creativity is fundamentally about generating new ideas and new forms, and much of this is dependent on new labor pools who bring forth fresh ways of interpreting the world. And so it is the cycle of a depressed and then thriving economy that makes for a constant entry of new forms of art and culture and the people who produce them and then the marketplace where they can be bought and sold. But such a cycle has ceased to exist in New York, and certainly no one would wish a recession upon New York to provide cheap housing for a wave of young artists. But policymaking must take its place such that new creative people are actually able to move into the city and afford rent and studio space, and that neighborhoods that have been home to dense artistic communities do not all go the way of SoHo, replacing art galleries with Banana Republic. In other words, policymaking must cultivate the density, low barriers to entry, open nightlife and social environment that have been the pivotal forces in maintaining New York City's creative edge. From zoning that helps (not hinders) nightlife districts to creating more subsidized housing and studio space for artists, designers, and musicians to more city support for cultural events such as Fashion Week and the Whitney Biennial, policymaking can facilitate many of the mechanisms by which the cultural economy operates most effectively. Such a policy perspective is unconventional—it is not about dumping money into public art or giving grants to artists and designers by way of tedious grant proposals and applications that take so much time that most artists would rather spend painting or designing. Instead, what this approach asks for is actually engaging with the city and the very built environment in which art and culture thrives. We do not normally think about policy incentives for art, culture, and nightlife, and yet without these industries New York would not be New York. Their presence not only enriches the city, it creates and defines what New York is to the world. And, as such, policy and government must work to sustain it.

That art and culture can be optimized through policy and government intervention bodes well for cities and regions that are invested in cultivating their own cultural economy. That creativity exhibits tendencies that can be supported through policy tells us that

Eleven Spring Street near the Bowery in Nolita, a former carriage and stable house that has become a world famous landmark of graffiti and street art. Plans to turn the building into condos include gutting the building and removing all of the artwork on the façade. Photographer: Frederick McSwain. © Frederick McSwain. Used by permission.

places that want to further establish their cultural advantage have a means to do so.

The case of New York City has broader implications for the study of the creative economy and of economic evolution more broadly. As a case study, it can teach us something about the broader world of creative production. Or rather, how does creativity happen in the first place? What makes creative people innovate? And why does creativity concentrate and flow to some geographic spaces? What are "scenes" and how do they matter to cultural production and economic growth? To what extent are the informal structures of creativity and its broad social life important elements of its production system and creative economic development? I'll return to these themes—what New York City can do to support its cultural economy, and how other cities can find inspiration in the New York case—in the final chapter of the book.

Through the use of nearly one hundred interviews with those in art and culture from the famous and the almost famous to the unknown—the wildly successful and those hoping to just make ends meet—this book aims to understand how creativity happens in the first place and why it happens where it does. It is a lesson and story for New York City but also for art and culture more broadly. As such, it is a story about icons such as Diane von Furs-

tenberg, Quincy Jones, Francisco Costa, Marc Jacobs, Ricky Powell, Zac Posen, and the Talking Heads, and graffiti writers such as Futura 2000, Lady Pink, DAZE, and Lee Quinones, but also one about the struggling, young artists with small loft studios in Brooklyn and on the Lower East Side and the aspiring designers emerging out of the Fashion Institute of Technology or Parsons. It is a story about up-and-coming creative workers, along with the long-standing artists who paved the way and established New York City as a global creative hub.

Most fundamentally, this book is about New York and the creative people who live there, people from seemingly dissimilar worlds who share similar qualities in their creative production and social patterns, and in their need to live in New York. Their stories tell us about the very nature of art and culture and the places and spaces that cultural producers inhabit and diffuse creativity and ideas within. It is the story about how New York City makes creativity and, just as important, how creativity makes New York City.

Andy Warhol exemplified these dynamics more than anyone. He understood but also encapsulated, in both his work and his Factory, the collective nature of creativity: that fashion, art, film, music, and design did not reside in separate spheres—that instead they were constantly engaging each other and sharing ideas and resources across creative sectors. In his work, Warhol translated commodities into art, whether soup cans or dollar bills. But he also understood the inverse: that art and culture could be translated into a commodity form—what he called "business art," a central tenet to contemporary creative production. Warhol also saw the significance of the social spaces in which these industries and creative people interacted—his Factory merged cultural production with a social scene. And he demonstrated that this scene was instrumental in generating real economic value for those who participated in it, both through the merging of ideas while at a Factory event and the way in which the Factory cultivated economic value through its social cachet. And thus, the social and economic dynamics exhibited within the artistic and cultural world are very much the Warhol economy.

Much of this book is devoted to understanding how contemporary cultural industries and workers interact with one another, the city and different industries, but first it is important to see the trajectory and history of art and culture in New York, an overview that the next couple of chapters will give. Punk may have defined the late 1970s and '80s and hip-hop and a return of rock and roll may be the music du jour, but how musicians produce music, engage with other musicians and artists, and network their careers may not be a product of their genre or time period but instead indicative of how creativity emerges and is transmitted to the public at large. What we want to know is if processes by which Diane von Furstenberg's wrap dress, Jay-Z's new single, or Mark Rothko's paintings are generated, distributed, and evaluated exhibit similar tendencies. This retrospection and compression of the history of art and culture in New York City is useful: looking at creativity through time allows us to see if there is an overarching pattern by which cultural production operates. Understanding the history of New York allows us to view the present and the past and their relationship to each other, and gives us the perspective to discern the fads from the fundamentals of how and why creativity happens in New York City.

Chapter 2

HOW IT ALL BEGAN
From the Rise of the Factory to the Rise of Bling

Some of us remember and forever idolize Madonna lounging in that white wedding dress on a rowboat in Venice in her "Like a Virgin" video.[1] Maripol is the genius behind that look. Along with being a stylist for Madonna, Blondie, and Grace Jones, Maripol was a fixture in the 1980s Lower East Side and East Village party scene. Using her Polaroid camera, she documented the hip, the depraved, the famous, and almost-famous—from the platinum vixen Debbie Harry to a regal Grace Jones to Madonna in a hot pink wig and a young and brooding Vincent Gallo.

On a late May evening in 2006, I went to the SoHo Grand Hotel for Maripol's exhibition, accompanying the book release party for *Maripolarama*, a collection of her Polaroids from the 1980s party scene. Co-hosted by the fashion designer and gallery owner Agnes B, the party swelled to capacity within an hour. Attendees of the event poured out onto the balcony, the patio, and West Broadway's sidewalk. Maripol was there in a brightly patterned dress under a shock of deep brunette hair, talking to her admirers and friends from the '80s and today.

Some of her subjects came—the brash young things in the photographs transformed by the intervening decades. They mixed with the young artists and designers in their twenties and thirties—a girl with hot pink earrings made from duct tape and another dressed all in white with a belt that flashed programmed digital sayings on its buckle. There were Mohawked punks and glamour girls, men and women with dreadlocks and beautiful cheekbones, fellas in throwback jerseys and girls in tapered jeans (reminiscent of 1980s Jordache but purchased for $250 at an Intermix boutique). Writers and artists and old-school graffiti stars and actors and fashion designers remarked that they hadn't seen a party like this since back when Maripol was documenting them. Here, the old guard met the new and made it clear that understanding New York's creative scene today requires appreciating its roots.

Economists call this "path dependence," but the rest of us might just say "history matters"—small decisions made in the past can have large effects on the present. Institutions, like New York's fashion, art, and music scenes, sustain themselves over time. Today's creative establishment finds its roots in the people, the movements, the institutions, and the scenes that have been here before. Historians and economists often point to a crucial "historical moment" that is the watershed moment for a city or a region to gain a competitive advantage. In New York, many point to World War II and the influx of refugee artists as a critical point in the city's cultural economy. The influx of artists created an impetus to establish schools, venues, galleries, and neighborhoods that support their industry, thus encouraging new flows of artists into the city, more creative ideas, more artistic moments, and so forth. Equally important, the 1970s depression of New York City's economy made it possible for artists, galleries, musicians, and music venues to afford to be in the same places, most notably the East Village. In fact, the 1970s marked the true beginning of the convergence of artistic and broader cultural production that we observe in the 2000s. Put simply, the social and economic dynamics that establish a city's advantage in a particular field (whether art in New York or automobile production in Detroit) often reinforce themselves over time, creating a "lock-in" advantage over other places.

By the same token, the cultural history of New York affects the cultural present. Modern artists have rethought, reinterpreted, revised, and creatively deconstructed earlier visions. The Dada art movement of the 1910s stimulated the neo-Dada and graffiti of the 1960s and '70s. Marcel Duchamp's 1917 "ready-made" urinal is industrial designer Tobias Wong's inspiration for his contemporary "readydesigned" products from his "this is a lamp" chair to knock-off Burberry buttons. The early 1900s apparel manufacturing firms on Seventh Avenue led to the showrooms for fashion companies today. The literary bohemian enclave on the Lower East Side in the middle 1800s has been revived, first in the East Village art movement of the 1970s and '80s, then in the establishment of CBGB in 1973, and most recently in the hipster bastion that the neighborhood became in the late twentieth century.

The Original Bohemians: 1850 to World War I

"New York in the 1910s was a writer's city, literature the paramount art form. Downtown, books and magazines were the chief forms of entertainment and obsession, not painting or music, and bohemian conversation sooner or later settled on what the talkers were reading that week," writes Princeton University historian Christine Stansell. Beginning in the 1850s, New York City had established itself as a leading center of publishing, the city's defining cultural form at the turn of the century. While much of literary bohemia was not involved in large-scale publishing, the concentration of the industry within the city generated an outpouring of journalism, left-leaning magazines, literary journals, poetry, and the like that allowed the city to perpetuate writers' ideas on a more global level.[2]

The clustering of writers, journalists, and poets formed strong, politically inclined groups that provided the intellectual outlet where they often discussed how their writing was positioned (and relevant) in the world at large. Magazines such as Margaret Anderson's *Little Review*, which published works by William Carlos Williams, and the *Masses*, edited by Max Eastman and published in the Village, were filled with the writing and sentiments of the time and also were politically liberal. (But with a cost: Anderson, for example, was arrested for publishing installments of James Joyce's *Ulysses* in the magazine, and Eastman, along with other journalists such as John Reed and Randolph Bourne, was criticized [and almost put out of work] for being against World War I, when popular media were supporting it.)[3]

Early bohemia, most notably, was associated with a social cause, what Stansell calls a "politicized sociability"—writing and art affected and informed politics (and vice versa). While part of this inclination manifested itself in literary publications, it was also evident in the support that New York bohemia gathered for the labor movement and the working class. Writers and artists took part in the 1912 Lawrence, Massachusetts, textile workers' strike, for instance, and used their close ties to the media and publicity to back the laborers. This sensibility also crept into journalists' sensationalistic writing about other countries' socioeconomic plights, including books like John Reed's 1914 *Insurgent Mexico*, which, directed toward a popular audience, was a culmination of his research and adventures reporting on the revolutionary civil war in Mexico.[4]

From the late 1800s to 1920, writers clustered in and transformed Greenwich Village. In 1911, the Ferrer Center on St. Mark's Place served as a socialist and cultural outpost, attracting the king of Dada art, Marcel Duchamp, and the photographer Man Ray (the two met each other there and continued a lifelong friendship and artistic collaboration), along with the poet William Carlos Williams. In 1912, active efforts to merge art, culture, and politics were found in the establishment of the Liberal Club and the socialite Mabel Dodge's weekly salon. The clustering of writers and publishing and printing firms (Alfred Knopf, Albert Boni), fostered the expansion of the industry. Dodge's salon, for example, was located near Washington Square, while the cafes and bars within the neighborhood were often the meeting places for literary bohemia, from Ernest Hemmingway and F. Scott Fitzgerald to Dorothy Parker and Theodore Dreiser and publishers like Knopf and Boni. The literary bohemia, while dominating New York's artistic scene, also influenced other industries, particularly theater. Floyd Dell's "Liberal Club Players," for instance, drew largely from the writing scene.[5]

Turn-of-the-century New York flourished as a center of cultural movements, with its intrinsically social and heterogeneous nature on full display. Other creative industries were also getting their start: Most notably apparel and fashion manufacturing were gaining ground and Broadway was up-and-coming as a prominent theater district. The music scene, dominated by blues and ragtime, was centered in Tin Pan Alley (West 28th Street between Broadway and Sixth Avenue) and was a harbinger of the flourishing of jazz in the 1920s and 1930s.

Art, while still fledgling in New York (it would center in Paris until it moved to New York with the Abstract Expressionists in the

1940s), nevertheless contributed to the bohemian scene in the 1910s. The influx of World War I European refugees, most notably Marcel Duchamp, who arrived in 1915, invigorated the New York art scene. Already Duchamp had made his mark with his *Nude Descending a Staircase* at the 1913 Armory Show. The Dada movement of the mid-1910s through the 1920s, which included poetry and theater but most saliently the visual arts, reacted against traditional conceptions of art, with the key players being Duchamp, Man Ray, and painter Francis Picabia. Its centers included Alfred Stieglitz's gallery, 291, and Walter and Louis Arenberg's studio.[6]

Fashion design had a markedly different trajectory from the other visual arts. It has always been, to a greater extent than art or literature, more linked to an economically valued production system—fashion is, after all, and not so insignificantly, about making money. Not just apparel production but the fashion design process itself is oriented toward creating economic value (markedly different from the traditional sentiments of poetry, music, and so forth, and certainly at odds with the spirit of Duchamp's work). In that vein, fashion has moved on a different timeline than other creative industries. With the invention of the sewing machine in 1846, "ready-to-wear" designs were being produced with ease, and by 1880 New York was dominant in apparel manufacturing.[7] By 1900, the garment industry accounted for a quarter of the city's manufacturing, with 134,308 dressmakers, tailors, and factory garment workers, over double the number of carpenters, joiners, painters, and glaziers combined, with most of the industrial activity being located in the Lower East Side. Big department stores like Macy's, Lord & Taylor, Henri Bendel, and Bergdorf Goodman were all established in the mid-1800s.

The same period saw the fashion industry's rise as a creative and design-oriented sector. Two of the industry's most elite and significant magazines were established in the nineteenth century, *Harper's Bazaar* (1867) and *Vogue* (1892). *Women's Wear Daily* (WWD), the industry's trade publication, appeared in 1910. Also during this early period, the Pratt Institute established its fashion design program (1888) and the Parsons School of Design was founded (1897), setting in motion the ability of the city to create skilled individuals in merchandising, designing, and producing for the industry. Despite the expansion of the fashion industry within New York City, the design inspiration remained decidedly Parisian, with most clothing designs, instructors, and concepts coming from Europe's fashion capital. It was only after World War II that, as the geographer Norma Rantisi puts it, New York "ascended" as a world fashion capital.[8]

Between the Wars: Jazz, Dada, and Ready-to-Wear

The 1920s were the heydays of jazz and the beginnings of American fashion as we know it today, bringing pivotal changes to New York's music and fashion scenes. Jazz came into its own in the 1920s, flourishing particularly during the Harlem Renaissance (1920–1940) in places like the Cotton Club (founded in 1923), the Savoy Ballroom (1926), and later the Apollo Theater (1934), where legends such as composer and pianist Duke Ellington, trumpeter Dizzy Gillespie and vocalist Ella Fitzgerald performed. Ellington's hits "Take the A Train" (a reference to New York's subway line) and "Don't Mean a Thing If It Ain't Got That Swing" solidified his presence in the jazz world and also propelled New York City's position as a center of jazz. During the Harlem Renaissance, informal events were used to raise money for rent, and bootleg alcohol was the basis of "rent parties" (a practice not so dissimilar to the 1990s house music and Ecstasy drug-fueled parties known as "raves"). During the 1920s and 1930s, there were over one hundred entertainment venues in operation between Lenox Avenue and Seventh Avenue in Central Harlem, propelling Harlem into one of the most important black cultural and creative centers in the world. Jazz also appeared in the Village at venues like Small's and the Village Vanguard. New York City continued to be a great center of jazz well into the later half of the twentieth century, counting John Coltrane, Miles Davis, Sonnie Rollins, and countless others—famous and less so—as significant contributors.[9]

Even as bohemian New York transformed from a primarily literary scene to a more music-oriented community, fashion continued its successful trajectory from apparel production to apparel design. While Paris—and particularly Coco Chanel and Jean Patou—remained the dominant inspirations for clothing production and design worldwide, the 1930s brought the first inklings of New York fashion talent. In February 1931, a group of fashion leaders, Helena Rubenstein, Elizabeth Arden, *Vogue* editor Edna Woolman Chase, and Eleanor Roosevelt held the first meeting of the Fashion Group, organized as a "force" in propelling women's careers in the industry.[10] By 1938, the first issue of *Vogue Americana* hit the stands, and the establishment of the Costume Institute created greater links between fashion and performing arts. By the early 1940s, the Fashion Group had become the Fashion Group International and brought with it a new focus on American designers. Media outlets like the *New Yorker* and the *New York Times* were promoting American style, with the latter's permanent installment of its semi-annual *Fashion of the Times* in 1942. Around this time, the Council of Fashion Critics established the now-celebrated Fashion Week.[11]

Fashion

The outbreak of World War II was instrumental in promoting New York as a fashion hub. The July 1940 Nazi occupation of Paris closed off the city from New York City buyers and the press, forcing them to look elsewhere for both inspiration and clothing.[12] The war also inspired a certain patriotism that oriented the industry toward American designers. The confluence of these different factors—increasing the appeal of New York fashion—combined with the already established apparel production system to make New York City an unstoppable force. Post–World War II Paris never fully regained its crown as fashion capital of the world.

Several factors set the stage for New York art making a splash in the global art community after World War II. First, several of the most important formal institutions of art were founded: the Museum of Modern Art (MoMA) in 1929, the Solomon R. Guggenheim Museum in 1937, and the Whitney Museum in 1931, which is responsible for the Whitney Biennial, an event that features lesser known but promising American artists. Second, and arguably even more important, was the Works Progress Administration (also known as the Works Projects Administration or WPA), which ran from 1935 until 1943 under Franklin Delano Roosevelt's New Deal. The WPA gave artists projects to create public art and murals under the program's Artists' Project. The program employed over 5,000 artists, with New York accounting for nearly half of the parti-

Art

cipants.[13] Most important, the program was instrumental in establishing artists' careers and reputations, and for creating a network or community within the art world.

In fact, this government-sponsored program first established the type of network structure that artistic communities still use today to find jobs, disseminate information about their work, hear about emerging artists, and interact with one another. As the art dealer and curator Jeffrey Deitch explained to me in our discussion of the WPA, "[The] Depression really fueled creativity . . . these structures [community, network and so on] were developed through the WPA." Many of the artists who would later be known as the Abstract Expressionists worked on WPA programs—most notably, Jackson Pollock, Mark Rothko, and Willem de Kooning, among many others. It goes without saying the WPA left a significant legacy in the structure of New York's cultural economy and its accompanying social and economic networks.

After the War: The Rise of New York City

The period following World War II was undoubtedly the watershed moment for New York's artistic and cultural movements. As art historian Norbert Lynton asserts, "America dominates the story of art from the 1940s to the 1970s"—and New York could be substituted for America. During the war years, benefiting from the occupation of Europe, New York designers and artists shifted the spotlight away from Paris and onto their own creative endeavors. The war had also encouraged significant European artists to come to America, Mondrian, Ernst, and Dali to name a few.[14] The late 1940s and early 1950s solidified the cast of Abstract Expressionists or what art critic Harold Rosenberg later called—with reference to artists such as Pollock and de Kooning—"Action Painters." Their work, the first designated American art form, was also known as the "New York School" and was characterized by a tendency to be extreme, nontraditional, and uninhibited,[15] with bold colors, broad strokes of paint, and new ways of using material. Consider for example Pollock's technique of using the brush to drip paint, but never actually touch the canvas.

Even though the New York school of Abstract Expressionists exploded onto the scene by the 1950s, many of these artists had been working steadily during earlier, more uncertain times and, by the time they achieved fame, they were also reaching middle age. As Jed Perl, the art historian and *New Republic* art critic, points out, "It is easy to forget that while the late 1940s and early 1950s were the time when careers really began to take off, for the artists whose work defined the Abstract Expressionist style, 1950 was also rather late in the day. The artists who had started out in New York in the 1930s had lived through periods of stark poverty and mind-boggling uncertainty."[16] Part of the explosion of New York art can also be attributed to the sheer concentration of major galleries and the influx of artists, many of whom spent time in the same institutions from MoMA to Hans Hoffman's School to the Cedar Tavern to the Tanager Gallery to the Artists' Club.[17] The New York School also made an active point of detaching itself from Europe, most saliently marked by de Kooning's famous speech at the MoMA, "What Abstract Art Means to Me," in which he made a sweeping break from European influence on American art forms.[18]

Another point that this brief look at the Abstract Expressionists should make clear: this community both survived and flourished because of the formal and informal structures available to them within the city—structures that proved pivotal in cementing New York as a global center of art and culture. The Cedar Tavern, the Artists' Club, and the Hoffman School all were located in lower Manhattan between 8th and 10th Streets, within a few blocks of each other. They offered the informal environment where, as the critic and playwright Lionel Abel pointed out, there were "ideas in the air."[19] As Perl explains, "No single idea was promoted at the Club, but there was a fascination with how ideas bumped up against one another or slipped into one another or appeared or disappeared . . . The Club was an absurdist clearinghouse for ideas, and the artists were glad to speak their minds as intellectual currents whizzed by."[20] Jerry Harrison, the guitarist and keyboardist of the Talking Heads, explained: "[At the Cedar Bar] artists were talking about painting theory . . . Fist fights over whether Picasso was still relevant . . . People don't stop talking when they go out." Artists' studios, most located on 10th Street, were also instrumental in the exchange of ideas and knowledge on art, as was the MoMA as a formal institution for relaying important information to artists. The Club, also known as "Bill de Kooning's political machine," was a place both hailed and criticized as a venue to advance ideas and platforms for New York's art community.[21]

The heady days of Abstract Expressionism were also exciting times for the intermingling of cultural disciplines, a dynamic that continues to be of even greater importance into the twenty-first century. Great writers Frank O'Hara and John Ashbery not only hung out with the artists in cafes and bars but also often gave talks and wrote reviews, poetry, and essays about their work, reflecting the interactive relationship across culture and how the different creative fields supported but also reviewed and evaluated one another's work. By this time, artists were becoming famous with the public at large. Franz Kline was traveling on a train when a fellow commuter came up and asked him if he was the famous painter. "It was understood that Kline would be recognized at the Cedar," Perl explains, "but the very idea that here, in a busy commuter train, an artist would be recognized, that suggested an escalating level of fame."[22]

While Abstract Expressionism remained of preeminent importance into the 1960s (with Joseph Cornell's "collage" pieces and the Eames brothers' photography and design), simultaneously, Dada had returned full force.[23] The "neo-Dada" and Pop Art movements, most distinguished by Jasper Johns, Robert Rauschenberg, Andy Warhol, and Roy Lichtenstein, were distinct in their incorporation of pop culture (Lichtenstein's comic strips) and modern materials (Warhol's silk screens), which gave way to the punk-graffiti-postmodern art forms of the 1970s.

But even before the ultimate confluence of creative production in the 1970s, Andy Warhol was making headway with his midtown "Factory," his studio from 1963 to 1969. By the time he was shown by the star-maker gallery owner Leo Castelli in 1964, Warhol had made the artist's world one of glamour and celebrity, a trend that continues. While the Factory was ostensibly Warhol's place for making his silk screens, it was also a hangout for soon-to-be famous musicians, actors, and the like, including Mick Jagger, Lou Reed, Truman Capote, the tragic socialite Edie Sedgwick, and the famous transsexual (and Warhol's muse) Candy Darling. Not coincidentally, the Factory was also an amphetamine den. Warhol's Factory was not just a bastion of diverse creative forms. It was also a place where the eccentric could feel at home, a precursor to New York's nightlife scene of the 1970s and 1980s. Or as one commentator put it, "While drag queens and transsexuals had previously been viewed by society as just depressing weirdos, Andy Warhol made them sexual radicals."[24]

The period immediately following World War II was also significant for the resurgence of New York's literary scene, with the establishment of the Beat writers, a term coined by Jack Kerouac in 1948. While many of the Beat writers met and produced work in New York City in the 1940s, particularly Kerouac, Allen Ginsberg, and William Burroughs, the scene gained world recognition after John Clellon Holmes's 1952 *New York Times Magazine* article, "This is the Beat Generation," and with the smashing success of Kerouac's 1957 now-classic tale of bohemian lifestyle, *On the Road*. Ginsberg's *Howl* (1955) and Burroughs's *Naked Lunch* (1959) also came out of the Beat literary scene.[25]

Dovetailing with the Beats' congregation in New York from the 1940s through the 1960s, New York's music scene built on its legacy as a center of jazz with the introduction of bebop, along with the rise of such seminal jazz musicians as John Coltrane, Dizzie Gillespie, Charlie Parker, Miles Davis, and Nina Simone, who all continued to play at the Village Vanguard, Small's, and the Village Gate, along with the Apollo Theater in Harlem. At the same time, folk music was concentrating in the Village by the 1940s, most notably in the performances of Woodie Guthrie. Folk peaked in the 1960s with the explosion of Bob Dylan, Joan Baez, and Joni Mitchell onto the music scene. Folk music, like the literary movement of the early twentieth century, was very socially conscious, protesting inequality and war and promoting civil rights (the latter a cause that the jazz vocalist Nina Simone also embraced). Members of this more recent group also took up residence in Greenwich Village, spending time in many of the same cafes and clubs that jazz musicians, painters, and writers of the time were frequenting, in particular, the Cedar Tavern. This tendency for artists and musicians to share the same space and to merge their work and social lives marks today's cultural economy as well.

Fashion had not yet formally entered the mix, being still removed from traditional conceptions of bohemia and creative production. The Fashion Institute of Technology (FIT), established in 1944, became the preeminent fashion design school. By the 1950s, the Tobe Report, established in 1927 as a weekly fashion consulting report for retailers, was devoting more and more space to women's fashion in New York City. And while advanced technology both in manufacturing and transportation enabled production to move to Pennsylvania and New Jersey, design and pattern making remained in the city, particularly concentrated in the midtown Garment District.[26] As Dorothy Shaver, vice president of Lord & Taylor, commented in 1952, "Little more than twenty years ago, the word 'American' and the word 'designer' had not even been introduced to each other. Today they form an accepted and respected phrase in almost every language."[27] The geographer Norma Rantisi astutely remarks, "The fashion pyramid was leveled and New York's place in the new international constellation was firmly established."[28]

With this dense concentration of designers and their associates and a new edge over Paris, New York designers were beginning to advertise themselves as just that. By the 1960s, New York designers such as Calvin Klein, Ralph Lauren, and Bill Blass were running their own operations and creating their own identities as designers heralding the beginnings of cultural commodification and celebrity in the fashion world.[29]

The 1970s Through the Early 1980s: Postmodernism, Punk, and the Downtown Scene

Deindustrialization, the oil shocks of the 1970s, and New York's economic recession left the city in deep social and economic decline, with massive unemployment, fiscal crisis, and depressed rents and real estate. The same period was marked by national social unrest. From Watergate to the Vietnam War to the aftermath of the civil rights movement, America as a whole was significantly dissonant in its identity and social values, and New York more acutely than most places. New York reacted to what Jimmy Carter later infamously called a "malaise" with darker and more chaotic art forms. Explaining why New Yorkers moved in this direction instead of toward a kinder, gentler reaction—say, one of free love—that gripped other parts of the country, Ron Kolm, an author, editor, and downtown New York fixture, explained, "You couldn't drop acid and take the A Train."[30]

Marvin Taylor, the director of New York University's Fales Library, is a leading expert and archivist on downtown New York. In 1994, he began the Downtown Collection—which contains photos, writings, music lyrics, and artwork, among dozens of other artifacts—at Fales, documenting the New York art scene from 1984 to the present. As Taylor writes in *The Downtown Book* (partly a culmination of much of the work from his Downtown Collection), "New York in the 1970s was a dark and dangerous place. By 1975, the city would be bankrupt and sold down the river by President Gerald Ford," as indicated by the notorious *New York Daily News* headline October 30, 1975: "Ford to City: Drop Dead."

Ironically, these same factors also created an environment that allowed artists to cluster in the same neighborhoods, paying rents so cheap that instead of working a second job, they were able to focus completely on performing and exhibiting nonstop in rock venues, clubs, galleries, and cafes. Hilly Kristal, the founder of CBGB, explained to me, "When there was a recession in the 1970s, it was really easy for them [different types of artists] to overlap because rents were really low. . . . Always an overlapping of creativity, for many years. I think many artists are musicians and vice versa. Patti Smith is both a musician and a poet. Ginsberg was always in here [CBGB] performing. It's a natural state and always has been." Places like the nightclub-restaurant Max's Kansas City, established by Micky Ruskin in 1965, became centers not just for the now-prolific punk music scene but for the art world, too, where famous artists would have their own table, or, as Jeffrey Deitch explained, "You could walk in and find yourself at a table with Andy Warhol, at a bar with . . . Jeff Koons."

The downturn in the economy that negatively affected much of society was significantly positive for creativity in the long term. The director Tony Silver, best known for his cult hip-hop documentary

Style Wars, told me, "New York was wide open at the time. Anything was possible. . . . If you lived in New York at that time, graffiti was already everywhere and it had been for ten years. Intermittently it had been exciting, beautiful and wonderful, and much of the time a symbol that we had lost control. There was this sense that things were out of control. The city had lost the ability to service us. There had been serious headlines in the papers about the crisis in New York. And how the city was decaying. So this was a sign of hope at the time—from the street."[31]

The bleak social and economic conditions were essential in solidifying New York City's position as an artistic and cultural hub. The creative community could actually live there, coexisting with a rawness and ambiguity about where the city was going to end up. The abandoned industrial warehouses were being reused as galleries, studios, and nightclubs, while cheap rents allowed artists to concentrate in particular neighborhoods, first SoHo in the mid to late 1970s, and the Bowery and the East Village in the 1980s. And while it was one of the worst social, economic, crime-ridden times in the city's history, the mid-1970s through the mid-1980s was also one of New York City's greatest creative moments.[32]

Fueled by cheap rents and large studio spaces, the "downtown scene" below 14th Street became intrinsic to art and culture. The art historian and curator Roselee Goldberg defined the creative map of New York: "the demarcation between Uptown and Downtown was another reality. Below Fourteenth Street was a distinct parcel of urban geography."[33] While uptown had the MoMA and other formal art institutions, the new wave of music, art, and writing was happening in another part of the city. It was happening downtown.

But what exactly was happening? Most significantly, the cultural world was shifting from modernism to postmodernism. Strict adherence to art forms and the definition of culture and cultural products were now being reconstructed completely—it was not that just anything was art, but anything had the *potential* to be an art form. In earlier periods, jazz and Beat writers had dominated downtown, but the scene was quickly evolving into a more diverse, cacophonic, oddly fused medley of sounds, graffiti, painting, design, and performance. It was here in the 1970s that art, music, fashion, and design collided into what we now can observe as an all-encompassing cultural economy.

Andy Warhol and Keith Haring with his Pop Shop, while irreverent and chaotic, were also trying to make art accessible.[34] Broadly speaking, New York as an art center continued in importance with the increasing rise in popularity of Pop Art, neo-Dada, and the introduction of postmodernism. But other artists such as Jeff Koons and Julian Schnabel were also quickly gaining fame, with Schnabel showing with influential gallery owners Mary Boone and Leo Castelli in 1981.[35] Simultaneously, the art scene was changing and becoming more closely entwined.

Nightlife became the nexus for all different types of creative people. These seemingly disparate artistic realms saw an increasing fusion of creative fields, with art performance becoming an active part of nightlife, which was becoming instrumental to the production and dissemination of creativity—and its role only intensified as nightlife became the center of artistic performances ranging from music and cabaret to live painting, drama, and dance.[36] Many of the artists who would arrive on the scene in the 1980s congregated in New York and engaged in the city's creative scene during the mid-1970s and early 1980s, particularly "street artists" Jean-Michel Basquiat (part of the graffiti duo SAMO), Keith Haring, DAZE, Futura 2000, and Lee Quinones.

The clubs didn't just play music but were often filled with artwork and live performance art, where designers, graffiti writers, punk rockers, and writers all hung out in the same place. The clubs and the party scenes were so wild and new that, as Lee Quinones put it, "The scene was so good it was like getting a new piece of ass every night." The Roxy, for example, was a punk haven until 11 p.m., when hip-hop DJs started spinning. As DAZE explained to me, "Then [Afrika] Bambatta started DJ-ing at Mudd Club"—and the punk kids stuck around to hear him play. Or as Carlo McCormick, editor of the illustrious hipster *Paper Magazine*, and a downtown author and expert who was there participating in all of it, remarked, "All modes of cultural production were in the same room sharing the same space." The connection between those producing art and culture and the audience coming to watch was seamless, McCormick noted. "There was no distinction between performer and audience," he said. "Everyone was a participant." Art performance, an almost absent part of contemporary nightlife, was intrinsic to the creative scene and included performances not just by rock bands but artists like Matt Mullican, Fab Five Freddy, and the breakdancing group the Rock Steady Crew, all performing at the Kitchen (formerly the kitchen at the Mercer Arts Center).[37] From Keith Haring to cabaret singer John Sex, artists of all types participated in performances in nightclubs such as Pyramid and the Roxy in the East Village, and Danceteria, north of Union Square. Goldberg describes the postmodern New York art scene: "The thrill of co-opting these late-night, off-the-street venues, which were explicitly *not* art venues, generated an exuberant performance scene with its own animated cabaret style."[38]

Places like the Mudd Club were both galleries and nightclubs, where artists not only mingled with each other and their audience but also cultivated their reputation and gained recognition. Other clubs, like Max's Kansas City, which was both a restaurant and nightclub, were hangouts where the most famous and the unknowns from all creative fields mingled. Haring and Basquiat were very much involved in the nightlife scene, working as DJs and installation artists. Many artists worked in other types of creative production: Patti Smith as a poet and musician to Patti Astor as actress and gallery owner. As McCormick put it, "Little known fact, I would meet Jean [Basquiat] and he would have this big pipe and he'd fill it with this flaky heroin and we would smoke it and he was a DJ there [at Pyramid]"—along with being an installation artist and graffiti writer. Nightlife allowed a blending of different cultures and the beginnings of artists' ability to use their creative skills in a variety of realms—a tendency that became increasingly important through the 1980s into present day, as culture and cultural production became increasingly commodified.

Part of this scene was the mid-1970s punk rock explosion, and later the post-punk New Wave sound, with CBGB and Max's Kansas City fostering the movements. Punk, with its aggressive sound and affection for hard drugs, captured the dissonance of the era, developing a new type of music, which while referencing the 1950s, sounded fresh and edgy. As the urban lore goes, Television, the seminal punk band with Richard Hell, Richard Lloyd, and

Tom Verlaine, convinced Hilly Kristal to let them play at CBGB, at the time a folk and bluegrass club. And punk rock was born.[39] Other bands like the New York Dolls, the Ramones, Patti Smith, and the Talking Heads played at the Kitchen, Max's, the Mudd Club, CBGB, and the Mercer Arts Center. The Mercer Arts Center, with its several performance spaces, housed off-Broadway plays along with music performances, the New York Dolls having their own residence in the venue's Oscar Wilde Room.[40] New Wave, which evolved from punk, dominated the scene by the late 1970s into the mid-1980s, with the Talking Heads, the Ramones, and Blondie leading the scene, which continued to center around CBGB. New Wave, as the photographer Nan Goldin captured in her famous work *The Ballad of Sexual Dependency*, was immersed in hard drugs and aggression. These art forms remained symbolic, or not yet produced for money. That would come soon enough.

Other art also flourished in the same spirit—not of hard drugs and aggression, necessarily, but of blurring the line between performers and audience, and among art forms. While fleeting, the loft jazz movement caught hold during the same period (it was all but dead by 1980), with Sam Rivers, along with Studio Rivbea being key players.[41] More tellingly, at least for our purposes, the scene also witnessed the introduction of hip-hop. A confluence of dance, rap music, and graffiti art forms born from New York City streets, hip-hop would gain global popularity in the 1980s and 1990s. Graffiti saturated subway trains, and breakdancers could be found in basketball courts around the city, along with rappers and DJs who held "block parties" in city streets. Part of the hip-hop scene made it into clubs, most notably with Afrika Bambatta DJ-ing at the Roxy and the Mudd Club and the Rocksteady Crew breakdancing. The hip-hop scene also drew from beyond its own borders: Bambatta attracted punk rockers, while legendary rock band Blondie incorporated then-graffiti artist Basquiat and Fab Five Freddy in their music videos and lyrics.

The most important point to make about this moment in New York's cultural scene is not the drug use or pre-AIDS free love (of which there was plenty of both), but instead the links between different modes of art and culture, how they shared the same institutions and neighborhoods in spreading their products and applying their creative skills to different types of art. As Ingrid Sischy, editor in chief of *Interview* magazine, explained, "[There is the] assumption that fashion and art are enemies, but that wasn't always the case. We're not saying it's the same form, but they are running on parallel tracks. Sometimes the dialogue is 'I hate you,' sometimes the dialogue is 'I love you' sometimes it's 'You're interesting,' sometimes it's 'I want to rip you off'." In that vein, DAZE remarked to me about Blondie's use of hip-hop icons in their new wave lyrics and videos, "Deborah Harry [Blondie's vocalist] didn't see the differences in culture, but instead the similarities." Not only did creative people, from punk rockers to pop artists, live in the same parts of town, but they went to the same after-hours venues and participated in the same performances. And nightlife operated in two significant ways—as a support structure for the creative community and also as an institution by which cultural forms were performed and evaluated. While nightlife ostensibly operated as an entertainment form—and could be easily dismissed as such—its meaning and significance go far deeper.

The importance of the social component to cultural production, the central tenet of this book, was crystallized during these crucial years. Fashion designers publicized their lifestyles (what they did, where they went) through interviews, as evidenced by the star status that Gloria Vanderbilt and Calvin Klein attained through this approach.[42] Further, fashion houses embodied a whole lifestyle—transcending just fashion—in the products they sold, as most obvious in the cult of Ralph Lauren or Calvin Klein. "It was not a time of guitar solos, arias, perfect objects in sterile cubes . . . the formalist separation between mediums and strategies, or the once-unquestioned authority of the singular artist's hand and vision," McCormick noted. "The point is," he continued, "that you don't listen to the lyrics without keeping time with the beat, you don't go into a room without seeing who else is there, and you don't go to a show without at least acknowledging that—beyond all other subjectivities—the rules of perception might have a lot to do with what drugs everyone was on, and who left together."[43]

In the late 1970s and early '80s, New York's cheap rents, abandoned warehouses, and horizontal, ambiguous relationships across art and culture gave rise to the true establishment of New York's creative scene. The pieces had existed earlier, no doubt. But now, art and music and fashion could no longer be looked at in separate compartments—they were sharing too many ideas, materials, and spaces both socially and in their art forms. The scene could engage in what the French sociologist Pierre Bourdieu calls "restricted" cultural production, artists could produce art for art's sake (what Bourdieu would call "symbolic capital") with no real regard for economic reward.[44] These two factors, the horizontal relationships across art and culture and the fusing of different creative forms, along with the freedom for creative people to engage in restricted production, established one of the greatest moments in New York's artistic and cultural history.

Much of this scene manifested itself most vividly in the East Village art movement of the mid-1980s, "when glamour and sleaze were nearly indistinguishable, and the boy next door was an androgynous, foot-high-peroxide-pompadour-sporting singer named John Sex," as the New Museum described its 2004 tribute exhibition to this time period, *East Village USA*.[45] Jerry Harrison, of the Talking Heads, said, "Being recognized in the East Village was more important than getting [one's] picture in *Time* magazine—it was truly underground." The East Village teemed with galleries, artists, and musicians, with many of those working, showing, and performing all living in the same densely packed neighborhood.[46]

And Harrison was correct—for a moment. By 1984, Walter Robinson and Carlo McCormick's celebrated article in *Art in America*, "Slouching Toward Avenue D," acknowledged the larger art world's encroachment on the bustling subculture.[47] Part of this evolution was the movement of New York street art (graffiti) from the South Bronx and the Lower East Side into the homes of international art dealers and on the radar of art enthusiasts worldwide. The FUN Gallery, opened by Patti Astor in 1981, became the pivotal spot for graffiti artists to show their work.[48] And there was one more thing: creativity, it was becoming increasingly apparent, was very marketable. And nothing seemed more marketable than the scene that had been lurking in Jerry Harrison's subculture for so long.

The Mid-1980s to Today: Culture, Commodification, and the Conquest of Cool

The shock of AIDS as something far more mysterious than cancer combined with the ravages of crack, cocaine, and heroin to severely subdue the sexual liberation and drug experimentation that accompanied New York's artistic scene. But the buildup of dense creativity that fermented from the mid-1970s through the 1980s culminated into the ultimate watershed moment for New York's creative scene in the mid-1980s: New York City became the premier global creative hub of fashion, music, art, design, and these worlds collided in the insomniac, coke-fueled, disco-lit world of nightlife. Artists were no longer producing art only for their friends, living in run-down walk-up apartments, or just trying to make it. They had arrived, and they were selling their creativity on the global marketplace. Downtown party boys like Marc Jacobs and Stephen Sprouse stirred the imagination of the international fashion world, while hip-hop artists, once relegated to street block parties were becoming mainstream, with broad popular appeal.

The mid-1980s marked the start of the increasing translation of culture into consumer products, or what the UCLA geographer Allen Scott terms the "commodification of culture."[49] In other words, the street scene, the flamboyant creativity, the fusion of different art forms, was no longer just flourishing as "restricted" cultural production. It had untapped economic value and worldwide demand. While culture and capitalism have long been linked together—from the selling of classical music to the scoring of movies—the degree to which this merger was occurring was far quicker, more extreme, and all-encompassing than ever witnessed before.

This transformation of New York's art and culture from bohemia to a creative economy was perhaps most evident in the rapid rise to stardom of graffiti artists and hip-hop musicians. While distinctly different in their styles and future trajectories, the graffiti artists Haring, Basquiat, Quinones, and Futura would become an intrinsic part of the New York art scene. (Basquiat would die of a heroin overdose in 1988, Haring of AIDS in 1990, while Quinones and Futura have continued to be recognized not only as pioneers of the graffiti movement but world-famous artists in their own right.) The artists who originally produced graffiti became dominant in avant-garde, pop, and contemporary art along with design-related products (which Futura became especially involved in).

By the mid-1980s, graffiti increasingly translated into big money. And anyone could have seen it coming, although few did. Warhol's Pop Art and Blondie's incorporation of hip-hop subculture in its increasingly popular mainstream music were the beginnings of the intersection of culture and cash as we know it today. After Basquiat exhibited at Mary Boone in 1984, she sold his pieces for up to $20,000 each. Shortly afterward, Christie's auctioned one of his paintings for $20,900.[50] By 2001, fashion designer and artist Stephen Sprouse was designing graffiti-splattered bags for Louis Vuitton that were selling for hundreds if not thousands of dollars, and selling out of boutiques and department stores across the world. Building on the increasing market demand for cultural status symbols, through the 1980s and 1990s fashion designers slapped big logos on their clothing and accessories (Gucci, Tommy Hilfiger, DKNY, Calvin Klein).[51] Hip-hop music, once strictly an urban-based street level culture originating in New York City, gained global credibility with the establishment of *Yo! MTV Raps*, performances on *Saturday Night Live*, the establishment of hip-hop record labels (Def Jam Records by Russell Simmons and Rick Rubin), and the increasing stardom of rappers like the groups Run-DMC and the Beastie Boys.[52] Cult movies like *Style Wars* (1985) and *Wild-Style* (1983) glorified the gritty subculture of hip-hop and graffiti.

Some of this transformation manifested itself in the increasing expense and elitism of nightclubs, from Danceteria to the Mudd Club to Palladium to Studio 54, where as Carlo McCormick explained to me, "At Studio 54 you pretended you were holding coke and gay . . . you pulled up your shirt to show your track marks to get into the Mudd Club." No longer a free and open cultural environment, nightlife became increasingly exclusive, letting in only those creative producers who were also linked to the cultural marketplace or the culture of cool, while wannabes were left on the wrong side of the velvet rope.

Indeed, the nexus of art, culture, and nightlife had become synonymous with glamour and celebrity, but also a professionalization of the cultural production system, in stark opposition to the earlier punk attitude. Jeffrey Deitch commented, "This mixture . . . In the '50s the Abstract Expressionists, late '50s into early '60s with Beats . . . With Pop [Art] begins the connection between fashion, music, art and then into the '60s you really see it with Warhol's Factory, the best example. Mid-'70s, the punk music scene connecting with that [the creative scene] into the '80s with the Mudd Club, and graffiti and hip-hop connecting with that to some extent. Then, things got really professionalized, you didn't have the same scene, where you could walk in and find yourself at a table with Andy Warhol . . . it became more upscale. Before, everyone was at the same dive bar—it became less democratic."

The art and culture scene still congregated in nightlife, though it became less about performance and actual artistic production and more about the networking and the exchange of knowledge necessary to establishing oneself in the field. Michael Musto, the decades-long nightlife columnist for the *Village Voice*, explained, "People actually had to go out of the house to connect with other people, which made for a teeming nightlife scene populated with networkers and freaks (not mutually exclusive groups, by the way)."[53] From musicians and their backers (Madonna, the Talking Heads, hip-hop moguls) to artists to designers (Marc Jacobs, Stephen Sprouse), nightlife continued to be the node of creative exchange with, as Musto points out, "The parade of artists, designers and professional partiers prancing around me, desperate to be noticed."[54] The professionalization of creativity also broke up the scene. As Jerry Harrison put it: "[Creativity worked] all around the fact that there was a club, people wanted to go to hear original music, bands play . . . didn't have to play cover songs to make money, professionalism kills the scene, fragments the community." Part of this splintering related to some of the less desirable side effects associated with the scene—drugs and AIDS. Jeffrey Deitch explained, "The fluid scene was not thriving, some of it has to do with AIDS, all of the people who put it together, the club entrepreneurs, magazine writers—they died. A whole creative gay community died, this had a tremendous effect from the mid to late '80s to 2000."

Meanwhile, the increasing economic rewards for cultural production (platinum albums, hip-hop clothing companies, contemporary artwork being sold for millions of dollars, the ability of nightclubs to charge highway robbery for entry) meant that artists, in the broadest sense, were becoming well aware of the potential to transform their symbolic capital into an income, but on the flip side some of them would inevitably be left out. If you didn't measure up in the marketplace, you didn't measure up. And New York would no longer provide for the inexpensive agglomeration of free and open creativity. High rents pushed artists out of Manhattan and far into Brooklyn and Queens.

Nightlife's function changed significantly. No longer was it an open community dedicated to being an outlet that cut across class lines, where the only entry requirement was creativity. As Musto explained to me, "It is a bizarre contradiction. [Nightlife] is a place for bohemians and people living on the fringes and also a billion dollar industry. Ever since the advent of bottle service, it's really been a goldmine industry for some of these kinds of clubs . . . everyone is trying to cash in on it. Really right now it is a lucrative situation to jump into." He continued, "Speaking in terms of New York, in the eighties, there was a downtown literally and it catered to those people [bohemians]. People who owned Area didn't even care if they made money; they wanted to create this artistic, creative club. The way it evolved New York became shiner and glitzier and no longer for starving artists. It became more of a soulless experience but more of a lucrative experience. You don't see art on the walls anymore, let's put it that way."

The artist Steve Powers commented, "That seemed like a lot of fun. Now there are no drugs, no sex in the bathrooms. Back then there was new music." Clubs began to demand high covers and $300 bottle service from patrons, and had exclusive guest lists. (These expenses continue to skyrocket.) Nightlife continued to make or break careers but rarely because of the performance within the club. Performance art became how creatively one could appear in gossip columns. Fame and links to famous people generated cultural value. (Again, this trend has continued on the same trajectory.) Nightlife, while still essential and intrinsic to the creative economy, transformed from a place of raw cultural production and a dense creative community into an increasingly cost-prohibitive site of networking and career building.

Cultural producers understood—and quickly—the links between their symbolic capital and economic gains, which is how rapper Diddy and singer Jennifer Lopez managed to create clothing empires, Stephen Sprouse painted graffiti-covered bags for Louis Vuitton, and artists like Futura and Lee Quinones designed sneakers for Nike and Adidas, respectively. Indeed, the creative scene of the late 1980s through the 1990s was a far cry from the bohemia of the early 1900s, far less involved in social movements and more, out of necessity and demand, focused on commodities and high-profile publicity, a trend that continues into the twenty-first century. Some artists will always make outrageous and sensationalist work that sells for millions (Jeff Koons' hilarious *Michael Jackson and Bubbles* sold for $5.6 million in 2001).[55] But more markedly, the late 1980s and 1990s brought about a very frank conversation among creativity, culture, and the marketplace. The director Tony Silver expressed it like this: "There are many types of commodification. Is it a commodity? Is it art? Is it from the streets? What is it? You can't untangle this stuff—you can't escape it. It is a very complex subject. Hip-hop is both a commercial juggernaut but also a chance for kids all over the world to invent their own form. Both things can coexist."[56]

While creative New York today is still the city of high rents and strict guest lists, it has again become a significant commentator on the social issues of the day. The new century has produced an intersection between some of the earlier conceptions of bohemia into the later twentieth century notions of commodification. Many of the mass social concerns, from drugs to discrimination to poverty to AIDS, have had inadvertently large impacts on the creative community. Designer Marc Jacobs has used his clout to connect the creative world to liberal politics with his participation in the political group Downtown for Democracy. Jacobs collaborated with the group to make clothing with political statements, which has sold in Barney's and his West Village boutique, particularly during the 2004 elections. In recent years, New York designer Kenneth Cole has shaped his entire advertising campaign around supporting liberal social issues, from AIDS research to same-sex marriage. Hip-hop musicians, particularly Diddy, have been pivotal in rounding up the youth minority vote with their "Vote or Die" campaign, and Russell Simmons is a spokesperson for People for the Ethical

Treatment of Animals (PETA). While these designers and musicians are still selling clothing, they have directed at least some of their production toward social causes of their choice, a modern-day bohemia of sorts.

Art, surprisingly, has not been as active on the social front. Jeffrey Deitch commented, "This is a question many people ask me. We have many challenging things going on in the world today; every artist is opposed to Iraq. You would think art today would be very political, you see some of that, of course, but for the most part you don't. Artists are involved with building this alternative world, childlike, the art is not aggressive . . . [though] it may change quite quickly." But fashion and music also have been largely uninvolved in larger social issues—a very different cultural scene than the politically charged and socially conscious 1850s and 1960s.

All this said, the larger cultural community in New York has recreated its scene. Street art has returned with a fever, with mega-exhibitions in galleries across the city (for example, Twist showing at Deitch Projects, Ryan McGinley's photography on the graffiti subculture at the Whitney Museum) and the scene flourishing in bars in Williamsburg, Brooklyn, and on the Lower East Side. And the integration of art, music, and fashion seems more entwined than ever before. Not only do artists, designers, and musicians find themselves mingling at the same bars and clubs, from Lotus to Stereo to Bungalow 8 to Max Fish, but they have used the increasing commodification of culture to produce cross-disciplinary work and collaborations. From artist Ryan McGinness's soccer balls on fashion designer/talk show host Isaac Mizrahi's program to artist Matthew Barney's recent work *Drawing Restraint 9* with his wife (the musician Bjork) to designer Cynthia Rowley showing her fall line at Deitch Projects, the fusion of creativity is ubiquitous and increasingly generates value across global social and economic realms. Then again, maybe it never really changed. As Ingrid Sischy remarked, "I don't know if New York has changed. We're always being told, 'Oh, you can't live here' [but] you *always* couldn't live here [when I first came to New York]. I lived in half a room. I know we're being told it's being run by money and power, but go to a gallery opening run by two 21-year-olds and feel the vibrancy. Yes, it used to be in SoHo, now it's Chelsea. You go to Mercury

Lounge on Houston—maybe it's not CBGBs but there is still a crowd cheering or booing. Some of the people who come here will make it and some won't." Or as the fashion designer Zac Posen explained: "Like the West Village, prior to that SoHo was the cultural center for creative success. I think obviously geographically we are on a small pincushion, [with] artists and creators moving to different neighborhoods. Every generation has its own neighborhood. It moves through the city. Everyone wants to be where the cool people are."

The "New" New York Scene

My friend Brooke and I had just left Ryan McGinness's art opening in SoHo and were heading to his studio for the after-party. On the border of Chinatown and SoHo, where many artists and designers set up shop in the vast warehouses left over from manufacturing's heyday, Ryan's studio was six flights up in an enormous space that took up almost the entire floor. Ryan had renovated the entire studio: Minimalist white walls, hardwood floors with just a smattering of brightly colored textures in the kitchen and office area. With no doors, the rooms seamlessly blended into one another. Dozens of Ryan's ethereal and whimsical paintings and his richly colored graphics hung on the walls.

When we arrived, the party was already in high gear. There was a lot to celebrate—his art opening had been a spectacular success. People milled around drinking cocktails and Red Stripe beer, and eating gourmet apricot Rice Krispie treats and edamame from the hip Nolita restaurant Rice, all served in take-out cartons—a quintessential blending of high and low brow—or "nobrow"[57]—that Ryan effortlessly conveys in his art and personality. The party itself was a medley of different people, from fashion designers to fashionistas, artists to art dealers, and graffiti artists to those who write about and photograph them, along with the many people from other worlds who hung out in the now very stylish, street-art-meets-high-culture scene, reminiscent of the graffiti art movement of the 1980s.

Jeffrey Deitch, who has advised artists from Jean-Paul Basquiat and Keith Haring to Jeffrey Koons, is the veritable gatekeeper of the scene. Art dealer and star-maker, Deitch not only owns his highly influential Deitch Projects gallery, which has presented exhibitions by Yoko Ono, Barry McGee, Larry Clark, among over one hundred others, but has also been the curator and advisor for sensationalist productions and exhibitions. For example, Deitch almost went bankrupt from bankrolling Jeff Koons' "Celebration" series.[58] He also was responsible for Vanessa Beecroft's performance for the Louis Vuitton store opening party in Paris in the fall of 2005. Slim and petite with a full head of wiry salt-and-pepper hair and his signature light-framed circular glasses, Jeffrey leaned against one of the windows, always surrounded by friends, fans, and artists hoping for a chance for a show. In a small sequestered area of the studio, fashion designer Cynthia Rowley's baby lay peacefully on a blanket sleeping soundly, oblivious to the carnival surrounding her. This confluence of creative people partying, celebrating, exchanging ideas in a historical Chinatown warehouse—once a vanguard of the city's manufacturing economy, now renovated into a spectacular studio—is the nexus through which New York City's creativity perpetuates itself.

Art dealer and star-maker Jeffrey Deitch with the burlesque luminary Miss Dirty Martini at the opening of "Womanizer" at his Grand Street Deitch Projects Gallery in SoHo, January 2007. Photographer: Melissa Webster. © Melissa Webster. Used by permission.

In the last 150 years, New York City's creative scene has been focused and refocused and reconstructed over and over again and yet, whether it is Duchamp's Dada, Duke Ellington's jazz, Bob Dylan's socially charged Greenwich Village, Warhol's Factory, or the pop-street-high art of Ryan McGinness, art and culture exhibit similar tendencies regardless of what genre or form they take. They are social and fluid and operate without boundaries across different cultural forms, and work best when there are low barriers to entry for all types of culture and when they are not inhibited by social or economic restraints. But why New York's art and culture should matter to the city as much today as 150 years ago is a far larger issue than its scene or coolness factor. That these industries provide jobs and revenue and real economic advantage to New York City is the other big part of the story, and a topic I will now turn to.

Chapter 3

BECOMING CREATIVE

For most, where Blondie played their first show or where Marc Jacobs hangs out is utterly irrelevant. The inexhaustibly cool creative world is a concept, not a reality, and not one that most people—even New Yorkers—ever enter. So it's a wonder why we should care at all about creativity and culture, which for all intents and purposes doesn't affect our lives, our economy, or really anything we do.

Unless it actually does. Creativity isn't worth writing a book about if not for the assumption that it means something more significant. Art and culture aren't just the cool kids dressed in black hanging out around St. Mark's Place or the surrealist exhibition at MoMA—though they invariably have an impact on us and define the New York experience. (The black nail polish craze of 2006 no doubt gave props to those goth and punk kids in the East Village who had been wearing it for years.) But more important is the idea that art and culture have a place alongside finance, law, and big-headquarter corporations in contributing to New York's livelihood.

Most see New York as transforming from a trading port city to manufacturing, and in the 1980s to finance and corporate headquarters. And in all respects, New York has been a leading global city in terms of its sheer size, economy, and prowess in industry. When the manufacturing economy came to a screeching halt in the 1970s, most industrial cities from Detroit to Chicago to Pittsburgh were left as hollowed out centers of unemployment, crime, and decay. New York had its downtrodden moment too—from the mid-1970s to the early 1980s—but it lasted less than ten years before the city once again rose to the top of the global hierarchy. As urban economist Edward Glaeser has remarked, "All cities, even New York, go through periods of crisis and seeming rebirth, and New York certainly went through a real crisis in the 1970s. But while the dark periods for Boston, Chicago or Washington, DC, lasted for thirty or fifty years, New York's worst period lasted less than a decade. . . New York's history is one of almost unbroken triumph."[1] Part of New York's ability to be a dominant player in the world economy is its ability to reinvent itself by becoming a leader in industries that also happen to be powering the world economy (whether assembly-line manufacturing or the stock market).

But what New York has always had (especially during its down-and-out days) is a dense cultural community of bohemians and creative professionals, from poets to fashion designers to filmmakers, that has remained stalwart—and has even thrived—through the city's economic and social ups and downs. What comes as a surprise when one looks at the data is that New York's true advantage over other places as a cultural stomping ground isn't just ethereal and aesthetic. Creativity provides real jobs and real revenue to the city. New York's advantage over other places is not in the sectors that we traditionally think of—finance, law, corporate headquarters. Other cities can easily match these. But fashion, art, music aren't just cool. They are economic drivers. In turns out that New York needs culture for more than just its hip factor.

Culture has also helped the city in an inconspicuous way. While culture does generate employment and revenue, it also acts in an intangible way, operating as an attractor of diverse people and firms that are drawn to New York not just for business but also for its energy and creativity. Culture is often treated as an amenity and thus a lure for professionals and workers in other industries who want to live and work in a culturally vibrant place.

Art and culture's role in New York's economy lies in the city's position as a dense hub of idea-driven, high-human-capital industries and workforce. Scholars have argued that New York's dominance is primarily a function of its ability to cultivate a single industry cluster (finance and professional services, with the second supporting the first). Yet the city's greatest strength is actually in being a diverse mix of strong, highly skilled occupational and industrial clusters, what Glaeser calls "skills" or what Richard Florida calls the "creative class." The city's concentration in high-level human capital is fundamentally what saved it from becoming one of the desolate wastelands of the manufacturing economy—as was the fate of Cleveland, Detroit, and Pittsburgh. This position of being a center of human capital–driven industries traces back at least a century. Even in the midst of its manufacturing heyday, New York was also a prime location for skilled labor and producer services ranging from finance to clerical work.[2]

As Raymond Vernon sagely predicted in 1960 in his prescient book *Metropolis 1985*, ". . . The Region's forte is in providing a site for industries to which skilled labor is critical, whereas industries tend to avoid the New York Region when their prime need is low-wage unskilled labor." Vernon argued that New York was a great center for firms that relied on what economists call "external economies," or economies that emerge as a result of firms and industries who depend on outside resources and services (such as accountants or legal services) for their production processes. External economies is the difference between a manufacturing firm that does all of its production internally and relies on its own resources versus an investment bank that may contract out for a variety of different services from computer scientists to graphic designers to lawyers. Firms that rely on outside resources (or external economies) locate where professional services or production plants locate (and vice versa) in order to produce their goods and services. In this respect, much of New York's success in culture and otherwise is a result of the solid support structure that service industries and workers—from busboys to administrative assistants to couriers—provide, allowing the economy to run smoothly. While these industries often fly under the radar, they allow the city to efficiently and effectively compete in the world economy. Media, for example, while a skilled industry in its own right, also acts as a crucial distribution service for cultural industries. If not for the sophisticated and integrated network of publishing, TV, and radio with the city, New York culture would remain decidedly in New York. Instead, the city's media sector operates as an effective global distributor of New York-produced creativity, disseminating the city's ideas into the world marketplace.

New York as a center of external economies industry and global advances in transportation and technology was a harbinger for the New York that we know today. Raymond Vernon forecasted the fate of New York City. "The increased speed of travel to New York, in our view, is likely to encourage the growth of clusters of office activity in that area, rather than otherwise," he wrote. "The reasons for this expectation are illustrated by the problem of the central office elite. This problem is to maintain two links in the chain of communication: to maintain an easy flow of facts and decisions from headquarters to branch plants . . . and regional sales offices and to maintain an easy interchange of ideas by the elite headquarters personnel among themselves and with their outside advisers . . . The most probable outcome of the increased freedom offered by swifter air travel will be the further concentration of the office elite at a few headquarters cities. This tendency will be fortified by the use of high-speed electronic data-processing machines. For these machines will contribute to the centralization of data-processing and decision-making at fewer points in the structure of the giant company."[3]

Vernon was certainly partly right, but he could not have anticipated the extent of his prescience. It was not just the centralization of office space, but the transformation of the world economy from producing widgets to producing ideas would also require that people be located in close proximity to one another in order to trade their ideas and knowledge. And while art and culture have always been central to New York, Vernon could not have predicted how much of a global juggernaut that cultural commodification would become, and that being able to transform culture into a product for the marketplace inherently required a clustering of creative production, and that much of this would happen in New York City.

Why Culture Matters

Many people think New York has art and culture, but how many of us, really, think they drive the economy? Not many. Probably not even the artists themselves.[4] As the regular storyline goes, New York may be known for its artists, musicians, designers, and so forth, but they are certainly not essential in the way that finance or law is in providing lots of jobs or in contributing to the city's competitive advantage. The city, it would follow, is not dependent on cultural industries for its survival. Art and culture are more the icing on the cake, enhancing New York's reputation as a global hub of all things.

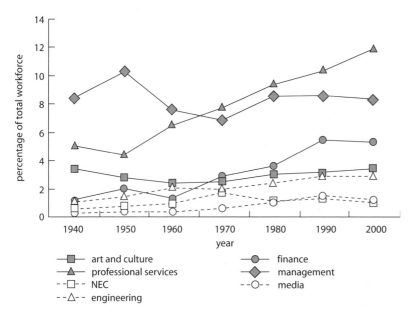

Figure 1. High-skilled Human Capital Industries in NYC, 1940–2000 (by occupation). Source: *U.S. Census of Population, PUMS data, 1940–2000.*

But culture does matter to New York City's economy, and the city does depend on art and culture not only for quality of life but also for jobs and revenue.[5,6] Culture is an employer (from galleries to recording studios), and contributes to an atmosphere that helps the city draw workers and businesses that seek out places with a vibrant creative community and the amenities it provides. Just looking at employment, the cultural sector has witnessed a continuous increase in its presence within the total workforce since 1940, peaking in 2000 (the latest census data available) at 3.56 percent (see figure 1 and appendix).[7]

Art and culture combined form the fourth largest employer in New York City behind management and professional service occupations, and just behind finance in its proportion of the workforce. That art and culture jobs are almost as dominant as financial occupations is indicative of their (often neglected) importance to New York's economy. Art and culture have witnessed a steady increase in employment over the last sixty years, indicative of both their potential for future growth (it has not declined yet) and their ability

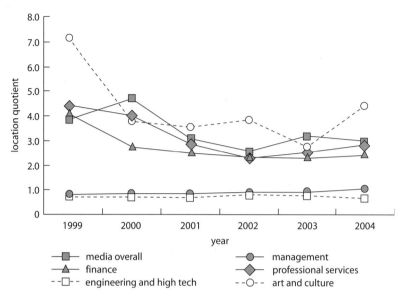

Figure 2. High-skilled Occupational Clusters in NYC, 1999–2004 (by location quotient). Source: Bureau of Labor Statistics, Occupational Employment Statistics 1999–2004.

to remain consistent despite fluctuations in the metropolitan economy—a somewhat surprising result given that most economists believe art and culture are luxuries and are often the first to go during economic hardship.

Art and culture are New York City's crucial competitive advantage—meaning they form the sector in which New York has a unique lead over any other city. In order to measure this, I used a method called a location quotient, which allows us to see how New York compares to other places and where its strengths and weaknesses lie (an LQ over 1.00 is more concentrated than other cities, while an LQ of 1.00 means it is average, and an LQ of less than 1.00 means it is less concentrated).[8] For this reason, LQ is a useful tool for economic developers and policymakers, giving clarity to what makes New York different and distinct.[9]

Unquestionably, the occupations that are most concentrated and reflect the greatest regional competitive advantage are art and culture (see figure 2). Fashion designers, with a 15.98 LQ, boast the highest concentration, almost triple that of all occupations, including those in finance, law, media, and management. Across all fields and industries analyzed, New York's greatest advantage is within the cultural sector. In 2004, the New York metro was over four times more concentrated in art and culture than any other city, indicating a broad sweeping strength in creative production.[10] Only Los Angeles and San Francisco even compare, with the latter significantly lagging behind New York's dominance. Generally, most artistic and cultural occupations in the region possess location quotients of at least 3.00, with several boasting concentrations over 5.00. In addition, despite the ongoing perception that Los Angeles is the overwhelming leader in film production, the industry's location quotients in New York are just behind and at times ahead of those for Los Angeles. Particularly, New York is closely following Los Angeles in film and video editors and producers and directors. In part due to Broadway's dominance in live theater, New York ranks higher than Los Angeles in set and exhibit designers and makeup artists.[11]

Making Its Move

New York City is an educated and idea-driven town, and the industries that power it require acute skill sets. Yes, industries like finance, CEOs and headquarter offices, law, public relations are important, but the key is that art and culture are the leaders in this broader significance of skills and ideas on the city's economy.[12]

From the 1970s to the early 1980s, as manufacturing plants shut down in droves, and business moved from North America to South America and China, cities lost their central functions. Undoubtedly, New York experienced disastrous economic conditions as well, as neighborhoods from the Lower East Side to Williamsburg closed manufacturing shops and became vacant and crime-ridden. However, unlike many industrial cities that remained stuck and unable to shift gears from manufacturing to a more human capital–driven, or in Daniel Bell's term "post-industrial," economy, New York City was already beginning to make the shift even in the midst of industry's downfall. As early as 1970, human capital–based industry was taking up a significant portion of the workforce, indicating that even within manufacturing and working-class industry, many of the occupations were of a high human-capital nature.

With the decentralization of the production process (most manufacturing was moving off shore while the headquarters remained in central cities), even within industries that were more labor-intensive (e.g., the apparel industry), the cities and regions that possessed the innovative, skilled occupations (e.g., the management, the designers and so forth) were the ones that rose to the top of the world economy. New York City already had a head start in this domain. Overall, its industries and occupations were becoming more and more idea-driven, and when the industrial economy broke down, a human capital–intensive or "skilled" economy was there to take its place.

Even with the rise of human capital as the backbone of economic growth, which human capital and industries were most important remained up for debate. New York City's ability to sustain its position as a leading player is a part of the long-standing debate on what factors influence city growth and why some remain on top of the global heap. Off the top of our heads, most of us think of Tokyo, New York, London, and Paris, and maybe Berlin or Los Angeles as the most vital urban economies in the world. And many urban scholars are fixated on why these cities are the leaders in the world economy and on unearthing the characteristics that these urban centers share. Scholars have argued that New York City is a global city as a result of its position as a world center of finance, business services, and management.[13] As the University of Chicago sociologist and leading globalization theorist Saskia Sassen concisely remarks: "National and global markets, as well as globally integrated operations, require central places where the work of running global systems gets done."[14]

Ideas and skills matter, but which ones matter the most? Art and culture clearly contribute far more to New York City's economy than traditionally thought. Further, they are symbiotic with other industries, most notably media—where culture provides skill sets, while media operates as a distribution network for creative production. What's clear when we compare culture to finance, management, law and so forth—the industries we generally point to as leaders of the city's economy—is that creative industries are not just a part of the broader idea city, they are its raison d'être. Looking at each of these industries in turn, it is apparent that art and culture are not just a part of the city's economy—they are indeed creating New York.

Media Town

From the *New York Post's* Page Six to the *New York Times* and the *Village Voice* to the major book publishers located near Rockefeller Center to Madison Avenue's advertising firms, New York as much as Los Angeles (albeit in a different way) is a world center of media production. Media plays an important role in New York's cultural economy, particularly because it is the public (and creative) face of many other skilled sectors, ranging from finance to the arts, and because it is the distribution network that transmits New York culture to the world. For these reasons, media could easily be merged with art and culture, because so much of its activity is inherently creative and about culture. Yet, media as its own industry is worth taking a look at, partly because it operates as a hybrid—being creative, yet applying its creativity to other industries. Public relations, broadcasting, editing, and other communications services are all instrumental in the success of translating messages, ideas, and products into marketable forms. As an industry, media ranks third behind finance and professional services (see appendix).[15] This result is indicative of the large and diverse workforce that participates in the media industry, from public relations to advertisers to graphic designers.[16] Its position has remained generally stable over the past sixty years. Media-related occupations (like public relations managers or advertising agents) are hard to classify, as many of the occupations within this sector overlap with other industrial and occupational sectors, particularly art and culture.[17]

Many of the occupations within media demonstrate a consistently high representation within New York, almost three times more concentrated than other sectors (see figure 2 and appendix).[18] Only Los Angeles has as significant a concentration of the media industry.[19] Besides Los Angeles and New York, no other metropolitan area has any significant hold on the broadcasting and television industry.[20] And besides New York and Los Angeles, only Washington, DC, and Chicago also boast significant representations in media-related occupations. Media, it is worth emphasizing, is essential to art and culture. While New York has always been a cultural hub, media has been the conduit responsible for transporting the city's creativity into the global marketplace.

CEO City

The towering skyscrapers glittering Manhattan's skyline define New York City. Each of these tall steel buildings houses a multitude of global powerhouse companies, from Sony to JPMorgan Chase to any number of banks and consulting firms that run many of the major financial and management activities in the world economy. And within these buildings are the powerful CEOs and top-level management that orchestrate the big deals, mergers and acquisitions that keep the global economy humming along. This mythology of Manhattan has also been a part of how urban scholars have defined New York. For several decades, scholars have been pointing to the concentration of managerial and executive occupations as a signifier of a global city.[21] Much of this line of argument has posited New York City as the quintessential example of this type of economic strength. Management occupations are very important to the different human capital–driven industries, representing almost 10 percent of the total workforce and second only to professional services (which includes law, medicine, and education; see figure 1).[22]

Indeed, management is ubiquitous in the New York economy—part of this is because many different industries require management-level workers, and especially because New York has traditionally been a hub for upper-level corporate activity. From Whole Foods grocery stores to Goldman Sachs, managers of all forms are needed to guide everything from the company's vision and aggregate goals to the quotidian activities that keep things moving.

Yet despite its position as a significant employer, New York does not maintain a competitive advantage in managerial and CEO occupations, which notably are not concentrated in the city (see figure

2). Relative to other large metropolitan areas, New York's very average concentration in chief executives (hovering at 1.00 LQ) ranks below Boston, Charleston, South Carolina, Chicago, Raleigh-Durham, San Diego, San Francisco, and Washington, DC.[23] In fact, while New York possesses an LQ of over 1 for several of the management occupations, it does not rank number one in any management occupation, indicating that several other major cities are more dominant in top-level management and executive occupations. These results indicate two things. First, management is an occupation that is present everywhere because all types of industries require it and thus it is not place-specific—therefore, although a lot of New York's workforce participates in management occupations, so do lots of other people in other metropolitan areas. Second, looking at the location quotient, other places are more dominant in this field. In other words, even if management is required everywhere there are firms and industries to be managed, it appears that more of this management and running of companies is happening in places other than New York.

Corroborating this result, the New York metropolitan region has been losing Fortune 500 companies for the last fifty years. In 2000, the New York Consolidated Metropolitan Statistical Area (CMSA), which is a broader (and more forgiving) geographical unit than the metropolitan region, and includes parts of Connecticut, Pennsylvania, and New Jersey, was home to only 14 percent of all large corporate headquarters in the nation, down from 16 percent in 1990 and 31 percent in 1955.[24] Today, New York hosts not one main office of the nation's top twenty retailers.[25] Thus, although New York has a large number of managers, so do lots of other cities. Our image of New York as the United States' preeminent center for management is more myth than reality. Management is certainly not distinctive to New York.

My Bonus Is Bigger than Yours

Every year, we hear the stories of mega-bonuses on Wall Street. Most people think finance is the great powerhouse of New York's economy. Yet this perception is misleading. In terms of those who actually work in financial positions, it is the third-ranked occupational sector, with 5.41 percent of the total workforce in 2000. Certainly, this is not insignificant, and its presence in the metropolitan economy has been one of steady increase over the last sixty years, peaking in 1990 (see figure 1), but it is not quite as overwhelming a force as we would presume before looking at the data. As an industry (which includes all the assistants and paralegals who work for a financial company, along with the chefs in a corporate cafeteria), finance is far more formidable (the second largest employer behind professional services). But this is primarily because financial firms require a diverse group of workers who are not necessarily working in financial occupations per se.[26] Those who are actually running the show, so to speak, are not as represented as our perception of New York would have us believe.

Looking at New York's competitive advantage, we see the same results. Overall, the city is almost 2.5 times more concentrated in finance than other cities, but this advantage has been declining over the last several years.[27] While occupations within the sector possess concentrated location quotients, it is important to note that finance, often considered the New York region's stronghold, is not as represented as some other occupational clusters (see figure 2). In other words, the depiction of New York as uniquely centered on finance is unsupported. In comparison with other U.S. metropolitan regions, while New York maintains top rank in securities, personal financial advisors, and financial analysts, Boston, Chicago, Washington, DC, and San Francisco are close behind in these categories and leading in others such as actuaries, budget analysts, financial examiners, and general financial specialists.

Corroborating these findings, the city's share of the nation's security jobs has declined from 36 percent in 1987 to 23 percent in 2002. Between 1990 and 2002, the securities industry grew by just 0.6 percent in New York City, while New Jersey experienced a 248 percent job expansion in the same years, indicating that finance is becoming increasingly decentralized, seeking out locales outside of New York City. While securities employment does not dominate the New York economy, it accounts for 20 percent of all the wages in the city,[28] which means that the city economy (and tax revenues) may be too dependent on an industry that is only robust at the top tier. Overall, these results indicate what some economists have been positing for several years—finance appears to be losing its hold on New York City's economy.[29]

Lawyers, Guns, and Medicine

But doesn't New York have a bunch of lawyers, judges, doctors, and others who work in professional services? Anyone who has watched endless reruns of *Law & Order* would certainly get that impression. Isn't New York what sociologist Saskia Sassen calls a "postindustrial production site"?[30] In the post-manufacturing era, where economies are driven more by ideas, innovation, and human capital than actual physical production of goods, it is places that produce high-level services that are particularly important to the global economy.[31] These professional services are based on skilled human capital and are related to education, law, and medicine. Finance and management are tightly linked to these services, as these different industries help one another and need one another in the production of their own services and innovations.

Sure, professional services are a formidable force within the New York regional economy, possessing the greatest proportion of the total workforce of all human capital–intensive industries, a position they have kept since 1960. As a whole, they are the second largest force behind the service sector, and the largest high-skilled employer, representing almost a quarter of the workforce (see figure 1 and appendix).[32] Between 1960 and 1980, professional services truly took over, and part of this increase is due to the decline of manufacturing, which was once the city's economic powerhouse. But it is also indicative of something else: As New York's manufacturing declined, human capital–based occupations were already in motion to take over as the economic driver of the region. Professional service occupations' percentage of the workforce (the lawyers, doctors, teachers, judges, and the like) increased almost 2.5 times between 1940 and 2000, while the industry as a whole increased four times in that same period, with medicine and education leading the pack.[33, 34] Law, however, lags significantly, disputing common perceptions of New York as a predominantly litigious city.[35]

In terms of its competitive advantage, New York is over 2.5 times more concentrated in professional services than other metropolitan areas, particularly faring well in medicine and education, indicating that one of the city's greatest strengths is in high-skilled services.[36]

That said, dominance in these occupations is not significantly greater than in other leading metropolitan regions, and overall employment figures indicate a general decline in the last several decades. From 1970 to 2000, the city's percentage of the region's employment in professional and business services declined from 60 percent to 45 percent, a 25 percent decline overall.[37] The results in finance and professional services run parallel, and indicate a general trend that, although the city still possesses an advantage in these occupations, their concentrations have declined and overall these industries are not as dominant as we have assumed.

Where It All Began

New York's long-standing advantage is being a great center of high human capital. This strength in ideas and skills is what saved it in the 1970s and continues to power the city today and into the future. But to really understand New York's position as an idea city, we must take a look at history. Idea-driven industries may be at the forefront of New York's economy today, but even hundreds of years ago, they were significantly present. What's more, part of New York's success in skilled occupations is reliant on the city's unique advantage in service sectors—from high-end professional services that crunch numbers to the basic operations from retail to clerical work that keeps top-level transactions running smoothly. Looking back at New York City's economy over the last several hundred years shows us that ideas and creativity—and the dense and integrated service network that facilitates it—have always been in its DNA, along with being the city's true economic advantage.

The very early data tell us very little other than that New York City was becoming the central hub of activity within the state. In 1790, the city had almost a quarter of the state's population (23.5 percent), a proportion that would decline before it peaked at 60 percent in 1940. To put it into perspective, from 2000 through

2004, the region had a stable 42 percent of New York State's population. Data from the 1790 tax returns, which give occupational information for landowners within Manhattan, reveals to some degree the composition of the New York economy.[38] Of the 4,483 landowners, 10 percent were skilled, almost a quarter were working class, while over a third of this population was involved in the service sector. Farming then (as now) is nonexistent for the most part.[39] As New York was a thriving port city at this point, the concentration of service is an indication of the trade of goods. The sizable labor representation is a harbinger of the manufacturing industry, which by 1820 was taking hold of the city in the form of sugar refinery and apparel production in particular.[40]

Finance, one of New York's central industries, took root early. Even though in 1820, 3,872 people worked in commerce (approximately a quarter of what manufacturing employed), by 1840, the financial industry had increased its employment more than three and half times. During the same time, New York City possessed 50 percent of the state's financial industry, a number that has steadfastly increased over the past 160 years. For example, in 2002, New York City represented 69 percent of the state's employment within the larger "finance and insurance" industry, indicating that New York City continues to be the central hub of financial activity within the state.[41]

Come Together

The large, trendy loft spaces in SoHo, the Meatpacking District, the Lower East Side, and Williamsburg that poor artists once inhabited and where celebrities and bankers now reside, originally housed the production and warehousing activities of New York's manufacturing industry. It was this beginning, primarily feasible due to its port and geography, that allowed raw materials to come into the city and then be transformed into high value-added goods. Manufacturing possessed a remarkable supremacy over the metropolitan workforce, so much so that even in 1890, when New York City was still only Manhattan, manufacturing employed more workers (499,185) than financial and insurance companies did in

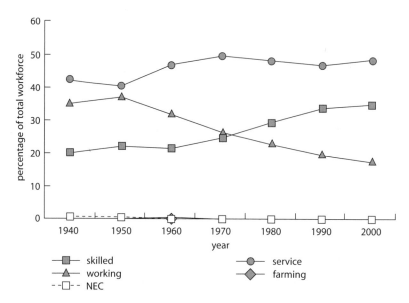

Figure 3. NYC Economy by Occupational Classification, 1940–2000. Source: *U.S. Census of Population, PUMS data 1940–2000.*

2002 (430,265), in a much larger New York that includes five boroughs and approximately 8 million people.[42] Despite New York's role as a manufacturing hub, such concentration was short-lived. Even as early as 1950, New York City's working-class employment (which was primarily composed of manufacturing) began to decline (see figure 3).

But New York has always had a lot going on in services. The service sector was remarkably present even during the time period that we usually associate almost solely with manufacturing. In 1940, during the heyday of manufacturing, the service industry made up 43 percent of the New York economy, while working-class occupations made up 36 percent. By 1970, service occupations were the most dominant sector of the region's economy, capturing half of the workforce, with working class (still primarily driven by manufacturing) at 26 percent.

Skilled occupations were not as prominent in New York in 1940, capturing about 20 percent of employment. But something very interesting occurred in 1970: the proportion of working-class occupations intersected with the proportion of skilled occupations and switched places (see figure 3). Today, working class occupations make up less than 20 percent of the region's employment, while skill-driven occupations make up 35 percent of the economy.[43]

This switch of roles in 1970 from a working-class to a skill-driven economy is indicative of the overall economic restructuring and decline of manufacturing that occurred in urban centers around the world. Yet, unlike many cities that took a substantial hit, New York was lucky to have a booming service industry that was already more prominent than manufacturing. In addition, New York as a "skilled city" was on the rise and supplanted manufacturing as the city's economic driver.[44] Because New York has always been a global hub of something, the service support structure to transmit information, goods, transactions, and the like is equally important in maintaining this edge.

Services, defined as clerical, food, hotel, and retail/wholesale industries—in other words, those industries that provide quality of life or support—were as important as manufacturing and, until 1970, the service industries outperformed human capital–intensive industries as well (see appendix). In fact, service has maintained dominance over all other industries for the last sixty-five years, and more than likely beforehand as well (we just do not have the same solid data for the period before 1940).[45] This makes sense. So much of New York City's efficiency, its attractiveness for businesses and tourists alike, has to do with the city's ability to provide services ranging from office support structure to entertainment, from restaurants and dive bars to Bergdorf's and vintage stores.[46]

No matter what, when people come to New York City, whether for business or tourism, they need places to sleep and eat, so it makes sense that hotel, retail/wholesale, and food-related occupations have remained a relatively constant part of the workforce for the past sixty years.[47] The success of the many different industries that have dominated New York's economy has been a result, in part, of the strong service industry that supports them directly (e.g., office work) and indirectly (e.g., in the form of amenities, consumption, and so forth).[48] Conversely, the success of other industries from art and culture (which draw tourists) to finance (which generates more disposable income) provides a reason for the service industry to exist at all.

New York's original advantages over other cities are increasingly being supplanted due to the decentralized nature of many industries, mirroring the story of manufacturing. By way of example, from 1956 to 2002, while wholesale trade continued to represent a substantial part of New York's economy (even increasing its industrial proportion), the distribution of this industry reflects the growing decentralization of trade both within New York and in the nation as a whole. In 1956, wholesale trade employed just 1.30 percent of New York's workforce, yet accounted for 39.3 percent of all national employment in this sector.[49] By 2002, wholesale trade had increased to 5.38 percent of New York's employment, yet it constituted just 3.39 percent of U.S. employment within the industry. This transformation points to a general increase in the importance of trade to New York's economy but a decreasing comparative advantage over other metropolitan areas, due to the dispersal of wholesale trade to other parts of the country. What happened with wholesale trade indicates that the advances in technology, transportation, and information exchange have made it easier to produce and exchange goods and services in lots of different places—thus driving many industries to locate where the cost of business is cheaper. Certain industries, like trade and manufacturing, that are not "place-specific," that is, they do not require being in particular places to conduct business (and do not depend on external economies) may, and more likely will, go to the place that is most cost-effective. This trend is reflected in the increasing loss of New York's competitive advantage in manufacturing and trade (from dominance to virtually nonexistent representation) over the past fifty years. Indeed, this also speaks to the need for New York to find another reason why it is a crucial place for firms and people to locate. And it has. New York, once a great bastion of trade and manufacturing, is increasingly a city powered by ideas and skill sets, and the people who need to live and work in close proximity to exchange them.

The Idea City

Today, New York City's real competitive advantage and unique position as a global city lies in its skills and ideas, and particularly, its position as a great center of art and culture. While trade is still prominent in New York, it is now not just the physical exchange of goods but also that of ideas, professional services, and knowledge. Overall, New York City is successful due to its ability to capitalize upon its diverse economy and mix of industries, an observation that harkens back to the great urbanist Jane Jacobs' acute observation that diverse economies are essential to perpetuate growth.[50]

New York's gain in skilled, human capital–intensive industries in the 1970s could be initially attributed to the decline of manufacturing (i.e., as manufacturing declines as a percentage of the workforce, inherently skilled industry gains proportional representation). However, if we look at the service industry as a whole, it did not increase proportionally to skilled industries, indicating that it is not strictly a default proportional increase, but that indeed skill-based industries were independently on the rise during this time period. Ever since this pivotal time period, human capital–based industries, from finance to art, have remained stable in their position within the New York economy, both in terms of rank and approximate percentage, reflecting the permanence of skilled labor as a vital part of the New York economy and also the strength and longevity of each sector within the skilled economy.

There are many ways to look at the economic dynamics of a region, and the location quotient is a simple way to see New York's standing relative to other cities. The insights gained from the numbers are important considerations in setting economic policy that aims to sustain and further maximize New York's competitive advantage and position as a leader in the world economy. Specifically, it is in the arts, design, and media where the region possesses its greatest strengths and possibilities for prosperity. Simply put, it is art and culture that make New York "different," and also more attractive, than other places. As art and culture are recognized as central to the growth and success of cities, cultivating and supporting these industries becomes intrinsic to the region's economic optimization. This policy directive is not to diminish the importance of contribution to gross domestic product (GDP), employment figures, or tax revenue, of which the financial industry continues to dominate.

Using location quotient analysis along with looking at workforce proportions teaches us something about the difference between

New York's employment versus its "distinction" as a metropolitan area along with telling us something about the general nature of particular industrial sectors. For example, while the financial industry employs approximately 10 percent of the total workforce, its location quotient reflects a much smaller advantage, indicating the ubiquity of the industry throughout the country. Art, culture, and media, on the other hand, employ slightly fewer workers than finance, yet they have a much larger location quotient, reflecting the centralized nature of their industries. This is true not only in terms of their prowess relative to other cities, but also as formidable and significant employers in their own right. New York is dependent on art and culture to provide thousands upon thousands of jobs for its workers. The sheer dominance both in terms of location quotients and ranking compared to other large metropolitan regions indicates that New York's distinction and competitive advantage are above all as a great center of cultural production. In other words, in order to fully participate in the art and culture economy, you pretty much have to be in New York (or Los Angeles)—a point that has also come across clearly and repeatedly in my interviews with artists, designers, and musicians who that live and work in the city.

New York City has always been a leader in whichever industry is powering the world and national economies. This chapter further reiterates New York's importance as a great global center, and also its remarkable ability to continue to reconfigure and reinvent itself. Today, New York is powered by ideas and skilled human capital skill sets, represented both in employment and concentration.

Yet within this sphere, we see that art, culture, and media are what truly make New York unique and distinct within the global economy. Further, the cultural industry's advantage appears to be growing. In 2001, there were over 150,000 jobs in arts and culture, a 52 percent increase from 1992. In those same years, employment in TV and film and commercial theater has almost doubled.[51] Undoubtedly these numbers have increased. So not only does it appear that New York City's true distinction is as a global city is in creativity, but that the region has demonstrated its ability to expand this advantage.

These two significant findings—New York's position as a global hub of ideas, and particularly its cultural dominance that continues to grow—emphasize a crucial need to understand how the artistic and cultural economy works, and why New York is so conducive to its social and economic dynamics. This book aims to provide a deeper understanding of how art and culture "happen" and why New York is so central to their production—a topic long ignored in the social sciences, and one that will be examined in depth in the following pages.

Chapter 4

On a beautiful, sunny weekend day at the end of April, the sky bursting with a periwinkle blue that made the chance of clouds or nighttime seem impossible, my best friend, Marisa, and I were walking through the West Village on West Fourth Street hoping to stumble across the Marc Jacobs store. I knew the boutique was on Bleecker Street, but given the sinuous streets in the Village, that didn't really give me much of a clue to our destination. I looked around and met eyes with a well-dressed older man.

"Sir, you wouldn't happen to know where Bleecker is?" I asked him.

"Sure," he replied. "It's just a block down there."

"Thanks, we're looking for the Marc Jacobs store," I explained.

"Oh, yes, that's right down there on the corner," he said, "Actually, I know Marc. I live near him down here in the Village."

Marc? He called him by his first name. Clearly, they were friends, or at least acquaintances. Marc Jacobs, the long-standing darling of the fashion world, with his tousled, thick, chocolate-brown hair, and his penchant for wearing hooded sweatshirts, had a knack for making the 1940s schoolmarm dress look positively sexy. He was easily the most prolific and widely acclaimed American designer since Ralph Lauren, and maintained a sense of prestige and nonchalant couture long after the latter sold out. Marc Jacobs was the picture of modern American fashion. I loved him.

"You know Marc Jacobs?"

"Oh yes, we're friends. I'm Giles, I make jewelry."

Within seconds, I started explaining my research project and how I would love to interview Marc.

"Well, Marc, he would be good, and I think he'd be up for it," Giles replied. "I'll see him this weekend. Give me your contact information and I'll pass it along to him and tell him about you. I really think he'll do it for you."

For months I had been trying to get hold of Marc Jacobs—calling his main offices, sending emails to my friends who worked in fashion, grilling interviewees for possible contact information, and all to no avail. And here, on a sunny Saturday afternoon of shoe shopping, I had literally run into my opportunity to interview him. And so this story goes for the millions of artists and designers and musicians and other creative producers living in New York City who are hoping to find their success, their industry breakthrough.[1]

It's easy to see why interactions like this are important. But to understand their larger impact, especially in today's city, it's useful to explore how cities and their economies have changed over the last thirty years. The dynamics that power today's economy make the structure of city life and its random exchanges and run-ins all the more important and meaningful.

In the 1970s, cities across the country watched their economies grind to a halt. Manufacturing, the bread and butter of the U.S. economy beginning in the late nineteenth century, was rapidly (almost overnight) becoming obsolete in Western economies. From New York to Pittsburgh to Detroit and beyond, urban centers, once driven by high-level manufacturing production that supplied thousands of jobs and billions of dollars in revenue, faced a serious crisis. Increased globalization and technological advancements, which made it easy to transport materials across the world, meant that manufacturing firms were able to set up shop in developing countries that offered cheap labor and abundant resources. Countries like Brazil had perfected more advanced technologies in steel production, making Pittsburgh's and Cleveland's steel mills antiquated and comparatively expensive. U.S. cities were no longer competitive sites for manufacturing. Many of them rapidly became wastelands of urban decay, beset by massive unemployment and fiscal hemorrhaging, with abandoned plants and mills and hollowed out downtowns that bred crime.

At the same time, something curious was afoot. Despite an overall national crisis in the manufacturing economy, some places had managed to not just survive but do really, really well. In Silicon Valley, outside San Francisco, and through Southern California, business was booming. And while it did involve production, this was a different type of industry—primarily technological (and in the case of Southern California entertainment-related) in its content. Simultaneously, while New York City was in a deep fiscal crisis, it too was making gains that were dampening the impact of the manufacturing industry's decline. As manufacturing plummeted in New York, other types of industries—finance, management, entertainment, and service—made strides, taking the place of the city's manufacturing industry and catalyzing an almost complete recovery of the city's economy by the mid-1980s.

These new industries were inherently different from manufacturing in what they produced. They were equally different from one another as well. And, most tellingly, despite the overall depression of the U.S. economy, they proved robust and strong. Their success lies less in the differences in what they produced (whether computers, accounting spreadsheets, or designer clothing) and more in how they produced it.

In 1973, just before the collapse of the manufacturing economy, Harvard sociologist Daniel Bell wrote a seemingly clairvoyant text on the transformation of the global economy. In *The Coming of a Post-Industrial Society*, Bell argued that the base of the economy would shift radically, from manufacturing to information, science, and technology, and be oriented toward providing services. In Bell's view, post-industrialism would become the overarching framework under which society and economy would operate. Look again at the industries that were doing so well while the manufacturing economy declined—science, technology, finance, entertainment, and so on—and consider how radically they differ from the manufacturing that drove the American economy—the world economy, really—for the previous one hundred or so years.

Steel mills and assembly lines didn't run themselves. They required workers. They also required a small group of people who were instrumental in creating innovations in production technology or making decisions about new products and structuring the work environment. But Bell's post-industrial economy—the kind of economy that dominated places like Silicon Valley and, by the mid-1980s, New York City—comprises industries prized for their ability to continually innovate and create new, advanced ways of doing things. And the places that have high concentrations of innovation and the people responsible for it were most successful—which explains why in the midst of the decline of manufacturing, Silicon Valley, highly concentrated in engineers, computer scientists, and design specialists (the human capital behind innovation) was economically robust and exhibiting great possibilities for even more growth. New York City, while suffering from the collapse of its industry, was managing to recover faster than other metropolitan areas because it had already begun establishing human-capital-driven industries, from finance to entertainment. Put another way, the post-industrial economy's existence depends on human capital.

Innovators (whether designing semiconductors or graphics for an album cover) need skill sets to do their job—skills that they're likely to learn formally rather than just on the job. So to tease out the relationship between "human capital" and urban or regional productivity, economists often use base educational levels (bachelor's degree or above) as the proxy. In numerous analyses, Edward Glaeser, an energetic and quick-thinking economist at Harvard University's Kennedy School of Government, has tested the relationship between human capital and economic growth. He found out that high human capital in both 1980 and 1990 predicted for even greater concentrations of a skilled labor force and greater economic productivity in the decades that followed.[2]

Richard Florida, a professor of public policy at George Mason University in Virginia, has thoughtfully and cogently expanded ideas about the role social and human capital plays in economic growth. When I first met him in 1999, when I was an undergraduate at Carnegie Mellon University in Pittsburgh where he was then teaching, Florida had started thinking about the differences he observed between cities that were more or less economically vital. Florida had already gained repute for his exploration of the decline of mass production and the rise of high-technology industrial districts in Japan and Silicon Valley, but his study of cities and economic growth took him in a new direction. In a more nuanced view of the "human capital" argument, Florida concluded that successful cities had high concentrations of creative people, what he subsequently termed the "creative class," a much broader category than just artistic and cultural workers.[3] But who are these creative people? It's not so much how much education they had (although that often served as a predictor of how innovative or creative any individual or class of individuals might be in their work lives) as much as it was about what people did with their human capital and how they used their creativity and ideas. Florida used occupational categories instead of educational levels to test each city's performance. For example, an artist, writer, or musician may not have a bachelor's degree, but the jobs themselves require constant innovation. Superstar innovators like Bill Gates are college dropouts, yet masterminds in technological advances for society. Florida's data confirmed that cities and regions with more people in innovative occupations had the economies that did the best overall. Florida's thesis explained a lot of what was going on in Bell's post-industrial economy: People drive growth because their ideas and creativity are integral to innovation, which fuels economic expansion.[4] Places with more people who participate in idea-driven industries and occupations see more economic productivity.

The way the post-industrial economy produces goods and services is markedly different from that of the manufacturing economy. Manufacturing relied heavily on large independent firms that housed their entire production system—from the conception of an idea to the labor to the assembly of a product—within each individual firm, and often located in the same building or plant. Much of the manufacturing economy was inherently "autarkic," a terrible word for self-sufficient, meaning that each firm depended on itself to produce goods. Silicon Valley's technology firms and New York's financial industry operated under almost the exact opposite organizational scheme. Increasingly, these post-industrial firms were engaging in what economists and geographers call "flexible specialization," a term Michael Piore and Charles Sabel coined in 1984. Piore and Sabel argued that the post-industrial economy rested on smaller, specialized firms that relied on one another for different parts of the production line, with each contributing its part to a variety of different goods and services. Another label for this type of production is "vertical disintegration": products rarely passed through a company from top to bottom without ever seeing the outside. Instead of producing all the parts for a computer, now one firm produces the microprocessor, another the hardware infrastructure, others the various sound and video cards, others the software, and so on. Such linkages reduced the risk of investing in a new product—risk was now diffuse among the many firms involved. This organization also allowed for greater product differentiation, because firms could be a part of lots of different types of goods, or at least create different versions of a general prototype.

But the other thing that happened, almost by accident, was that all this transferring of parts and divisions of labor and so on also lent itself to exchange of information and knowledge among the people doing the transactions. People talked. They compared notes. They changed jobs. And when one engineer or designer meets with another to talk about how a new computer's design will fit with the hardware inside, or whether a particular fabric will work with a designer's spring collection, chances are they exchange a lot of ideas—even ideas not necessarily directly related to the task at hand, from the names of other pattern makers to what is going on in Milan's fashion industry. That exchange of knowledge ended up translating into new ideas and product innovations—innovators applied ideas in new contexts, worked to fix problems that plagued firms as a whole, built incremental knowledge that led to break-throughs.[5] As people engaged with others outside their own firms, they often bounced ideas off one another, brainstorming about new products, sharing information about emerging technologies. As people became dependent on one another because of the actual divisions of labor involved in making new products, they discovered that "nonmaterial capital"—human interaction and the sharing of ideas—is equally important to the survival of the company or industry. Economic geographer Michael Storper calls this "untraded interdependencies," and they are crucial in understanding why some places did better than others in the new economy.[6]

Annalee Saxenian, a political scientist and urban planner who is now the dean of the School of Information Management Science at the University of California, Berkeley, explored one of these differences, comparing the success of Silicon Valley with the apparent failure of Boston's Route 128. Route 128, a circumferential high-way that rings Boston about ten miles out from the city center, dividing the city from its more far-flung suburbs, had been the leading producer of high technology for much of the century. But almost overnight in the 1990s, Silicon Valley came to the fore while Route 128 declined. It was not only that Silicon Valley started producing more, but also that it became a leader in innovation in the semiconductor and microprocessor industries. Saxenian interviewed dozens of those who worked in the high-technology industry, from computer programmers to venture capitalists to managers, and those who ran the trade associations that high-tech firms belonged to. What emerged was a distinct difference in how the high-tech industry operated in the two places. Route 128's approach recalled the organization of the manufacturing industry—large, independent firms wary of sharing information with other firms for fear of losing ideas, increasing competition, and declining as a company. Contrast that with Silicon Valley, which fostered a more cooperative, interdependent environment where much of the work was done through decentralized networks of production among lots of smaller firms— a perfect example of Piore and Sabel's flexible specialization.

The Valley's decentralized, cooperative environment helped spawn more innovation and encouraged firms to use the same information and resources in different ways. Much of this dynamic is formalized in what the economist Paul Romer has called "endogenous growth," the ability for wealth, production, and divisions of labor to come from within a particular place without external inputs.[7] Unlike a piece of equipment that becomes less productive over time, as it requires maintenance, isn't compatible with new technology, or ceases to produce products that consumers want, knowledge exhibits increasing returns. It continues to build upon itself and become more productive as firms or individuals interpret the same information in new ways. Instead of becoming less useful over time, one piece of knowledge has infinite applications (or nearly so). But the only way to optimize knowledge and information is to allow more people to attain it. This open and decentralized information sharing is the central distinction between Silicon Valley and Route 128, and why the former was able to be in a state of constant innovation.

Part of what was so interesting about Saxenian's exploration of Silicon Valley was where these exchanges of knowledge occurred. Sure, some of them were happening in boardrooms and offices, but Saxenian discovered the unexpected importance of informal environments, like associations, restaurants, and bars. Prime among these was the Homebrew Computer Club. Its founders advertised it on bulletin boards: "Come to a gathering of people with like-minded interests. Exchange information, swap ideas, help work on a project, whatever." Within several months, the club had over five hundred members. Over the past several decades, as Saxenian reports, Homebrew members have founded more than twenty computer companies, including, most famously, Steve Jobs' Apple and Bill Gates' Microsoft.[8] Or, as Saxenian explained, "The region's social and professional networks were not simply conduits for the dissemination of technical and market information. They also functioned as efficient job search networks."[9]

In the Valley, informal collaboration, information, and ideas outside the workplace proved just as important as the interactions that happened at work. The Homebrew Club used to hang out at the Oasis, a local bar; Google's $1.65 billion purchase of YouTube happened at a Silicon Valley Denny's restaurant. The sheer concentration of like-minded and complementary workers makes these interactions, and the places they occur, meaningful. As Harvard Business School professor Deborah Strumsky and her colleagues discovered, a metropolitan area's ability to generate patents (a pretty good proxy for innovation) is closely linked to the sheer number of inventors located in that metropolitan area.[10] But the real surprise, something that's taken as common wisdom now, was the importance of the industrial and organizational cultures that firms in the Valley embraced. The two worked in tandem, and resulted in lots of like-minded engineers sharing lots of ideas. They may have worked for different companies, but they were focused on what sociologist Pierre Bourdieu called "restricted production": more than making money, they aimed to create ideal computers. The dynamic operated successfully because it had the dense formal structures of labor pool, firms, financial institutions, and so forth that made possible the informal engagement simply because all of these people were sharing the same space. As the seminal economist Alfred Marshall wrote, "So great are the advantages which people following the same skilled trade get from near neighborhood to one another. The mysteries of the trade become no mystery: but are as it were, in the air."[11]

Saxenian's findings in Silicon Valley echo observations that the great urbanist Jane Jacobs made about cities some forty years ago concerning the role of place and the built environment in facilitating the types of environments and interactions that spur innovation. It's useful to start with a little history on the evolution of Jacobs' ideas. Jacobs despised contemporary urban planning, with its knee-jerk tendency to impose physical order on the apparent chaos of the city. Such planning, she argued, dampened creativity, spontaneity, and organic, authentic urban life. In her 1961 book, *The Death and Life of Great American Cities*, Jacobs turned the entire fields of urban planning and urban sociology on their heads. City planning was then focused on creating high-rise housing projects and big parks, both of which stunted the natural composition of urban life. Jacobs argued that these types of projects did not foster the environments that allowed for consistent and spontaneous human interaction, in other words, the social places where people actually interacted. Parks, considered an elixir to urban blight by city planners of the day, became desolate after dark, often encouraging crime and vice, while housing projects rarely engaged with the city around them and were hardly ever located in places with grocery stores, dry cleaners, and coffee shops—the basic components of city life and the very settings where humans interacted. Jacobs' central tenet was that city plans failed to incorporate and encourage the organic nature of human interaction, which smothered the randomness of city life and the possibility of people running into each other. In her 1969 book, *The Economies of Cities*, Jacobs called the social and economic outcomes of these interactions "new combinations"—the very stuff that was going on in Silicon Valley. She believed that a city's structure and its broad avenues and small streets must be amenable to serendipity: the unexpected meetings and social exchanges when streets lend themselves to a variety of functions, what Jacobs called "mixed uses," housing, restaurants, stores, and so forth. Independent physical structures hindered city life in the same way that "autarkic" firms hindered innovation on Route 128.

The very observations that Saxenian and Jacobs made about successful places—critical mass and robust social connections—are the backbone of social network theory. These interactions or "new combinations"—where they occur, how they occur, and which ones are more or less meaningful—have become the central concern of disciplines from sociology to organizational behavior to economics.

More theoretically, scholars have been concerned with answering the broader question: How does human interaction advance careers, disseminate ideas, and fundamentally propel economic vitality? In the late 1960s, Mark Granovetter, then a doctoral student in Harvard University's sociology department, wrote a paper discussing the importance of what he calls "weak ties." As the story goes, Granovetter submitted the paper, "The Strength of Weak Ties," to the *American Sociological Review*, a top journal in the profession, where it was, as he explained to me, "indeed rejected, and very vigorously so . . . I still have the reviews, though I have no idea who wrote them." One of the reviewers so kindly told Granovetter, "Of the innumerable problems with this paper, I will enumerate the first eight." Not to be discouraged, Granovetter resubmitted his paper to another top publication, the *American Journal of Sociology*, where it was accepted and has become one of the most widely cited articles in the entire field of sociology. It lays out the fundamentals for present-day social network theory.[12]

As he told me, Granovetter's theory was a convergence of several different intellectual avenues he had pursued. First was his undergraduate work in science, where he had observed the importance of weak ties in hydrogen bonds in chemistry and Van der Waals forces in physics. As he put it, weak ties "played the role of pulling together otherwise disconnected chunks of the physical world." Second was a lecture he had heard from the Columbia University sociologist Harrison White, who argued it was more effective to pass information through people who were seventh or eight closest to you than those who were more closely tied to you. Third was Granovetter's own dissertation research on finding jobs, where his interviewees were telling him they got their jobs through acquaintances rather than friends. Granovetter identified a pattern across a wide array of disciplines: the ties farther away, not closer, were most influential. And the central point of Granovetter's article reflected this. He argued that the relationships most important in career mobilization and information transference were not those rooted in strong trust bonds but were the linkages between people who are not in close connection to one another. These relationships, the "weak ties," play intricately influential roles in success.

For example, your tie to your doctor (who is probably not personally close to you) is far more important to your health than your friendship with your cousin. Your ability to get a new job is more likely dependent on a wide network of acquaintances who are plugged into a wider network of other acquaintances, further increasing your chance that someone knows someone who is willing to give you a job. As Granovetter puts it, "The contention here is that removal of the average weak tie would do more 'damage' to transmission probabilities than would that of the average strong one."[13] He argues that people with great numbers of weak ties find themselves in the best position to "diffuse innovation." Sounds a lot like the Homebrew Computer Club. "[T]he analysis of processes in interpersonal networks provides the most fruitful micro-macro bridge," wrote Granovetter. He continued, "In one way or another, it is through these networks that small-scale interaction becomes translated into large-scale patterns, and that these, in turn, feed back into small groups."[14]

The more people you are acquainted with, the more likely it is that your information will be diffused and the more economic and social opportunity it will bring. Conversely, remaining linked to a small clique of close acquaintances—say, coworkers in your department—will constrain the spread of knowledge to within that group. You in turn will be less privy to knowledge outside of this insular world. Silicon Valley had more weak ties.

Ten years later, Granovetter wrote another (maybe even more famous) article that examines how socialization interacts with economic production. "Economic Action and Social Structure: The Problem of Embeddedness" argues that economic functions, from doing business to discouraging malfeasance, rest in the construction of social norms and social networks that regulate how people behave. Or as Granovetter puts it, "Most behavior is closely embedded in networks of interpersonal relations and that such an argument avoids the extremes of under-and over socialized views of human action."[15] While Granovetter was mainly concerned with how people establish networks of trust, his point can be applied to how socialization (and its ensuing networks and institutions) influences the creative marketplace.

How Creativity Works

No market relies more heavily on social networks than the exchange of cultural goods—like fashion, art, and music. Cultural industries and their products are driven by taste rather than performance. You buy designer X because others like him and he's appeared on certain tastemakers in the pages of certain magazines or at certain venues, not because his sweater will keep you the warmest. That's not to say that technical proficiency has no bearing on decisions, just that it's not typically the primary factor.

Why we choose to wear what we do or listen to particular music has a lot to do with "taste" and the ways that culture attains value. While initially such processes appear arbitrary, there are real mechanisms by which such taste and value are formed. In his astute book, *Creative Industries: Contracts Between Art and Commerce*, Harvard economist Richard Caves explores creative industries' (like art, music, and poetry) special economic properties. Creative products, Caves argues, may appear simple but are in fact complex, representing the marriage of many strands of research, production, marketing networks. The industries themselves incorporate innovation and meaningful new forms at almost every stage in the production process. Caves argues that there are several properties by which creative industries operate. First, they rely on what Caves calls the *motley crew* property, which entails the combination of diverse people, groups, and industries that work together to produce a good (think of the Hollywood movie industry). They also depend on the *nobody knows* property, which means that it is hard to predict how successful a good or product will be when it hits the market. Further, creative economies have a multiplicative production relationship: every input in the process must be present at the correct time to do its job. The relationships that govern both the input factors (e.g., clothing fabric, costumes, makeup), as well as the market, rely on contracts, most specifically incentive contracts and reputation. Incentive contracts reward those products that add value or become great successes. Producers are paid based on the good's outcome (for example, artwork that actually sells). Reputation works on two levels. First, it influences creative workers to put forth their best work in order to maintain or improve their reputation.

Sloppy or lazy work will undoubtedly be punished by disparaging critiques, which will influence the product's market success. Second, reputation helps alleviate some of the mystery associated with the *nobody knows* property. As art, movies, musical performances, and books are not easily gauged until they are actually experienced, the reputation of an artist often guides buyers to purchasing even if they do not know the satisfaction of the product before hand (e.g., Mark Rothko's paintings, Salman Rushdie's novels, or Bob Dylan's concerts).

Caves' characterization of creative industries ties in quite significantly to the importance of social networks and diversity of firms and labor pools in successful economies. Certain creative industries, like Hollywood's film production or the actual production of records, operate in a middle ground, requiring large-scale, permanent production and investment and at the same time adapting to changing technology, social issues, and fads.[16] Yet the actual recording of music, writing of songs, and so on (the innovational aspect of record producing) for the most part does not require huge production facilities or overhead costs. Here, innovation is amenable and dependent on firms' ability to instantaneously tap into the skill sets of their weak ties. Simultaneously, creative producers themselves depend on firms' instantaneous demands for these skills.

Cities and the Diversity of Weak Ties

So what does all this have to do with Marc Jacobs? The most important distinction of the cultural economy—what makes it so interesting to explore—is that while it is a part of the broader human capital economy, it is taste-driven, not performance-driven. People decide to do business together not because one's semiconductor runs faster or one's piece of property is more profitable, but instead because of what product they like best for whatever reason, a judgment that is primarily subjective. Because of the ambiguity over how to truly measure the success of a product—or even if its success is measurable—social dynamics play a determining role in dictating who to hire to do graphic design or what shoe design to send to production. The economy of art and culture operates in a constant state of "hypersocialization," where weak ties are extraordinarily important. And the social component to these decisions is why the geography of creativity—where creativity happens—becomes so meaningful. Put another way, *place matters* because the social networks are grounded in particular places where culture is produced and consumed.[17]

All of this high-flying social and economic theory points to why my serendipitous meeting with Marc Jacobs' neighbor on a New York City street is consequential. Understanding why New York remains a creative center is unearthing how the social networks within the city work to the economic advantage of artists and designers. Part of this involves actually pinpointing which social dynamics are more important, where they occur, and how, more broadly, the cultural marketplace operates outside of a traditional 9-to-5 firm. And this is why running into a friend of Marc Jacobs on a Saturday afternoon becomes economically meaningful.

Francisco Costa, the creative director for Calvin Klein, explained to me that New York is a marketplace and that fashion design is the ultimate intersection of creativity and economics. He noted, "New York is specifically designed for 'there is business and we're going to make this into a business' which is [after all] an American value. . . . There has to be the business, otherwise there is no point. If people aren't buying the clothes then you're in trouble." Moreover, the subjective nature of creative business makes the social realm the marketplace. As fashion designer Diane von Furstenberg told me, "The social life in New York is very work oriented. Go some place to support someone. There is a support system that weaves and creates the social." In the creative economy, weak ties (e.g., knowing that producer or that graphic designer who you met at a party or recognizing mutual acquaintances) carry great weight because within art and culture weak ties are economic opportunity. Lazaro Hernandez, a star designer of the fashion house Proenza Schouler (which he started with Jack McCollough) explained, it is not so much the physical suppliers (of fabrics, fitters, tailors) that are important, because they will come to you wherever you are. Rather, it is the network of people and industries, the editors, magazines, the public relations, and the celebrities that are essential to selling your product—people who are not personally close to you

Supermodel Alek Wek with fashion designer Diane von Furstenberg backstage at her 2007 autumn/winter show during Fashion Week. Photographer: Andrew Bicknell. Courtesy DVF Studio.

(and not even necessarily in your industry, a topic I will return to later) who make your career. In his book *Neo-Bohemia*, Vanderbilt University sociologist Richard Lloyd looked at Chicago's Wicker Park neighborhood and found that an important function of cultural social networks is the ability to engage with fellow artists who can be a source of critique, support, and collaboration. Similarly, Quincy Jones explained, "It's not musicology, it's sociology . . . It starts with the social. Like with bee-bop, rappers started rapping for each other. Same with jazz musicians, they care about what the jazz musicians think first. Can you play or can you not? Can you really play?"

One musician said, "[Social networks] that's why people come to New York. There is very little that gets done in New York [in art and culture] that is merit-based, they are actually network-based, it boils down to the same maxim: 'It's all who you know' . . . There are seven DJs like me [who have a similar style] but at any given time I will get a lot more gigs because I know more people."

As countless interview subjects noted, people are often picked for the freelance job or the gallery exhibition or the T-shirt design based simply on the premise that they know the person or firm who is hiring them (or the firm knows of them through an intermediary). This distinction between creative production and other industries (law, finance, and so on) is because within cultural production, evaluation of skill sets is subjective. It's not about GRE scores or where one went to school. Coleman, a DJ who regularly spins at Bed and at Bungalow 8 and has done the runway music for Gucci, Yves Saint Laurent, Alexander McQueen, and Zac Posen, bluntly explained, "Everyone [I got jobs with] was from knowing someone. None of them came from me calling up and saying 'Hey, I'm Coleman' . . . Cold calling? Forget about it."

As many of my interview respondents explained, those who you meet socially become those you deal with economically. Boogie Blind, one of the DJs for the now-defunct underground hip-hop group the Xecutioners, noted, "[You] run into them [people who provide economic opportunity] anywhere: record labels, shopping, studio recordings to get projects that turn into money." Or more broadly, as Daniel Jackson of the design and fashion company Surface to Air explained, "Informal social networks are probably the most powerful driver, pretty much everyone we work with we have a personal relationship with."

One DJ, Kevin McHugh, jokingly told me a story of how this happened for him. "I was out on a date three weeks ago, I was really bored. I went to get another drink and ran into someone from Creative Time [a public art organization] and he put me in touch with a music house, a place I was going to contact. I got in touch with them and now I am going to send a demo. . . . Where you socialize, your social life completely determines your worklife and vice versa . . . [We] all go to the same places after a gallery opening, [we] go to the artist's dinner [etc.]."

Or consider Beck, the alternative-rock star/polymath who gave us the international alterna-rap hit "Loser" in 1994 and since then has produced seven major label albums among other independent and movie soundtrack songs. How the hell did that happen? Beck, long a fixture in LA's music club scene, made his break when he was messing around and rapping into the microphone while the main band was setting up. As Beck explained to Joe Donnelly in a fall 2006 interview for *LA Weekly*: "What I used to do is, I'd get up and play my *quote* folk songs. I'd be at Jabberjaw or one of these clubs, and the audience would all be talking or people would be outside smoking cigarettes, and the real band that was playing would be setting up equipment—the band that people were there to see. So there came a point where you're being drowned out by people talking and all that, and you start doing things, like I'd put my guitar down and sing a capella, or I would stomp my foot and start rapping and make up rhymes. And it was really just out of desperation. I did this one night and this guy came up to me, Tom Rothrock [record producer and co-founder of Bong Load Custom Records, which originally released 'Loser' as a single], and kept saying, 'I like that rap you were doing.' And I said, 'Thanks, I was just making it up. And I would love to rap—why not?' He said, 'I know a guy who makes some beats.' I gave him my number and, you know, I don't know what it was, six months or a year later I end up coming by after work to this guy's house, Carl [Stephenson, who co-wrote 'Loser' and co-wrote and produced other Beck songs], who I did my first record with. You know, he had a beat, and I wrote some lines, you know what I mean? And I put some of my slide guitar on there and that was 'Loser.' The whole thing was just sort of ridiculously simple, how it came together, and probably one of the things I worked the least on, but, you know, the best-known thing."[18]

While Beck's story is about Los Angeles (also one of the world's prominent cultural hubs), the point remains the same for New York. Creativity becomes meaningful—economically and so-cially—because the right people are there to translate it into something real and something that is heard and seen. If Beck was rapping into a microphone in Kansas, we wouldn't have "Loser," or Beck for that matter. Being there, hanging out in the scene, matters.

Consider the story of Bill McMullen, who became the graphic designer for the Beastie Boys. As he explained, he had moved to New York to work at Def Jam Records and had become friends with one of his coworkers. His friend invited him to play basketball with a group of friends, who turned out to be the Beastie Boys. While he was not particularly skilled at basketball, he had always been an avid fan of the Beastie Boys, so he sucked up his pride and went along. After a few games, Adam Yauch, the lead singer for the band, said he had heard that Bill was a graphic designer and that they were looking for a designer for the cover of their new album, *Hello Nasty*. Bill didn't think twice, and since then has done the logo for another album and also works on their music video production.

These anecdotes get to an important point, one that appeared again and again in my findings: People hire people they know and engage with in a social environment. Most of the hiring I observed, both freelance and permanent, is initially based on a weak tie that was established in a social setting. Hiring is not primarily based on a strict competition between competing designers, musicians, and writers, but more on the ability for creative people to utilize their social lives to their economic advantage.

My interviews point toward two other intrinsically linked characteristics of the creative economy, characteristics that make its social dynamics so important. First—a point that Bill McMullen's story encapsulates—creative industries can be instantaneous in their demand for new product, often requiring new creative skills at a moment's notice. As I discussed earlier, while social scientists have noted that the new economy forces firms to acquire flexibility and new collaborations to keep up with changing consumer preferences, the dynamics of creative economies are far more capricious and flexible than many other human capital–driven industries. Cultural goods are both trendy and ephemeral (a pair of designer jeans has the half-life of one season at best), and the cross-fertilization that occurs within creative industries requires a diverse labor pool and set of resources.

Because creative production requires near-instantaneous access to skill sets, creative industries and people often need immediate acquaintance with and access to lots of different people. This goes both ways. Firms need freelancers and contract workers as well as a permanent creative labor force, while creative people need employment, both temporary and long term. A new advertising campaign, a new design competition, the city's annual Fashion Week, or even the Council of Fashion Designers of America (CFDA) award show can require last-minute skilled labor. They may even lead to permanent gigs. Regardless, firms have to know where to find the skills they need, and the potential employees have to make themselves known. Social networks are simply the best and most efficient way to do this. And social networks are all about who the people you know know.

The city operates as the instant marketplace for these exchanges. As interviewees explained it, you meet the "right" people at an event or party and then literally run into them on the street (SoHo, particularly near the border of Chinatown, is a hotbed for such contacts) or at another party. Bonnie Young, the senior creative director for Donna Karan International, simply put it, "By accident, by chance I met Donna . . . One of my friends was dating her daughter, we all met out . . . Donna said 'Come work for me!'" Or as Paola Antonelli, chief curator for architecture and design at the Metropolitan Museum of Modern Art, noted, she often finds designers and artists through informal nodes, "all the time, not just at a party but walking down the street." As one respondent explained, "[It is the] physical reality of the city. You run into people, see people on the street. Casual, quick relationships." Another interviewee affirmed, "[You] physically run into people . . . Everyone walks in the city. Everyone I know lives from 14th to Canal."

And this highlights another important distinction about the creative economy. It is simultaneously both systematic and unsystematic. Bill McMullen noted that opportunities arose only when he moved to New York. "When I lived in San Diego and I would bring my stuff to New York, no one would ever call. It's so much by chance, by running into people. . . . It's quick when people need things they pick up the phone and call but so much is just instantaneous and [they] need it now and it's just too much work to contact that guy in San Diego. . . . They may have the sincerest effort to call me but why would they when they can just find someone on the street?"

There has to be some sort of system, though, at least in performing the very quotidian tasks of getting projects together, in assembling the vast and varied "motley crew." But strong ties are rarely necessary, and, even more, are rarely feasible. Gillian Schwartz, the former art director for Kate Spade, explained to me, "So many options in New York, [and] you have this constraint of time so you feel the scramble, so you depend a lot on the people you trust creatively to direct you to the right person . . . Referral is the only way it will work. Which is a bummer because when I first got here I was like 'this sucks' because I couldn't get into the network." Gillian's comments point out both the need to have instantaneous access to a labor pool and its diverse skill sets, as well as the importance of having a social network to attain contact with other creative producers.

In that sense, New York creative producers are walking Rolodexes. They possess many weak ties, which allows them to elevate their own careers but also to place fellow artists with clients and firms who need them. As one artist noted, "There is this larger world of creative producers [who have access to you] . . . [someone might say to me] 'Saw that artist in this show/magazine . . . Do you know anyone who knows this person? [I] want to bring them into this project.'" Many other interviewees noted the same dynamic. They often run into people who explain their project on the fly and then ask if they know anyone who could help. The converse is equally true—that they are contacted as a result of one of their friends or acquaintances recommending their work for a third party's project.

People find success in creative industries by casting a wide net through their networks of weak ties, and by being open to the structured randomness that such ties bring. They use the ties, too, through being friends with creative people who will seek out their skills. By engaging their networks, creative people instigate the dynamics that propel their careers and bring them some measure of economic success. But where exactly do these networks actually occur and what sort of social world do cultural producers hang out in? If it's not boardrooms, then where does the real work of the creative economy happen? Well, it doesn't require a suit, but knowing the bouncer doesn't hurt.

Chapter 5

THE ECONOMICS OF A DANCE FLOOR

David Rabin is the owner of the much celebrated and celebrity-studded Lotus and the Double Seven, touted as the "VVVVIP room for Lotus." When I contacted him for this book, he placed me on the guest list for both venues and invited me down to Lotus for a 1 a.m. Thursday performance of the dance troupe Pilobolus. Around midnight, I arrived at the Double Seven, a seemingly mysterious and obscure lounge on 14th Street in the Meatpacking District. The door had all the accoutrements of the traditional New York nightlife scene: velvet ropes, big men in black suits, skinny women in skintight black pants and cocktail dresses, and big drapes announcing the entrance of the club. After a review of David's personal guest list, the bouncers let me in and I walked down the long dark tunnel into a small lounge lit dimly by candles, and complete with a bar covered in crocodile skin. Most of the women patronizing it were tall, modelish figures, and at a mere 5'8", I was feeling somewhat short and fat. The men there were dressed in the requisite John Varvatos button down and Rogan jeans, while bottles of vodka and freshly squeezed mixers were being delivered to the tables by beautiful bronzed servers, in black uniforms.

David appeared shortly afterwards, a friendly and attractive man wearing jeans and a T-shirt but somehow seamlessly fitting into the upscale lounge. We talked about the club and how excited he was for it to open (it was just twelve days old when I visited it for the first time) and then he said something important. "It's a little slow now, but we're hoping that come September, it [the Double Seven] will be the place for the Fashion Week after-parties."

About ten minutes later, David took me across the street to Lotus, where even at 1 a.m. on a Thursday night the club was teeming with beautiful women in designer jeans and men praying that they had achieved the right ratio of males to attractive females in order to get in the door. Avoiding the crowd, David and I slipped in a side entrance, through a hallway lit by fluorescent lights and stacked with dining room chairs (Lotus does double duty as a restaurant) which led us to a large, open dance floor with a gigantic disco ball sparkling across perfect blond highlights and expensive jewelry. Women teetered around on the crowded floor in three-inch high stilettos, perfectly balancing watermelon martinis while dancing to a remix of Madonna's "Holiday." Above and surrounding the dance floor were alcoves and small private table areas, where "bottle service" starts at $300, and the even more privileged clientele had the option of just observing or the option many took, dancing on top of the sofas and chairs, overlooking the entire crowd.

It is in this node of thumping music, chaos, and glamour that some of the most important business collaborations of the cultural economy occur. Club promoter and DJ Larry Tee explained it like this: "Night clubs are valuable. If you're in a vacuum, you don't get that collision of culture necessary for making new creativity . . . Nightclubs are laboratories for new fashion and new sounds and a way for creative people to get together." Lorraine Gordon, owner of the legendary jazz club the Village Vanguard, put it simply, "Any artist who plays here gets a big push on their career."

The dynamics that propel power business lunches and Silicon Valley's Homebrew Club are present within the cultural economy, and even more ubiquitously and more significantly. Ricky Powell, the photographer who was particularly influential in documenting the 1980s hip-hop and party scene, noted this importance in his own life: "Social [is] very important to me on a professional tip. I like to document while I'm partying, sometimes that's when you get the best shit." While many scholars have attempted, both theoretically and empirically, to understand how innovation occurs in the social, and the role of place in innovation, much of this research has been directed toward manufacturing and high technology.[1] It has long been noted that global business deals often occur in New York's social atmospheres like the 21 Club or the bar at the Four Seasons, while biographies and histories from Bob Dylan's *Chronicles* to the art historian Jed Perl's *New Art City* have recollected the importance of neighborhoods like Greenwich Village and SoHo and bars like the White Horse, Cedar Tavern, or the Artist's Club.[2] In fact, as the story goes, it was partially word-of-mouth around Greenwich Village of Dylan's impressive live performances in small neighborhood clubs that catalyzed his recording deal with Columbia Records in 1961. Yet, while there is a rich cultural history of the importance of informal places where creative people hang out, we know little about how "hanging out" translates into beneficial economic and social outcomes, even though it's almost common knowledge that it does. As the artist Steve Powers put it, "You know what they say . . . Deals are not made in the board room, they're made on the dance floor."

Many scholars have looked at the importance of informal social environments in propelling careers, innovation, and business, and while they have noted the importance of the social in the constructing of economic action, the actual placement of where this social dynamic occurs is left in nebulous space. In other words, they acknowledge its importance but don't quite point to where it happens. Further, the social realm is often considered a positive side effect—or what economists call a "spillover"—of the clustering of formal labor pools, firms, and suppliers.[3] It is not, however, considered a central force in driving economic growth or new ideas. But in the cultural economy, the informal social realm is the center of action, not a spillover of other formal production patterns or clustering of firms and labor pools. Social interactions are essential to the overall production system, and the very concept of what an "institution" is (it's not a university, the government, or a trade association) must be rethought with regard to the creative economy. Art and culture operate in a different capacity.

The Critical Mass of Creativity

How is it possible that many of those I spoke with keep running into people who happen to have jobs or projects for them? How is it that they are able to make a living from their random social networks? How come a party or nightclub in New York City becomes a career or business opportunity? How is it that despite the fact that I found my interview subjects through vastly different sources, they all seemed to know each other—even those in different industries?

On one level, creative people hang out at the same bars, go to the same gallery openings, are in the same gallery openings for that matter, which is an important point that I will return to in greater detail later in this chapter. Ryan McGinness, a young and widely acclaimed artist, whom I had the chance to interview through another contact, had been in a show with both Futura 2000 and Lee Quinones, two graffiti artists I had also interviewed (I had found Lee and Futura through different contacts but they also happen to be friends). Ryan was also friends with several other of the artists I had interviewed even though I had come to know all of these different artists through various different sources. As Steve Powers remarked, "The social network itself is incestuous. Three of the people you mentioned [as artists I had also interviewed] we know or are doing projects with. They're the people who are going to make things happen and they're here [in New York City]." These types of relationships that I found just in my own research methods mimicked very much what is happening and what can happen due to the dense linkages of weak ties within these creative worlds.

Beans, a rapper, explained, "When you go to events n' shit, it's a pretty small town. Everyone knows each other." Valerie Steele, the chief curator and director of the museum at the Fashion Institute of Technology, summed it up in another way, "[In creative industries] people all know each other, they're all sleeping with each other."

These frameworks point to a critical mass of creativity, which explains why cultural producers are able to economically sustain themselves through these social ties. In a way, we can view the concentration of creativity in New York City in the way that Malcolm Gladwell describes the concept of "the tipping point" (also the name of his bestselling book). In other words, there is such a clustering of creative people in New York that a lot of global cultural production (from products to trends to new art movements) originates in New York City. As discussed in chapter 3, the creative economy is significantly more highly concentrated in New York than in any other metropolitan area; it has crossed the point of just having fashion designers or musicians or creative people to actually being the place where cultural ideas and trends emerge and where creative people have to be in order to succeed. There is not only a highly skilled workforce of creative producers but also a significant demand for their services in both creative industries (film, music, video, fashion) and crossover industries such as media and public relations. As the critical mass of creativity is not limited strictly to art and culture but also these other hybrid industries, the city also provides the formal institutions that offer permanent jobs and salaries to those with creative skills. The importance of a dense advertising industry in New York should not be downplayed. Many of the creative producers I interviewed had permanent jobs in one of these industries, such as Sam Wheeler, a musician but also a display designer for Barneys, or Claw, a graffiti writer and fashion editor for *Swindle* magazine (which was founded by Shepard Fairey, who also started the clothing company OBEY), or Stephen Blackwell, a musician and also editor for the indie music magazine *Death + Taxes*.

Further, the concentration of creativity leads to greater chances of more creativity happening. This seems obvious—more creative people leads to more creativity—yet it also indicates that innovation is not entirely capricious and unsystematic. The greater number of creative people lends itself to great possibilities for new innovations, artistic collaborations, and possibilities of discovery of new types of music, fashion, and art. As one musician explained to me, "The chances of a *SPIN* magazine writer being at a show in Kansas City is unlikely but here he could be out with his friends, not even working, and you can be heard by him. The chances of being seen by the right people is much higher." Or as Francisco Costa puts it, "I think the greatest thing [is that] New York is very small—we're always going to the same things, the same galleries, same shows, go to the same movies. There is a collective experience that is hard to get away from." Similarly, the fashion designer Zac Posen explained to me, "The social interaction is being part of the brain of the city—interacting with all different art forms, being interactive with different creative minds . . . Get to see your creations come to life—it's about when you catch someone wearing the bag, stomping in the shoes, twirling in the dress—becoming that Zac Posen woman."

New York City not only possesses a great density of creative industries and skill sets but a varied composition of them as well. It is not just "weak ties" but the dense concentration of different industries and occupations, the diversity of them, that enables many different types of projects and economic prospects. This concept draws back to the earlier discussion of the "motley crew" character-istic of the cultural economy. This incubator of different demands for creativity and the vastly different types of creative skill sets cre-ates a certain diversity of acquaintances that people and firms have access to. The demand for diverse skills matches this diverse and dense supply, which partly explains the great success of the cultural economy in New York. And part of this success lies in the way in which creativity is distributed—in other words, the media, by both offering jobs to artists and writing about and distributing informa-tion about creative industries, further affirms the city's position. As Alan Klotz, a gallery owner, explained to me, "New York is a conglomeration of a lot of people who care about the same passion and people think their passion is worthy to care about." Sally Singer, the fashion news and features director for *Vogue* magazine, put it this way, "Certainly the promotion of culture has been cen-tered here. If a tree falls in the forest and no one hears it . . . well, if it falls here it shows up in Gawker and in the newspaper. . . . Someone is going to make something and someone is going to think their coolness is in writing about it. And we are structurally invested in it. Money is its own art form, it's the whole Warholian curve."

This critical mass of creativity also allows a dense support system to form and encourages the emergence of artistic communities. Or as the guerrilla-street-artist-cum-international-sensation Shepard Fairey put it, "I never really looked at the market. My stuff really resonated with the people I liked to hang out with—the skaters and punks. Luckily I was recognized by people who are tastemakers." It was through initial support from a grassroots (albeit under-ground and subversive) community that Fairey launched his career. According to Robbie Guertin of the indie band Clap Your Hands Say Yeah, "[It is] easier to have more connections. In New York City, everyone is in a band and that really helps. Even Boston or other small cities for a small starting band there are only four or five places to go. In New York, we played in five or six places just in the Lower East Side. There is just more opportunity." Artistic communities often lack the cutthroat competitive spirit that many other industries display, and perhaps this has to do with the very diverse nature of creative goods (how can two artists really compete with one another when their product is aesthetically so different?). From the pre-gentrification days of SoHo to Studio 54, the artistic community has often been one of collective resources and solidarity.

Despite the increasing commodification of cultural production (that big corporations as opposed to small stores and galleries are running a lot of the creative marketplace) and the increasing limits on space and resources, the artistic community thrives in New York, and thus continues to attract cultural producers. As one musician put it, "Definitely an advantage to being here, in that you're friends with other people in bands here and you give each other the leg up." Gordon Hull and Daniel Jackson of Surface to Air talked to me about the Burger Club, which is a group of around forty people involved in creative industries who meet once a month to just hang out and eat hamburgers. Another young artist explained that just having other artists around to talk about the difficulty of trying to get work and establish oneself is comforting and supportive.

Futura 2000 told me the story of how, when he was first starting out in the 1970s and '80s, Basquiat, a fellow artist who was already receiving wide acclaim, gave him money so that he could go get more art supplies. Tobias Wong, a young, controversial artist and industrial designer, explained that the artistic community in New York is so important because he "need[s] the dialogue, [to] see other people's work, respond to theirs, hear their response to mine." This type of artistic community speaks to more than just agglomeration. These linkages of friendship and community are made possible by having a critical mass of creative producers in a particular geographical space.

Nodes of Creative Exchange

If the social is the market, or at the very least, the social begets the economic, then where exactly does the social occur in the first place?

Often, these social interactions take place in the exclusive lounges and bars in SoHo or the Meatpacking District (the ones not frequented by "bridge and tunnels" or regular New Yorkers) or on a

Sunday afternoon at Café Gitane in Nolita or at the tirelessly hip Bungalow 8 or Passerby or during dinner at Babbo or the clandestine basement restaurant, La Esquina.

The original point of meeting is in a particular place, and as most interviewees expressed, a social, entertainment-related, environment. It is this intersection of weak ties and social life that is most distinct to the artistic and cultural economy. Indeed, there is a marketplace for cultural goods, but due to their subjective nature, it is largely influenced by dense social networks which are often how an artist gets into the marketplace, why one piece of art is considered brilliant while another is not, and how gatekeepers (those who valorize goods) and creative producers engage.[4] Howard Becker, a thoughtful sociologist who wrote *Art Worlds*, highlighted the significance of the gallery and the museum, the formal institutions that act as the marketplace between creativity and commerce. While these institutions are important, there is a different type of institution—that of the club, the lounge, the rock and roll venue, and more intangibly "the scene"—that becomes embedded in the economic exchange of creative producers. Or as Jared Hoffman, president of the famous live band venue, the Knitting Factory, explained to me, "There is no doubt that there is a network of art and culture and that it focuses on certain institutions at certain times. The Knitting Factory has been fortunate to be in that position for fourteen years."

The Importance of Nightlife

When I first began this research, I knew there was significance to the role of clubs, restaurants and bars in the establishment of dense, vibrant urban areas. I also knew that artistic types were partial to hanging out in coffee shops and that some neighborhoods were more vibrant than others due to their mixed uses and diverse amenities, an observation Jane Jacobs made some forty years ago. The great sociologist Daniel Bell predicted the rise of intellectual communities that would exchange ideas in social environments. I knew of "industry parties" and that celebrities and high-profile creative producers often showed up at the same clubs and restaurants (as reported in the *New York Post*'s Page Six), which made them hip, cool, and difficult to get into. I also knew that while many a club comes and goes, there were some that remained stalwart in the entertainment world. Restaurants like Mario Batali's Babbo and clubs like Lotus and Bungalow 8 continue year after year to be the hosts of fashion after-parties, music release events, and celebrity birthday parties (all nexuses of creative people from different industries). Part of this is what the University of Chicago sociologist Terry Clark calls the "city as entertainment machine." Clark has spent the past several decades collecting data on entertainment and amenities, and argues that amenities and entertainment are essential in driving growth as attractors of talent.

But what I kept finding out when I talked to people was that it was not just about creating places for people to hang out or be entertained. It was not just that celebrities and creative people hung out in these places and got drunk, snorted coke, and danced all night. These places are also the sites of meaningful social and economic interaction—they are nodes of creative exchange, which forces us to look at entertainment venues in a totally different way.[5] While Ed Glaeser and Terry Clark have viewed cities as becoming concentrated in amenities such that they are sites of consumption, part of what is occurring in these nodes of creative exchange has less to do with consumption and their role as amenities in attracting people. Instead, it is about how creative people use these places as ways to advance their own careers and the cultural economy more broadly.

The Bungalow 8 and the SoHo of the creative industries are the Marshallian industrial districts of the Industrial Revolution. And they are speaking the same language—there is that something "in the air,"[6] as Marshall put it, these are places where knowledge is exchanged in the most casual but significant capacities. It isn't just over social engagements like dinner or power lunches but through music venues, gallery openings, and DJ nights that real knowledge and collaborations and product review are occurring.

Nightlife is economically meaningful in the creative world. As Quincy Jones explained, "Because it's about interacting. People interacting with each other, it's very important." And particular places are especially significant for specific industries. Places like

APT and Cielo in the Meatpacking District and Table 50 and the now-closed CBGB are huge sites for musicians, while the restaurant Indochine is a big fashion industry hangout. Other places like Happy Valley, Passerby, Lotus, Stereo, Marquee, Soho House, and Max Fish are great centers for creative people across all industries. Francisco Costa put it this way: "Why do people go to Bungalow 8? Because there are people there that are interesting and she's—Amy [Sacco]—been able to create a space that you want to be part of it, you want to be there because you want to be there to see people that interest you." Or as one music manager said to me, "If you're in the music industry, the club is your work atmosphere." Daniel Jackson, designer and cofounder of Surface to Air, corroborated, "A Friday night at APT is where you meet someone and work comes out of it . . . certain places like Max Fish are centers with lots of creative producers." It is in these nodes of creative exchange that meaningful economic and social production emerge that is beneficial for firms and creative workers alike. "DJ culture is really interesting. It's a love-jealousy thing. They congregate together to discuss what they're playing, the places they feel comfortable playing, the gripes about DJ-ing, also trainspotting [looking at what other people are playing]," one interviewee explained. Another relayed that Coffee Shop in Union Square is used as a market where models are scouted and signed. As such, many of the waitresses are aspiring models and many of the customers are modeling agents. Several interviewees noted that on the last Monday of the month, underground DJ legend Bobbito Garcia spins records at APT and the music industry comes in droves to listen but also to trade ideas and talk shop. Q, the agent for the now-defunct Xecutioners, explained that he went to Cielo to try to get a major Drum and Bass DJ to work with his group, "Talking business while Roni is spinning records." Or as Ricky Powell told me, "One night these dudes invited me out for drinks. I didn't want to go, then I said [to myself] 'go'—so you're in their sites—that's business for me but it's fun."

Other interviewees spoke of less calculated efforts to mix social with economic but nonetheless experienced similar situations. As the rapper Beans noted of Fez, a long-established lounge in the SoHo/Nolita section of Manhattan, "Everything started from the Fez. Different people see you at one show and ask you to perform

The once-bohemian now celebrity and hipster hangout, 24/7 diner Florent on Gansevoort Street in the Meatpacking District. Photographer: Frederick McSwain. © Frederick McSwain. Used by permission.

. . . Meet various people 'I saw you here, I saw you play here' they want to book you. . . . Fez was like Minton's Playhouse for us. Playhouse was where bebop [originated] and Charles Parker [hung out] . . . where they could work out ideas. Fez was like that for us. It was poetry—that's where I met a lot of people who are consistently doing stuff now. Actress Sonya Sohn when she was a poet . . . Nas came through there. Met Mos Def there too." Or as musician Sam Wheeler told me, "A guy I play pool with all the time at one of the Williamsburg pool places happens to be the A&R guy for Columbia [Records]. Anywhere else in the country, I wouldn't be talking music with people who work in music and he's hooking us up with Columbia stuff and bringing the VP to our next show.

The people you run into out [in nightlife] are people who are doing what you are interested in and they can help you and you can help them . . . Socially, there is a scene, hot places to hang out that everyone wants to go to and everyone who is in the know to what is going on and who want to, they're going to be there." Sally Singer of *Vogue* summed it up simply, "In an industry such as mine that is intensely collaborative . . . you can make a dress but you need a pretty girl to put it on and a place to take her or nobody is going to see the dress. From a completely technical perspective, you need a community to execute this and that is what New York is." Or as Ingrid Sischy explained, "I think it's a combination of elements that makes it. New York seems to be such a vibrant place for, I guess, the cooking up of things. I think it has to do with the combination of the physical and the sociological—the physical structure of how we live, and the mix of people. We're packed into these holes; so much of our lives goes on outside of our holes. For many, many years I lived in a basement apartment. We meet out there in places of public exchange."

Club owners are sensitive to these dynamics, and many try to cultivate themselves as nodes of creative exchange. Legendary founder and owner of CBGB, Hilly Kristal summed it up: "Starting back when I started the place, I decided to make this a place where creativity was necessary and the only way people could play is if they played their own stuff. I found that there was a grand scheme of poets, writers, musicians and actors all here and they were all together and overlapping. . . . I think many artists are musicians and vice versa. Patti Smith is both a musician and a poet. Ginsberg was always in here performing. It's a natural state and always has been. Rock n roll club, we cater to originality." Jo Addy of the members-only SoHo House explained, "[It's about] creating an environment for likeminded people to socialize . . . Come to SoHo House for one night and you see everyone, do your five minutes of business. People don't necessarily want to talk business, inevitably they do." Further, Jo explained that SoHo House actively tries to establish a creative center, "It's not about the money [membership fees], it's about what they do. Might be someone who is not yet a famous director but we think they have potential and they will be mixing with the big boys. It's about what you bring to the club. If we let all the suits in it would just become the Four Seasons bar on a Thursday night." An interviewee who runs an exclusive club and asked to remain anonymous admitted that, "If you are a top designer, famous actor, you are on the top of the list [to get a membership]. If you are a banker you stay on the waitlist." Saidah Blount, who does public relations and events for APT, also shared that the club actively works to nurture a culturally rich environment, "[APT is] a place that takes all those elements, art, music, fashion, literature and puts it all together in a way that is digestible . . . I think one of the reasons Marquee [another club in the Chelsea area] misses it is that it only does nightlife and fashion . . . Amy Sacco mixed a lot of things together, book readings and fashion shows, built a place where you never knew what elements would be fused together . . . Understood the goal of nightlife is to mix it up."

Saidah went on to explain that particular nights, while informally so, draw in different creative producers: "[We get] young T-shirt designers and jeans designers, Rogan, Earnest Sewn kids, kids from Stussy and Bape. Gay fashion industry on Sundays . . . Young gay kids from Levis and Puma up to the big guys who work for Hugo Boss . . . They do [talk business]. Weird unspoken line but you'll say 'Oh, I'm working on a project' [And they'll say] 'Oh really? Drop me a line tomorrow' . . . talking shop is big but it's unspoken but talking shop happens." Many of these club owners' and event planners' comments point toward the ambivalent motivations that occur within creative industries: Creative producers are well aware of the significance of their social life to their careers but they are uncomfortable formalizing it or being overt. There is the unspoken understanding that business is being conducted without formally constructing events with the ostensible goal of doing business.

Formal Institutions

There are also the formal social events such as industry parties and gallery openings that are actively organized to promote greater collaboration across industries and also among those in an industry. Across the board, interviewees were open about how essential these

Artist Ryan McGinness painting in his studio. Photographer: Melissa Webster. © Melissa Webster. Used by permission.

social events were to their careers or rather, the social is constantly the nexus between art and commerce.

The artist Ryan McGinness explained the systematic way in which this occurs in the art world: "Artists go to shows to meet people who write about art, meet them again and again [at gallery openings and shows], pretty soon call them up and invite them to their show." It doesn't hurt that there are over 318 art galleries in Chelsea alone—tons more than SoHo had in its heyday. Between 10th and 11th Avenues on West 25th Street alone there are over sixty galleries.[7] This agglomeration of galleries (and their ensuing parties) creates the type of environment that allows art, commerce, and society to function as a broader economy. As Ben Dietz, a DJ who also works for *Vice* magazine, explained, "The reason it happens in New York more than anywhere else is because well, by virtue of a story . . . I got back from Australia, had no money and [was] skateboarding around town. Well, to preserve my network, I would go to art galleries and magazine parties, run into a lot of people there . . . [It's the] *Cheers* phenomenon in any number of different places." Total Eclipse, a hip-hop DJ for the Xecutioners, put it this way: "If you're a recording artist there are a lot of people who take interest, but it helps to be seen. Parties and functions make it a small world for artists to collaborate. A person may not like your music but if you're actively going to different functions and you actually meet then you can collaborate and make a whole new sound . . . Magazine parties, publishing parties. Publishing companies throw a lot of parties so artists can meet one another. Awards ceremonies are good too . . . When I met Pharrell at a magazine party . . . we finally met up at the *VIBE* magazine party. We just kicked it and hung out and then afterwards I started DJ-ing for him."

As one art director shared, "When I think about it, I met all these people [who gave me projects] at parties . . . like gallery openings or a dinner party or a barbeque. Honestly, like any social event." Another musician corroborated, "Bands I've been at a party with and they're like 'we should play a show together' and I gave them a demo and we play a show together."

Formal institutions and industry parties are also where jobs are offered. The same galleries that hold art openings also provide employment and economic security in a very tangible sense to those who work on the openings, curate the exhibitions, and run administration and management. Formal institutions operate as hybrids because they are the centers of official economic transactions (the selling of art, the hiring of a labor force) but also lend themselves to tacit knowledge exchange and informal collaborations and social networks that emerge as a part of a broader phenomenon that these formal and informal nodes of creative exchange offer, otherwise known as the "scene."

The Importance of Scenes

It was a cold evening in the early days of March when I met Lee Quinones outside a Cuban restaurant in SoHo. Lee was carrying two big bags of Adidas shelled-toe sneakers, a.k.a. the "Superstar," that he had recently been commissioned by Adidas to design. They were selling for thousands of dollars on eBay and were a prized collector item for sneakerheads. Lee, a slight man in his early forties, was born in Puerto Rico and grew up in the projects on the Lower East Side of Manhattan. Lee had an energy about him that teenagers would envy, and while he had staked his claim in the art world by being a major graffiti writer in the 1970s and '80s who then made it in a major way in art galleries around the world, he was also a bit of a poet, jiving and jamming with hip-hop colloquialisms and fast humor. Lee and I went to Lucky Strike and ate French fries for a while before we headed off to the SoHo-based Deitch Project's opening of Os Gemeos, a Brazillian graffiti duo, and the photographer and documentary maker David LaChappelle's "Artists and Prostitutes" exhibition. When we got to the opening, it was packed, the Jay-Z/Linkin Park remix was blasting from the speakers, the lights were off, and the space was mobbed. Inside were the provocative photos of LaChappelle, flickering through a movie projector. The crowd was spilling out of the gallery, creating a party scene leading down the street to the other art space featuring the bright, playful psychedelic paintings and installations of Os Gemeos. All the while, Lee was being followed by a film crew that was doing a documentary on his life.

The works of LaChappelle and Os Gemeos were impressive and startling, but the motley crew of gallery-goers seemed less intent on the art and far more interested in interacting with one another. And so we come to an interesting point about these nodes of creative exchange. They operate on two distinct levels: in a formal transfusion of information (the artwork, the opening, the movie premiere, the rock show) and as a place of exchange for the subculture that comes to the more formalized event.

Both formal and informal, these spaces act as particular "scenes." Scenes have dual purposes—on one level is their ostensible purpose (e.g., selling art, serving cocktails, being a live band

venue), on the other is what happens within the social life surrounding the venue. In other words, scenes provide the site for cultural production.

One of the most important contributions to this exploration is
Dick Hebdige's 1979 study of London punk culture, *Subculture:
The Meaning of Style*. Hebdige, now a cultural and media theorist
at the University of California, Santa Barbara, wanted to decons-
truct the way culture is borrowed, interpreted, and exchanged in
our daily lives, something that he argues is often overlooked. The
very notion of culture "extends beyond the library, the opera-house
and the theatre to encompass the whole of everyday life." Hebdige,
who spent much time actually hanging out in the London punk
scene in the mid-seventies, argued that young punk rockers were
borrowing Afro-Caribbean symbols, music and so forth in efforts
to form a resistant subculture and style that was "pregnant with

Artwork by Brazillian graffiti duo Os Gemeos on Bedford Avenue in Williamsburg, Brooklyn. Photographer: Frederick McSwain. © Frederick McSwain. Used by permission.

significance." One of his findings was the significance of particular places—from the London shop Sex to gritty working-class pubs— the importance of particular scenes—in the production of the subculture. Similarly, University of Chicago sociologist Terry Clark has made recent significant advances to the study of the relationship between scene and place, by articulating the types of amenities (from coffee shops to art galleries to bars) that indicate the presence of a particular scene or subculture.

The story of New York's cultural scene tells us that different geographical locations play different roles for particular types of creative expression, and these nodes act on several levels. There are the obvious sorts like galleries for artists and music venues for rock bands, but digging beneath these formal institutions, certain places become great sites of creative exchange within a scene. Even with the closing of music haven CBGB, the music is still being played in hundreds of venues stretching from the Lower East Side to Williamsburg to the East Village and farther uptown. As one *New York Times* writer put it, "There are no reliable statistics about the flux of the quality of clubs over the years, but in general the ashes-to-ashes principle applies: when one closes, another opens."[8] Drawing from what Hebdige found in the blending of cultural symbols in London subcultures, particular sites evolve and support different

scenes over time. CBGB, while initially a center for bluegrass and folk music, increasingly became a place for punk and rock and roll. Max Fish, a colorful bar on Ludlow in the Lower East Side, has become a center for different subcultures of creativity: "Max Fish, known as a skater bar, started out as an art bar, and then skaters . . . now [it is a] hang out for skaters, junkies, artists and fashionistas," one interviewee explained. Daniel Jackson discussed a more casual scene that acted in the same capacity as formal nodes of entertainment and scenes: "[Back when we were at NYU] we had a big loft on 17th and Broadway and we used to turn big events or 'happenings' at my place with art. It is immediately more effective than showing slides at galleries . . . [Our happenings] were fun and organic but also meaningful . . . [we] didn't set out to create an underground art scene but we did anyway." The "Writers' Bench" at the 149th Street subway stop on the number 2 line has historically been the site where graffiti writers congregated and evaluated each others' "train bombing" (massive graffiti pieces on the outside of trains) as the trains went by. Or as Colt45, a graffiti artist on the NYPD's Vandal Squad most wanted list, explained it, "We [his graffiti crew, TC5] hang out at the same bar all the time and they [other rival graffiti crews] don't care . . . they have beef with us but they still stay away."

East Village beauty salon turned cocktail lounge, Beauty Bar, where you can get both "martinis and manicures." Photographer: Frederick McSwain. © Frederick McSwain. Used by permission.

Entire neighborhoods become scenes for particular cultural realms—Chelsea for art, SoHo for fashion, the Lower East Side for music and art, the Bowery for music—because they offer a fusion of the necessary formal events and dissemination of knowledge within the creative world and because they become the causal node for other types of creative economic and social exchange. And increasingly, the geographic boundaries of neighborhoods and "hangouts" become blurred as creative people tend to flock to the same places—the "scene" is that of "art and culture" as opposed to the stark demarcations outlined by Hebdige in London's punk scene, or what Clark found with regard to the different types of amenities

particular socioeconomic groups are drawn to. Instead, what can be observed is broader "creative scenes" that manifest themselves in diverse, open and amenity-rich places. In the same spirit, the great French sociologist Pierre Bourdieu characterized the many realms within art and culture as the "field of creative production."[9] In other words, the diverse people and institutions within the cultural economy operate in a broader symbiosis. So a place like Max Fish may historically attract street subculture, but it's still a place for art and culture in general.

Scenes, Nodes, and Gatekeepers

While I have discussed many of the important functions that places, particularly nightclubs and social venues, provide in terms of opportunities for projects, collaborations among different creative producers, and also the exchange of information, these nodes of creative exchange provide another crucial element to economic life—access to gatekeepers. Clark and Hebdige have allowed us to see the meaningfulness of scenes as both a symbolic form and a site for production. But the New York story tells us even more: What I found within art and culture was that scenes provided an economic function by becoming the nodes where cultural producers engage those who are responsible for selling and evaluating cultural products. Social scenes, while demonstrating fluidity, manifest themselves in space and it is at this junction where the social produces the economic. As Jeffrey Deitch put it in a *New York Times* interview, "Let's say there's someone, a well-known collector, who sees it [a piece of art he or she likes] . . . and then we're at a party that night, and I'll say, 'Oh, I want to introduce you to that artist whose work you liked.'"[10]

I do not want to talk about gatekeepers to a great extent here because I will discuss their importance and role in the next chapter, but I think it is important at this point to recognize the significance of geography in how cultural products are valorized. Anyone who even glances at *US Weekly* or *People* magazine, the celebrity-obsessed blogs *Perez Hilton* or *Gawker*, or, in New York specifically, the *New York Post*'s Page Six or the *New York Times*' Sunday Styles section, knows the importance of particular places for highly influential people and tastemakers. These places are also the critical sites where tastemakers meet creative producers. Or as Ray Pirkle, who is responsible for the start of the hip and trendy SoHo Grand Hotel, Tribeca Grand Hotel, and the lounge APT, along with being the general manager for Amy Sacco's restaurant Bette, pointed out, "Very few people make the decisions that change people's lives and they tend to like to hang out together."

It is long known in the fashion world that the young iconoclastic designer Lazaro Hernandez of Proenza Schouler first met *Vogue* editor in chief Anna Wintour on a first-class plane out of New York City, where he passed her a note, and the rest is history. Is this an accident or just coincidence? As Valerie Steele of FIT put it, "How happenstance is it? If you're flying back and forth to Paris you put yourself in a position to run in. Accidents don't happen." Alan Klotz, the photography gallery owner, explained that photographers were constantly coming in to meet with him and engage him in the possibility of showing their work. The very day I was interviewing Lazaro, he was off to a dinner party at Calvin Klein supermodel Natalia Vodianova's house. Lazaro explained that these were often great events for meeting celebrity stylists who are the well known conduit for getting one's clothing on a celebrity and into the public eye.

Take Soheil Nassari, a young and successful pianist who has played at Lincoln Center, Carnegie Hall, and around the world. He said that he had played several different recitals and had unsuccessfully attempted to get major music critics from New York media to come to his show. One night while partying late into the night at Lotus, he met a fellow club-goer who invited him to the photographer Patrick McMullan's birthday party. At McMullan's party (held at Eugene), Soheil met Richard Turley. Turley was a contributing writer to the *New York Post*'s Page Six, the daily gossip page that documents celebrity antics. In the world of media and entertainment, getting on Page Six is something of a debutante ball—it means you have finally arrived into celebrity. They became fast friends, and Turley then invited Soheil to a *Gotham* magazine dinner hosted by Richard Johnson, the chief writer for Page Six. Soheil met Johnson and exchanged contact information. Johnson told him to email him any time Soheil saw celebrities doing silly things and Johnson would plug him in boldface on Page Six as well. Soheil couldn't believe his luck and has subsequently made it into the gossip column several times. His fame, he found, concurrently increased.

Countless other interviewees shared similar experiences of going to particular places where the opportunity exists to meet either influential people within their industry who either valorize their products through their editorials or galleries, or people who will put them in contact with gatekeepers. While many are motivated to socialize for business reasons, a lot is uncalculated and coincidental and occurs because of the critical mass of cultural people in the same geography. As Andy Spade explained, "There is a community of people that cross over. You tend to go to the same restaurants, the same clubs. You walk into Indochine on any night and see the fashion world. [At] Passerby, you're going to run into AsFour [fashion house] and so many people . . . People like to stay together, it's generated by word of mouth and underground. . . . I live right in the middle of the Upper East Side, where it is totally generic, but I don't go out there. But you know you might run into one of your neighbors at a Deitch opening. Go to Elaine's, it's uptown but it's still a scene. They party as hard as the Misshapes [New York–based

DJs with a cult following] but they just do it differently . . . I think people use it [nightlife] quite a bit. Sometimes we'll [Kate and Andy] attend a party and we'll end up meeting someone we'd do a collaboration with."

The Social Production System

What these different dynamics speak to is a broader agglomeration of social synergies, networks, and institutions that allow for knowledge, skill sets, projects, and evaluation processes to interact in a flexible, informal, and largely efficient social production system. For decades, economists, urban planners, and geographers have been looking at the geographic clustering of the formal, physical production processes (from wine making to film studios) and the highly skilled people who are associated with it. The social component of these agglomerations has largely been considered a positive spillover due to the dense concentration of people and firms within related industries being in such close proximity to one another.[11] What I found out is that the social is an important production system for disseminating ideas, valorizing goods and services, and distributing jobs and skill sets across the creative economy, in and of its own right. The social production process may be highly informal and unsystematic, yet its role in producing art and culture is invaluable. Further, artistic and cultural producers are fully cognizant of the system's importance in the optimization of the creative economy, and that their decisions to locate or remain within New York City are a function of their awareness of the need to be a part of the social agglomeration. As Andy Spade put it, "We came here for the creative stuff . . . we came here because of the magazines we read—*Interview*, not *Forbes* or *Fortune*. You can live in a 100-square-foot apartment and if you are around interesting people doing interesting things, who cares about a 3,000-square-foot apartment? I know I can't get this anywhere else, so I will compromise." This is not to say that the physical and formal components of the creative economy are not important. What it is to say, however, is that the social production system should be seen as a significant contributor (not merely a "spillover") to the long-standing robustness of New York City's artistic and cultural economy.

These results point to a new way of looking at geographical clustering. The physical and formal production system (from labor pools to supply chains) to which scholars attribute the success of urban and regional economies is only part of the story. Because so much of artistic and cultural production is idea driven, it is the social clustering that may matter the most. Other parts of the production chain may locate in other places, but the dense social scene is what propels the innovation and dispersing of new knowledge. Moreover, for the creative economy, the cultural labor pool appears to locate in New York because of the need to access the social dynamics, and this desire is often primary in why they choose New York over other cities. These findings have implications for other knowledge-based industries as well. Scholars have often looked at agglomerations first through a lens focusing on formal structures and institutions (from universities to R&D labs). We may, however, learn more about how knowledge-based economies optimize themselves by also considering the impact of their social structure, not as a spillover, but as an independently viable production system.

Spatially Bound Creative Chaos

While the types of engagements discussed in this chapter happen both formally in the shape of industry parties or openings or fashion shows and also informally by going to the hottest new restaurant, lounge, or bar, one thing becomes certain—these meeting points are spatially bound and very much a product of the geography of the built environment and part of a larger social production system. In other words, how the physical space of New York has been constructed and the spatial configuration of neighborhoods and the institutions within them have propelled New York's ability to optimize its creative economy. The dynamics within creativity happen in particular places that remain in the same metropolitan geography of New York City. Or as one DJ I interviewed put it, "It's not New York because of the MoMA. . . I would be nowhere I am [now] if I didn't live in New York City, like if I lived in Stroudsburg, Pennsylvania. New York City offers a higher opportunity to be exposed to hip-hop . . . Chicago and Detroit have only four or five successful people [DJs] . . . Don't have the informal resources. Know how people say you 'got lucky'? You put yourself in the position to become lucky." This quote, and this book more broadly, refute a common perception in the arts and culture literature: that a city's formal institutions, arts and culture policy, and funding capacities play the most important role in the location decisions of cultural producers. The interviewees I spoke with point to a completely opposite finding: formal institutions have not been particularly instrumental in artistic and cultural careers, even for those who have attained wide acclaim and credibility and have actually been a part of public art projects. As Tobias Wong commented, "Have you ever seen the applications for them [grants]?" and then went on to explain how long and arduous the application process would be.

Instead, what all of the creative producers that I interviewed emphasized was being in the same geographic space as those who are instrumental to your career and valorize your product and also other creative types with whom one can collaborate, share ideas, and attain new projects. Formal institutions' greatest use is their physical infrastructure that provides the nexus for art and economics to converge. While formal institutions (from galleries to foundations) do offer financial resources, many interviewees said that this type of support was not as effective or as ubiquitous as the general public may believe. Although formal institutions do provide important resources, it is the social world that propels the creative economy. Much of this fusion occurs outside of formal institutions and in smaller galleries and underground events. The most important thing is that creative producers—those who supply and demand, evaluate and valorize creative skills and goods—find a node in which their market can manifest itself.

While which creative product becomes successful may be somewhat arbitrary, and the path in which a creative person accesses those gatekeepers or watershed projects that make their career may be unsystematic and random, the geography in which this social production system occurs is not random at all. Or as Lazaro Hernandez remarked, "If you want to be in fashion, you must be in New York." So in many ways, the creative producers that flock to New York, despite high rent costs and increasing gentrification of their older artistic neighborhoods, come here to plug in to this spatially bound creative chaos. They come to plug into this seemingly chaotic network of suppliers, gatekeepers, scenes, and other creative producers to increase their chances of breaking into their industry. They are well aware that they will not run into gatekeepers on a small street in Kansas City, or even San Francisco, Chicago, or Washington, DC. They will not necessarily find the meaningful art community in a place that does not have a dense network of creative producers already in place. They know that their opportunity for projects and collaborations intricately depends on being where other likeminded people are and that they meet these people, who open doors and great opportunities—the chance to become a meaningful part of the cultural world—in the social life of creativity.

Chapter 6

CREATING BUZZ, SELLING COOL

I met the graffiti artist Claw at a Lower East Side coffee shop on East 3rd Street and First Avenue on one viciously cold winter day. The coffee shop's large windows revealed the sun and piercing blue skies, appearing as if it were a hot summer day. The Lower East Side, while the established hipster outpost, is still beyond the periphery of being completely gentrified like the rest of New York City. It still has that gritty, unkempt feel of the 1980s, complete with rampant graffiti and worn down apartment buildings and duplexes. Claw (and that's the name by which you address her), who has made a name for herself by being one of the most celebrated female graffiti artists of all time is not the type of woman you would anticipate scaling walls and running from the cops. Petite, personable, and beautiful, with an olive complexion and a tumble of auburn hair, part of her appeal is that she is both a bad ass and a beauty queen. And indeed, quite an appeal she has. Claw, while still "street-bombing"[1] (she showed me some of her work just a few blocks away), also has clothing lines with Calvin Klein and Ecko, and is the fashion editor for the indie magazine, *Swindle*. How is this possible, while still running away from the law and being a legend on the street? As she sees it, that apparent contradiction allows her to succeed both subversively and commercially. As Claw puts it, "I make a living just being the Claw."

Claw's ability to succeed illustrates three important characteristics of the cultural economy. First is the unique and symbiotic relationship that creative industries have with one another—artistic and cultural industries engage with each other in all parts of their production, from idea generation to hiring new workers to valuing a creative good. Graffiti, art, fashion, design are not as separate as we instinctively think them to be. And often their skill sets cross-fertilize in different creative sectors, allowing creative producers to participate in a variety of different types of culture throughout their careers.

Second, in the last several decades, we have witnessed an increasing "commodification" of cultural goods, which allows culture from punk to hip-hop to be sold in a global marketplace. But in this commodification process, creative industries and creative producers must engage each other and generate new products together on some part for survival, because creative goods are risky and inherently must attract fickle consumer tastes. As discussed before, the more people, firms, and industries able to participate in producing a particular good, the more diffused the risk. These dynamics emerge as a result of the taste-driven, uncertain nature of the cultural economy.

Third is the diverse process by which creative goods are reviewed and valued.[2] It turns out that the way in which value is generated, both culturally and symbolically, does not always go through the traditional channels of museum curator or fashion editor. Cultural producers often act as reviewers for one another.

What has become clear is that in both the commodification and production of culture, creative industries are not independent entities that work in their own vacuums. Instead, industries operate horizontally, engaging with each other through collaboration, sharing skill sets and labor pools, and reviewing and valorizing each other's products—and much of this often begins in the informal or social realm, film directors and musicians hanging out at SoHo House or the Metropolitan Museum's Costume Institute's annual gala that mixes high fashion with high art, and has every A-list celebrity, designer, supermodel, and tastemaker in attendance. That creativity is so fluid that cultural producers from one industry move seamlessly into another (e.g., Claw as graffiti artist and fashion designer, Beyonce and her boyfriend Jay-Z as hip-hop superstars and fashion designers) reconfigures both how products are valued and who values them. (It's not just *Vibe* or *SPIN* magazine that has the last word on music—we know that whichever bands designer Marc Jacobs or director Spike Lee mention in an interview are given instant cachet. That's why iTunes regularly uploads celebrity song playlists for listeners to download.)

Yet all the informal social exchange and sizing up of each others work, or the buzz that surrounds a gallery opening, would not amount to anything if not for the global media conduits that broadcasted the buzz into a forecast of which artist, designer, shoe, or album is about to break—and these media institutions are plugged into the scene because they are located in the same geography as the creative producers and goods they are reviewing. The Costume Institute's gala event is reported for weeks afterward in publications ranging from the *New York Times* to the *Wall Street Journal* to *Vogue* to art magazines. These formal institutions and media outlets that review creative products and cultural events play a vital role in translating informal, social review into meaningful valorization of cultural goods on the global marketplace (Why did Elle MacPherson wear that yellow dress? Hideous or fabulous? Was the Met's tribute to punk deserved, well-thought out? Who has more control over the gala—Anna Wintour, editor of *Vogue*, or the museum itself?) The answers to these questions often dictate the shape of fashion and art for the coming year.

The seamlessness of the creative economy also gives cultural producers flexibility in their choice of which industry to work in, and the choice can be several different industries at the same time, or changing direction mid-career. Graphic designers can work on record album covers and for fashion houses at the same time, while musicians are often actors and fashion designers simultaneously. But we have often, in our depiction of art and culture, categorized actors as actors and musicians as musicians and so forth. On a multitude of levels, this is not the case.

These valuable processes, from reviewing creative products to finding jobs in a variety of different industries, are the very backbone to creating meaning and value for culture, and they occur in particular places—and not the places that are traditionally thought of. Does W magazine really know what's going on with some small designer in Kansas? Maybe, but chances are slim. But W magazine editors are well aware of what everyone is wearing, what music people are listening to, and so forth on a Wednesday night at Bungalow 8 or Cabanas at the Maritime Hotel. Why? Because they are often there too, hanging out and plugging into the scene. New York City's overarching creative scene encompasses fashion, film, art, music, design, and all things artistic and cultural. And the scene is valuable because it's where creative industries interact with each other and generate value. Innovation and creative production processes are far more nuanced, complex, and symbiotic than what economists, sociologists, and geographers have previously thought. Cultural production revolves around three important concepts:

1. The commodification of culture,
2. The symbiotic nature of creative exchange, and
3. Creative review across the cultural economy.

We'll consider each of these in turn.

Commodification and the Conquest of Cool

Shepard Fairey is the man behind the "Andre the Giant Has a Posse" sticker campaign, which started out as a prank and became an international phenomenon. In 1989, stemming from an inside joke with his friend Eric about the wrestler Andre the Giant, Shepard created the first stickers while a student at the Rhode Island School of Design (Shepard's sticker boasts a 7′4″, 520-pound Andre with an expressionless mug). "The Andre stickers started as a joke," writes Shepard, "but I became obsessed with sticking them everywhere both as a way to be mischievous and also put something

Guerrilla street artist Shepard Fairey's wheat-pasted propaganda-style icon on Gansevoort Street in the Meatpacking District. Photographer: Frederick McSwain. © Frederick McSwain. Used by permission.

A Shepard Fairey wheat-pasted image from his OBEY street campaign located in Williamsburg, Brooklyn. Photographer: Frederick McSwain. © Frederick McSwain. Used by permission.

out in the world anonymously that I could still call my own."[3] Quickly enough, the stickers gained appeal and momentum, finding distribution throughout the punk and skater communities, first showing up in Providence, Boston, and New York City. And with the help of a mass of fans interested in supporting the campaign, particularly those in punk, skater, and hip-hop subcultures and gen-

A skater at Tomkins Square Park in the East Village. Photographer: Frederick McSwain. © Frederick McSwain. Used by permission.

The original Andre the Giant sticker from Shepard Fairey's international "experiment in phenomenology." Originally Xeroxed on paper in 1989. Sticker design: Shepard Fairey. © Shepard Fairey. Used by permission.

erally those who embraced anti-authoritarianism and anarchy, the stickers were showing up around the world fast, far, and wide. While the original intent of the campaign appears to be an abstract parody on the pervasiveness of the media (Andre stickers and stencils could be found *everywhere*) and propaganda (more obvious in his later OBEY Giant campaign), the cultish following and the carpet-bomb stickering of cities around the world is a part of what Shepard has called an "experiment in Phenomenology."[4]

Shepard's Andre the Giant Has a Posse campaign evolved into the OBEY Giant campaign. OBEY, which is similar in nature and iconic status but with an even larger following that features stickers, stencils, and wheatpasted posters with Orwellian propaganda-like graphics that are often marked by anti-Bush (as in George W.), anti-war, and anti-corporate sentiments. (Those interested in participating can order a variety of OBEY Giant stickers, sold in bulk, from his Web site.)

As interesting as Shepard's guerrilla subculture campaign is, even more so is its transformation onto the global marketplace. OBEY Giant is not just a sticker campaign, it's a large-scale clothing-magazine-screen-printing-art-producing operation that encapsulates, as Shepard puts it, the "many facets of capitalism and consumer-trend psychology that revolve around supply-and-demand economic theory."[5] OBEY clothing can be found on the backs of skaters, punks, hip-hop musicians, and kids who just like the way it looks. As Shepard explained to me, "The hip-hop kids like my stuff for one reason and then the punk kids with the skinny jeans and vintage T-shirts like my stuff for another reason."

Shepard and his company exemplify two of the most important characteristics of the creative economy: the intersection of fashion, art, music, and design, and the ability for such cultural expression to transform into tremendous economic and social value. "[My goal] is keeping what I am doing accessible. As you get farther and farther up—it's like a pyramid—it becomes harder for a younger artist [to emulate]," Shepard reflects. "I can make pieces that are expensive but I want to sell $35 screen prints and $25 T-shirts. Where I am coming from in my work is that art is empowering. I want people to be able to access me [the stickers, the T-shirts, the art]—it's a template that's easy."

Since his original "experiment," Shepard has started the indie magazine *Swindle* (where Claw is the fashion editor) and the OBEY clothing line, and he has shown his artwork in galleries around the world. In the Warhollian spirit, Shepard has done silkscreen portraits of Chuck D, Noam Chomsky, Debbie Harry, LL Cool J, Jimi Hendrix, and Joey Ramone (among others), he's done the album covers, movie and album posters for a multitude of outlets ranging from the Black Eyed Peas (for their album *Elephunk*) to DJ Shadow to the *Walk the Line* movie poster to a Black Sabbath band poster for Ozzfest, with many of these images having graphic and visual allusions to OBEY or Andre. Recently, he designed the artwork for a limited-edition set of commemorative vintage guitars for Fender. Shepard also DJs at "Dance Right," a weekly party in an old Mexican bar in downtown Los Angeles. All the while, he and his fans, followers, and friends keep up the sticker and poster campaign in cities around the world.

Part of Shepard's success is that he has always seen the fluid and marketable nature of culture. As he put it to me, "I can only speak from my own experience, but growing up in the South and feeling like I didn't fit in with the dominant culture. My mom was captain of the cheerleading team; my dad was captain of the football team. When I was fourteen I started skateboarding and listening to punk rock. It was athletic but also creative and rebellious. Individually, I was influenced by the graphics, the fashion, the music. If you look at what I do, it's all an extension of that—I didn't look at it as art, but as a signifier of my culture: the T-shirts, making my own [skateboard] ramps and my own stickers. It was a very logical extension to apply it to my own stuff and feed back into the very culture that gave it to me. I never saw the compartments [of fashion, art, music design]. I never started as a fine artist and felt like a 'sellout.' I went in the opposite direction. I really like the street artist—you didn't have to submit to a gallery or a magazine, you just went out and did it. . . . A T-shirt is a walking piece of art. When I do a record label's album cover, I am producing art that gives people pleasure while listening. I'll go through the front door, the side door, the back door to get my point across."

The importance of valorizing creativity has to do with the broader transformation of culture into what the cultural theorist

Dick Hebdige has called (drawing from Marx) "the commodity form."[6] In Hebdige's intimate exploration of London's punk culture, he argued that subculture was increasingly being translated into the broader mainstream through mass production, further making it a part of dominant society. The same can be said of contemporary cultural forms.[7] A walk into any department store will allow you to purchase clothing and accoutrements that conjure up anything from the 1960s mod culture to present-day hip-hop. Formally, this discussion over increasing translation of culture into consumer products has been termed the "commodification of culture" or what Thomas Frank has called the "conquest of cool."[8] Frank argues that 1960s hippie subculture has become a glorious tool for advertising and marketing, by allowing those who purchase bohemian artifacts to feel as cool as those who actually participated in the subculture itself. His central argument is that consumers are able to purchase the "coolness" that was once only a product of particular subcultures through the transformation of subculture into mass production of cultural goods (e.g., the tie-dye T-shirts and Birkenstock sandals embraced by the 1960s hippies can now be bought at your local luxury department store). As Frank puts it, "The bohemian cultural style's trajectory [has moved] from adversarial to hegemonic; the story [is] of hip's mutation from native language of the alienated to that of advertising."[9]

Hip-hop culture is probably the clearest example of this commodification. The commodification of hip-hop has allowed the mainstream to buy into its mythology as the voice of the marginalized, the edgy, and more broadly, the street, creating unique tensions in this transformation. Consumers of hip-hop culture are able to buy their street credibility. As such, many of the contemporary graffiti writers I have interviewed are able to use this credibility to sign with larger corporations such as Pepsi, Nike, and Heineken, which feature their work in commercials and advertisements.

Rob Walker, columnist for the *New York Times Magazine*'s Consumed section, has spent a great deal of time trying to understand these relationships, and their contradictions. As he puts it, "Between the underground world of graffiti culture and the very mainstream one of selling products to consumers . . . Can you call someone a maverick if he sells stuff to multinational corporations? Can

you call him a sell-out if he's willing to risk arrest for the sake of self-expression?"[10] Graffiti artists Futura 2000 and Lee Quinones, along with others such as Cope, have had business deals with Adidas, Nike, Converse, and Northface among other brands, leading to a certain "corporatization" of street culture—or rather these once subversive and transgressive cultures are now part of large corporate mass production. Both Futura's Nike and Lee's Adidas special edition graffiti-inspired sneakers have sold for thousands on eBay. IRAK, considered the most glamorous graffiti crew in New York City, boasts members like Dash Snow and Ryan McGinley, who have become world-famous artists and photographers, the latter documenting the lives of the subculture. Even though most members of IRAK do not write graffiti anymore (mainly because, as one member put it, many are on probation, in jail, or in rehab), they are still selling the IRAK name and continue to meet for "business deals." As one IRAK member put it, "We've been selling sweatshirts at A-life [a sneaker and streetwear store on the Lower East Side of Manhattan] for 180 bucks a piece." McGinley's photograph exhibition, entitled "The Kids Are Alright," depicting a graffiti world filled with drugs, bisexuality, and illegality, was shown at the Whitney Museum in 2003 (making him the museum's youngest artist with a solo show).

The same can be said of rappers and hip-hop musicians. Radio stations like New York City's Hot 97 advertise themselves as "strictly from the streets, yo!" while hip-hop musicians do fashion shoots and events for sneaker companies. Further, a listen to any of the music coming from Hot 97 or Power 105 reveals that hip-hop artists use their innercity origins (whether embellished or not) as a part of their mainstream music careers.

Consider Tupac Shakur, arguably one of the most respected and prolific rap musicians in the history of the genre.[11] Born in Brooklyn in 1971, Tupac moved to Oakland, California, where he later joined the group Digital Underground, first as a dancer and later as a rapper. He then began producing his own albums, each successive one becoming increasingly popular, and started a successful acting career, most notably co-starring in *Poetic Justice* alongside Janet Jackson and later appearing in *Above the Rim*. Increasingly, however, his private life and his musical production were intersecting for better or for worse. Tupac was arrested several times (for assaulting a rapper with a baseball bat, among other deviances) and incarcerated (for sexually assaulting a woman). Despite Tupac's private life problems, his music remained outrageously popular (his platinum album *Me Against the World* remained number one on the charts for four weeks while he was in jail). His thriving career was stopped short when he was shot in 1996 after leaving the Mike Tyson–Bruce Seldon boxing match in Las Vegas. He died six days later. Coincidentally, he was with Suge Knight (the producer of Tupac's label Death Row Records), who in 2005 was also mysteriously shot in the leg while in Miami. This long description of Tupac ties directly into how Tupac and his record labels marketed him. The fact that he was, for all intents and purposes, a thug—both in reality and in his hit songs—lent him the type of credibility that made him a world-renowned rapper. Being deviant, somewhat dangerous, and part of a rebellious subculture gave him cachet.

Tupac's draw to his original cultural landscape is central to hip-hop's credibility. Hip-hop musicians and graffiti writers systematically draw from inner-city culture in their efforts to establish their legitimacy in the marketplace. This marketplace extends from music to the accoutrements of hip-hop culture such as throwback athletic jerseys,[12] hats, big jeans, and expensive sneakers.

Embedded in the pervasiveness of hip-hop is the expectation that musicians will also participate in other forms of production. Part of this latter phenomenon has to do with the demand by consumers to commodify all forms of the culture. It is not enough just to listen to the music, but to also wear the gear and understand the character. As Q, the manager of the Xecutioners, explained to me, "You're not a successful rapper if you don't have your own clothing line or your own movie." Another respondent, who works for Power 105, a hip-hop station in New York City, elaborated this point. "Back in the 90s, Tommy Hilfiger wanted to go different and Grand Puba [a rap star] started wearing Tommy Hilfiger and he [Hilfiger] just exploded onto the hip-hop scene. New hip-hop artists see that as an opportunity to do this themselves so [one] saw Phat Farm [with] Russell Simmons. Back before, in hip-hop everyone was wearing Nautica, Ralph Lauren, and Tommy Hilfiger. Now people are wearing Ecko and Phat Farm [the latter designed by hip-hop mogul Russell Simmons] and you can find this stuff in Macy's."

Or, as Richard Lloyd of the 1970s punk band Television remarked on the changing times, "You have your hip-hop and rap people. What's the first thing they do? They put out a clothing line—that's almost the first thing they do . . . There are people wearing Roca Wear and have no idea that the money is going to some rap person or [they're] wearing Sean John. They don't know it's Puff Daddy, or whatever his name is now."

Starting in the early 1990s, rap musicians were able to sell $50 T-shirts and low-slung jeans, successfully commodifying, as *New York Times* reporter Tracie Rozhon explains, "What many young African-American teenagers had already started wearing: an anti-establishment style influenced by prison inmates, who wore their pants baggy and held up with a piece of rope."[13] These efforts to convert street credibility into cultural products have become big business. Sean Combs, the fashion designer formerly known as the rapper Puff Daddy and now just Diddy, has made a career out of using his street credibility to create an empire. "I come from Harlem, New York and one of the things Harlem is known for is style, making something out of nothing. Nobody has money but everybody knows how to dress." In 2004, Combs' empire translated into $400 million in sales of his namesake's clothing line. Russell Simmons, another rap mogul, sold his clothing line, Phat Fashions, for $140 million in 2004.[14] The reason the fashion lines are so successful is because they are a commodified representation of hip-hop culture. As Beans, a popular rapper, succinctly put it, "Sense of commerce, not necessarily anything to do with music. Does hip-hop sell clothes? Yes, it does."

Commodification provides options for cultural and artistic producers. As Combs himself has said, there is a "synergy" across his "clothing, music and lifestyle" empire.[15] This ability for creative producers to use culture to produce diverse types of creativity also establishes interdependent relationships across industries, for collaboration, resources, commodification, and certification of their creativity.

Mixing It Up

In 2004, the producer/musician/song writer/ DJ Danger Mouse remixed Jay-Z's 2003 *The Black Album* with the Beatles' 1968 *White Album* (whose actual title is just *The Beatles* although the album cover is all white, thus the nickname), and created *The Black and White Album* (popularly known as *The Grey Album*), and what pop critic Chuck Klosterman called "the most popular album in rock history that virtually no one paid for."[16] As DJ Danger Mouse himself explained to Klosterman, "One day I was cleaning my room and listening to the Beatles' *White Album*. I was kind of bored, because the other hip-hop work I was doing was really easy. Someone had sent me an a capella version of *The Black Album* . . . So I'm listening to the *White Album* and I'm putting *The Black Album* away, and I suddenly have this idea: I decide to see if I could take those two albums and make one song, just because of the names of the two albums and because they're perceived as being so different and because I've always loved Ringo Starr's drum sound."[17]

Blending seemingly incongruent elements has become a backbone of new artistic and cultural products. Cultural producers' ability to sell products in another capacity is possible because of the unique open and reflexive relationship that creative industries have with one another. As *New York Times* reporter Tracie Rozhon writes, "[Cultural production has become] an informal mini-conglomerate that has at times included businesses as diverse as music publishing and advertising and restaurants." Part of the emergence of these sorts of horizontal relationships has to do with the amorphous nature of creativity and also the ability of different creative people to share resources, ideas and knowledge to create what Jane Jacobs called "new combinations."[18] Often these new permutations translate into collaborations across industries and new cultural consumer goods—what the economist Joseph Schumpeter termed "creative destruction"[19] (although, writing in 1942, he wasn't talking about rap music). As Shepard Fairey recounted, "Chuck D came in last week and signed a print. I like Public Enemy and Public Enemy likes me and so there's a collaboration."

But what this example also speaks to is the symbiotic, interdependent relationships across creative industries, or rather, artistic and cultural production and commodificiation is not limited to one type of creativity. The cultural economy engages in what we can also call heterarchy, a term Columbia University sociologist David Stark coined to explain the way people in different departments within an organization are able to use their diverse skill sets and resources to create new problem-solving techniques and new innovation by actually engaging parts of the organization that would not normally interact with each other.[20] The same type of dynamic and organizational structure holds true in cultural production.[21]

Creative industries need each other for survival in the marketplace, to generate new ideas and new goods, and as I will discuss later, to valorize their products. Part of this is because just as commodification increasingly has to do with the cultural significance of place, so do the components that valorize these commodities. As fashion designer Diane von Furstenberg explained, "New York to me is like Venice, it is the center of trade—no matter what they sell, what they do, people come and show in New York. . . . [New York] is more than the center where people actually create, [it is] a marketplace. The truth of the matter is that this city is the city of trade, it has been like that since I've been here."

In the broadest sense, everyone knows that creative industries inspire one another. As Lazaro Hernandez of Proenza Schouler pointed out, "Fashion is a reflection of society and what is happening in culture, which is influenced by other creative industries and dynamics." And the examples are endless. As the industrial designer and artist Tobias Wong told me, he made a huge splash when he started creating "knock-off" Burberry plaid buttons, which he would hand out at art shows. Because of Burberry's intense dislike of fake versions of its signature plaid, Wong and those wearing the inauthentic buttons found the entire charade ironic. But the true irony was when Burberry knocked off Wong's fake Burberry buttons and used them in a major advertising campaign, essentially "knocking off the knock-off." Bill McMullen, the graphic designer for the Beastie Boys, who also makes T-shirts, explained to me that his "Full Metal Jackin'" T-shirt is a convergence of several different art forms—drawing from Stanley Kubrick's movie *Full Metal Jacket* but also from street culture, with use of the term "jackin" (stealing cars) and a big picture of an Adidas "shell-toe" sneaker (a shoe popular among hip-hop artists and musicians).

Larry Tee, the legendary nightlife DJ and promoter, is credited with helping bring the transvestite RuPaul to stardom along with reviving Brooklyn's Williamsburg neighborhood into the hipster magnet that it is today. Being a part of New York's nightlife scene for over fifteen years, Larry was able to relate a lucid account of how creative industries seek out inspiration from one another. As the house DJ for Williamsburg's nightclub, Luxx, Larry told me that fashion designers would come just to draw inspiration for their upcoming collections. "A lot of designers were coming to our neighborhood to look at our crowd. Hedi Slimane at Dior, Dolce and Gabbana, John Galliano would come to look at the crowd and dance [at Luxx] . . . catch the vibe because that's their job, to see what's going on in the air." Drawing from the crowd, these designers, particularly Dior, created a new men's line with a "new wave aesthetic . . . young skinny boys, glasses, skinny ties," inspired by the club-goers' attire.

Similarly, the new wave and punk music of the late 1970s inspired fashion, with designers such as Betsey Johnson and Vivienne Westwood making careers out of the ripped up, edgy punk look most crystallized by bands like Television and later the Sex Pistols. Richard Lloyd, the guitarist for Television, noted that Malcolm McLaren (who later managed the New York Dolls and the Sex Pistols) was so taken by Television's ripped clothes and "anti-style glamour of poverty" that he took the look back to London where he and his then-girlfriend Vivienne Westwood owned a clothing shop, Let It Rock (after returning to London, he changed the store's name to SEX). She began designing clothing inspired by the Television look (adding safety pins to make it wearable), creating "torn clothing that was marketable." But as Lloyd points out, "As soon as that happened—everyone wearing spiked hair and rings through their noses—that signaled the end. When you could buy the clothing at Bloomingdales it was over."

Creativity provides inspiration across genres and disciplines—inspiration that often leads to marketable goods (like punk rock clothing). This is, of course, nothing new. While there is no doubt that this latter, profitable result certainly propels those involved to continue to churn out more creative ventures, is not to underestimate the deeper artistic and cultural innovation that occurs. It is the *ability* to translate these new cultural products that are derived from the fusing of different types of creativity into economic value that makes the process particularly relevant to economic development and growth. In this sense, creativity lends itself to the same "increasing returns" within knowledge and human capital that the economist Paul Romer has articulated.[22] Where the creative field operates and produces is instrumental in understanding how it drives regional economies, how the creative production system operates, and why particular geographies are used as idea production sites.

But the fusion across the cultural economy and its ensuing increasing returns to creativity are only possible when there really is a critical mass of diverse creative producers engaging in the same spaces. Sometimes these places are clubs, other times it is just the ability to run into them or access them in an immediate fashion. As Larry Tee explained, "Only happens if there is a community involved. Ficsherspooner and the Scissor Sisters [two bands] by themselves couldn't get to the media. Putting on performance art, putting on fashion shows in my club . . . [We] mobilize community around good creative ideas."

Gatekeepers, or How Buzz Is Created

Another realm of functional properties has to do with how creativity gets the product sold. After production, creativity sells itself to consumers and attains economic value. Since cultural goods are essentially taste-driven, a whole different set of criteria for consumption and purchase exists other than those associated with performance-driven products. Central to this distinction is the fact that taste is somewhat arbitrary but is loaded with social meaning. From "keeping up with the Joneses" to owning the newly reissued Nike Air Force One, consumers mold their taste around conceptions of what is cool, trendy, high brow or exclusive or a myriad of other qualities that fall under the umbrella of "good taste."

The last hundred years have seen sporadic interest in understanding systems of culture and even less tangible frameworks explaining how creative production spreads throughout the broader society. In 1904, the great sociologist George Simmel wrote an article, "Fashion," in which he argued that fashion is a function of class differentiation and a way for elites to separate (and signify this separation) from mass society, along with being a signifier most obviously of "the present." As Simmel wrote, "Fashion always occupies the dividing-line between the past and the future, and consequently conveys a stronger feeling of the present, at least while it is at its height, than most other phenomena."[23] Or rather, think about what is trendy or cutting edge today. Often it alludes to the past (as when a design has elements of the 1920s or touches on 1980s punk rock) but yet has been revamped such that it is obviously a contemporary fashion—and something that will not be fashionable next year (in other words, in the "future"). We can also look at who is wearing what is fashionable. Mostly, it is actresses, musicians, celebrities, people with economic means and so on, thus a very tangible example of class differentiation. People who are barely paying their electric bills are not sporting the latest $300 skinny jeans or the Fendi Spy bag.

Some sixty years later, Herbert Blumer strongly disagreed with Simmel, arguing instead that fashion is a process of "collective selection" or rather that "fashion appears much more as a collective groping for the proximate future than a channeled movement laid down by prestigeful figures."[24] In other words, Blumer argued that fashion was not decided by some elite figure or upper hierarchy. Instead, the processes of creating what is "in fashion" are applicable to larger cultural phenomena. Specifically, trends and fads, while not "inconsequential," are somewhat arbitrary and determined by large groups in society rather than by those occupying influential positions (think Anna Wintour, editor of *Vogue*) on the cultural hierarchy. Part of this collective selection is formalized in an "intense process of selection," marked by avid reading of fashion publications, competitors' scrutiny of each others' lines, and the incorporation of other types of cultural production, such as fine arts, literature, and politics. More recently, Princeton sociologist Paul DiMaggio has argued that taste and cultural distinctions are cultivated through social structure (in other words, who you hang out with and where you hang out).[25]

For those interested in understanding why some cultural production is held in high esteem or sells for large sums of money, the question remains: If taste is arbitrary, how does a consumer actually form his or her idea of good taste? How does she know what shoes to buy, what music to listen to, what art gallery to visit? And if cultural and artistic success is unpredictable, who is most important in creating a more certain chance of success?

Understanding how cultural products are transmitted to a broader collective is a tricky task at best—but marketers, fashion houses, record labels, and department stores have been formalizing the process for as long as consumer goods have been sold. We may on one hand argue that how products become successful is hard to pinpoint, there are indeed particular methods that have been formalized. In 1972, Paul Hirsch, a sociologist now at Northwestern University, wrote a provocative article called "Processing Fads and Fashions: An Organization-Set Analysis of Cultural Industry Systems." In this article, Hirsch argued that cultural industries operate in a "highly uncertain environment" in which cultural goods are produced, yet it is difficult to know which ones will succeed.[26] For example, how do you know which music single will be a hit? Which new bag will Kate Moss or Paris Hilton tote about town? As such, cultural products demand a certain type of system in which the consuming public can be advised as to what products to select. In other words, firms that produce cultural items create highly sophisticated ways to distribute them and to create their value. For example, those he calls "contact men" are hired to formally diffuse information about and to distribute cultural products. Part of their job description includes influencing media gatekeepers and finding new talent to produce more creative goods—and cultural firms depend on this. As Hirsch puts it, "Entrepreneurial organizations in cultural industries require competent intelligence agents and representatives to actively monitor developments at their input and output boundaries. Inability to locate and successfully market new cultural items leads to organizational failure."[27]

In this vein, Rob Walker, the *New York Times Magazine* writer, notes that corporations are well aware of the importance of tastemakers and influentials in inspiring product purchase, so much so that they hire "word-of-mouth agents" and "trend-spreaders" to tell their friends what to buy. "The great mystery of 'Consumed' [Walker's weekly column] is, Why does a certain person decide to buy a certain thing?"[28] The answer lies in who else is buying that certain thing. This is where we arrive at the other crucial function of the networks and nodes of creativity, and that is, they provide the stage where products are evaluated by the tastemakers or gatekeepers responsible for sending signals to consumers regarding the worth of a creative good.

Cultural Gatekeepers

It seemed ironically befitting that in early April 2006, the *New York Daily News* broke the story that Jared Paul Stern, a *New York Post*'s Page Six writer, was allegedly attempting to extort hundreds of thousands of dollars from billionaire businessman Ron Burkle. Stern, as Burkle's recording of meetings seemed to reveal, was using the column's influence and penchant for ruining or catapulting careers and reputations, to get Burkle, the managing partner of Yucaipa Cos., a big company with holdings in media, supermarkets, and clothing companies, to cough up $220,000 so that the gossip column would no longer post unflattering (and at times inaccurate) information about him. The case, which involved the FBI and the

U.S. attorney's office as a part of the sting operation that brought down Stern, shed light on the intricate dealings involved in the making and breaking of a gossip story. For example, in the days that followed the bust-up, it was claimed that other high-profile gentlemen, including movie mogul Harvey Weinstein and business takeover tycoon Ron Perlman, were offering perks such as first-class tickets to the Oscars for Richard Johnson, editor of Page Six, and jobs to Johnson's fiancée, in part so that only flattering information about them would appear in the column. Those accusations turned out to be without merit, and all charges against Stern were dropped. (In retrospect, it seems doubtful that someone as powerful as Richard Johnson needed those kinds of perks, anyway.) But the story tells us something else as well: it sheds light on the influence of gossip columns in the rise and fall of careers, and the cognizance of this influence by those involved in the media and other buzz-driven industries (music, film and so on). In other words, despite the fact that many people view gossip columns as trashy and inaccurate, they are intricately important to the careers of those in the news—so much so that those writing the columns can theoretically extort thousands upon thousands of dollars and perks in order to preserve a person's reputation. As Julian Niccolini, an owner of the Four Seasons, explained in a *New York Times* article, "Of course I care about the column [Page Six]—everyone in my restaurant reads it. . . . It reminds people that you are open, that you are alive, and that you are part of what is going on," explaining that repeated postings in the column were essential for his business.[29] Or as *New York Times* reporter David Carr puts it, "Beneath its gossamer skin of celebrity sightings and innuendo, Page Six occupies a significant coordinate in the business cosmology of New York City. Scores are kept and settled on the page, deals are floated and brands, both personal and corporate, are forged and melted down."

Richard Caves calls them "certifiers," Howard Becker, "aestheticians," Rob Walker, "Magic People." Many know them as gossip columnists, fashion editors, and celebrity magazine writers. While each scholar has a certain nuanced perspective on their role, the general consensus is that those that function in these roles are those that assess an artistic or cultural product and as such assign a value. As Walker puts it, "But whatever the intentions and caveats of the various approaches to the subject, the most typical response . . . is to zero in on the segment that forms the bridge over which certain ideas or products travel into the mainstream—influentials, trend-translators, connectors, alphas, hubs, sneezers, bees, etc. Let's just call them Magic People."[30] Or as *New Yorker* writer Malcolm Gladwell, who calls these people "connectors," writes, "The success of any kind of social epidemic is heavily dependent on the involvement of people with a particular and rare set of social gifts."[31]

It's the *nobody knows* property of creative goods that makes these gatekeepers important. Independent experts or certifiers are essential to the process of creating cultural value because they signal buyers about superior products. As Richard Caves explains it, "Consumption of creative goods, like all other goods, depends on 'tastes,' but for creative goods those tastes emerge from distinctive processes. People invest in developing and refining their tastes for creative goods. They consume them in social contexts, and the 'buzz' that circulates among them is important for organizing production. Although nobody knows its fate when a new creative good appears, social contracts transmit consumers' appraisals at a very low perceived cost to them, giving 'word of mouth' its importance of a creative good's ultimate success."[32]

Bestseller lists, the Academy Awards, magazine photo spreads, and artist profiles in esteemed magazines all act to certify certain artists and their products so that consumers know what to buy. In more subtle (and sometime brazen) ways, TV shows, movies, and celebrities also certify particular products, artists, and labels. (Witness Manolo Blahnik's dizzying success upon being touted as the "It" stiletto by the characters in *Sex and the City*.) Artists desperately need the approval of these institutionalized peer reviewers (unless they have a subversive cult following) to make it to the market. As Caves notes, innovation is just creativity that hits the market. Certifiers are tastemakers, and a breakthrough innovation in creative industries is really "consumers' broad embrace of a novel style."[33]

Ultimately, success in cultural industries (as in humdrum industries, as Caves calls more traditional industry) depends on technological advances and economies of scale, but different from other industries, it particularly relies on a skilled network that picks winners, a point that Malcolm Gladwell made in his famous book *The Tipping Point*. Certifiers act to pick winners and as such give mass consumers the cue as to what to purchase in a *nobody knows* world. These certifiers have enormous power over consumption—they virtually define taste and create status associated with particular products. Creative industries must work fervently to catch the tastemakers' attention, as their livelihood depends significantly on their approval.

When University of Pennsylvania sociologist Diana Crane undertook a large survey of galleries in New York City, she found that key "gatekeeper galleries" were instrumental in catapulting artists' careers. In her book, *The Transformation of the Avant-Garde*, she points out that a limited number of galleries represented the most visible artists who were given the most exhibitions at other galleries and museums and were purchased most frequently by major museums. She notes that these "gatekeeper galleries" were most likely to have shown leading artists first. The galleries were star-makers in that the artists they chose to exhibit or represent often subsequently became successful in the larger market.

So gatekeepers, tastemakers, certifiers, or peer reviewers pick "winners" and speak to consumers at large. Specifically, these groups occupy a larger platform within the media—that of the "expert opinion" through which all cultural products must pass through. Paul Hirsch wrote, "The mass media constitute the institutional subsystem of the cultural industry system. The diffusion of particular fads and fashions is either blocked or facilitated at this strategic checkpoint . . . This output is filtered by mass-media gatekeepers serving as 'institutional regulators of innovation' (Boskoff 1964) . . . no product can enter the societal subsystem (e.g., retail outlets) until it has been processed favorably through each of the preceding levels of organization."[34]

Or more simply, as Zac Posen put it, "Anna Wintour matters big time . . . Absolutely. Media culture has sped up the growth rate of American brands, the speed of infatuation, the idea of new and more. But at the same time it's still make or break." Another interviewee explained, "[In New York, we are] a bunch of likeminded individuals but we need someone who tells us who is good and who is not good. And this is where Anna Wintour comes in. [She says]

I don't do the things you do but I'll tell you what is good. She becomes a node of the critical mass." It must also be said that there can be and are a myriad of different gatekeepers for each industry. Anna Wintour may be the prize, but the editors of *W* magazine, and *Marie Claire,* along with reviews in the *New York Times* Style section or your name in bold face in the *New York Post*'s Page Six, can all provide important openings for a fashion designer's career. Indeed, some of these people, like Ms. Wintour, actually have official jobs to validate creative goods—that of the art critic, the fashion editor, and the museum curator—and they act as the official gatekeepers and aestheticians in the creative economy.[35]

These dynamics can elevate as well as limit the creative success of a product. Saidah Blount, then the head of public relations and events at APT, illuminated the flip side when she talked about the failure of Theo, a trendy SoHo restaurant: "A bad review from the *New York Times* is literally the kiss of death in this town. It [Theo] got two stars instead of three [and closed down thereafter]." Or as Colt45, a major graffiti writer, explained, "There are some people in books, magazines and articles that haven't done as much as those who are virtually unknown. And this is fraudulent in the graffiti world: People who get access to the media without paying dues. *Subway* and *Spray Can Art*—if you were in those books you were considered well-known, but if you weren't, you weren't considered. Mackie wasn't in it, Futura was." The very ability to access a gatekeeper is half of the battle in getting one's products established. Colt45 is not the first graffiti writer to tell me that Futura was not nearly as prolific as the media, galleries, and films have portrayed him to be—but by all accounts, Futura was able to get into the gatekeeper network.

A display designer for Barney's commented, "As my boss says, 'No designer is going to pull out of Barney's.' We're one of those places that can make or break a [fashion designer's] career . . . equivalent in the music industry of pulling out of a major label." The significant characteristic of a gatekeeper is that it is their official job to evaluate the subjective and give it an objective creative value, a similar concept to Caves' "certifiers," they are the final word on the value of a cultural good. Gatekeepers and certifiers are the editors, critics, curators, columnists, and reporters whose job it is to inform the masses about what is good and bad in the creative economy.

If only it were as straightforward as presenting one's creative product to gatekeepers who in turn select what is good. Often, however, the relationship between the gatekeeper and the creative producer has much to do with how much a gatekeeper or critic likes the producer. Or rather, in the same sense that valorizing what is "good art" becomes subjective, so it is also impossible to ignore the social dynamic between a creative producer and a gatekeeper. During a conversation with an event planner for Power 105, a New York City–based hip-hop station, he explained to me that "the record label should have a good relationship [with the radio station]." I then asked him why some songs were played on Power 105 but not on Hot 97, its rival station. He replied, "Take Nas R Jones for example, he might just have a better relationship with 97.1 . . . There was a time when 105 wasn't very happy with R. Kelly because he bailed on concerts with Jay-Z. For a time, you wouldn't have heard an R. Kelly record [on Power 105] and artists know this too."

Valerie Steele, the chief curator and director of the Museum at FIT and a leading scholar on fashion theory, pointed out, "Marc [Jacobs] was helped by being the favorite of all the fashion editors . . . He was a cute, amusing boy . . . Someone like Tom Ford, very good looking, very charming, very sexy. Is he a particularly good designer? Not particularly, but he is marketable." Interview respondents emphasized the importance of creating a positive social relationship with gatekeepers. Gatekeepers, after all, are human beings, and the very fact that creative goods are subjective makes the relationships between the critic and the cultural producer particularly important to the success of a good (as I will discuss shortly).

The Magic Word of Mouth

In 2005, Clap Your Hands Say Yeah, a Brooklyn-based indie band made up of a group of friends from Connecticut College, produced a self-titled album. As Robbie Guertin, a guitarist and keyboardist for the band, explained, "We recorded the first record and we made

Pianos, a longstanding bar and live music venue on Ludlow Street on the Lower East Side. Photographer: Frederick McSwain. © Frederick McSwain. Used by permission.

Clap Your Hands Say Yeah playing at a sold out concert at the Henry Fonda Theater in Los Angeles. Photographer: Rachael Porter. © Rachael Porter. Used by permission.

2,000 copies [thinking] we'll have something to sell at the shows, maybe send to promoters." At this point, Clap Your Hands was a local indie band that played mainly around New York in places like Pianos on the Lower East Side. As both Guertin and another band member, Lee Sargent, explained, their initial audience consisted of friends and friends of their friends. So it came as a pleasant surprise when their self-released album sold out (they had to make thousands more) and Pitchfork Media, a leading online music reviewer, came banging down their door for a copy—and subsequently raved about the record. It wasn't long after that that David Bowie and David Byrne were spotted at their shows, and *Rolling Stone* magazine called them the hot new band in 2005, creating even more of a buzz. Less than a year later, Clap Your Hands embarked on a national and international tour. As Guertin told me, "They [Pitchfork] came to us and asked us for it. After Pitchfork reviewed it, everyone started reviewing it." But if you ask Guertin or Sargent, they'll both tell you: It all just started by word of mouth.

Clap Your Hands' success is indicative of several of the ways that culture gets evaluated. Most obviously, Pitchfork Media played an official role in validating and letting a broader audience know that the music is good. Combine that with sightings of the Thin White Duke (Bowie) and the Talking Heads' front man (Byrne) at their shows and you've got a potent formula of coolness and legitimacy that's impossible to beat.

There are also the tastemakers and influentials, people who may or may not have official roles as critics but are nonetheless influencing what other people buy. Clap Your Hands had a combination of both. As Lazaro Hernandez explained, "Muiccia Prada can dictate to people . . . Like if she says, 'heels are over, flats are back' then other designers may follow suit." But tastemakers are not necessarily famous, and their job is not necessarily that of an official evaluator of creative goods, yet they are a part of an influential sector of the population that conjures up a "buzz" about particular products. Pitchfork, David Bowie, and David Byrne heard about Clap Your Hands on the street—it was as simple, and complex, as that.

In this vein, marketing and advertising agencies, such as BzzAgent, have popped up with strategies that include hiring "cool" people to spread trends via word of mouth just by walking around purporting a trend or talking to their friends about it. BzzAgent's clients include Ralph Lauren, Lee Jeans, and Anheuser-Busch, among others.[36] Ben Deitz, of the alternative *Vice* magazine, explained to me that *Vice* maintains a database of influentials and tastemakers to run by ideas, events, and the like. David Rabin, the owner of the nightclubs Lotus and the Double Seven, conveyed a similar sentiment: When one of their new clubs or lounges opens, the owners have a list of tastemakers and cultural influencers to whom they send promotional materials, such that a buzz around the new opening is established.

Peer Review

Cynthia Rowley, the petite and quirky New York fashion designer who has an affection for eccentric prints and tailored bohemianism, met me in her West Village boutique one cold January afternoon. Cynthia, unassuming and gracious, talked with me for several hours about her work. One of the things she shared with me was the seamless relationship that her work had with art and music. She remarked upon this relationship both in terms of inspiration and also with regard to how her clothing is evaluated. As she put it, "It used to be the real fashion press that makes or breaks your career. Now, it's if Lindsay Lohan wears your dress" (though Lohan's tastemaker status seems a bit tenuous these days). On the same note, the bombshell actress Scarlett Johansson was a runway model for Cynthia's fashion show.

The flipside of this phenomenon is when the actress Hilary Swank changed her mind at the last minute about what she was going to wear to the 2005 Oscars, from Calvin Klein to a dark blue number with a very low-cut back by Guy Laroche. As Francisco Costa of Calvin Klein explained, "In the history of Hollywood, no actress will ever tell what they're wearing before the Oscars. I have to be honest, it [Hilary Swank's dress] wasn't working and it wasn't working because her mind was on what she had already picked two weeks before. Because in the last fitting, she looks back to me and says 'Is my back tan enough?' And you know, 'Hello?!!' My dress had a low back but not like a crack in the lower back [he laughs], so she knew she was going to wear that [the other dress]. All she had to say to me was 'Thank you very much, next time let's do something else.' Obviously she was feeling used, by being part of a contractual agreement [with Calvin Klein] she wasn't happy about . . . She agreed on a contract that, a year later, she wasn't happy about—it's not my fault! Why did she agree to it? She is a lovely girl, she really is. But you find they've got ten people vying for them . . . It's a big deal [switching dress at last minute] but it's like 'tough shit' [for the fashion house]! you know?"

In an intersection of the gatekeepers/certifiers, tastemakers, and heterarchies is a phenomenon called peer review. What is distinct about this concept is that the reviewers of cultural products are not necessarily within the confines of a particular industry (e.g., a music or art critic), that instead, these reviewers reside within the broader cultural economy—essentially, tastemakers from one industry are often tastemakers for another. Cultural producers in one industry may be reviewers for another—Kate Moss as model but also fashion critic. At the same time, unlike the concept of the tastemaker who operates on a range of different rungs of the social ladder, or the "word-of-mouth" among ordinary "cool" people, peer reviewers operate within the cultural economy and reside in the top level of their industry. It is this position that allows them the luxury of evaluating and influencing the economic value of products and people in other creative industries. By establishing themselves as legitimate artistic and cultural producers, they are given carte blanche to valorize creative production across other artistic and cultural spheres. Sally Singer, fashion news and features director of *Vogue* magazine explained, "Everything connects up. Certain industries have similar concerns. Especially since fashion has become big media. Especially since the supermodels. Before nobody knew the models' names. Then with the supermodel, fashion became a kind of giddy entertainment industry. Fashion is sold off the backs of celebrities, sold off the backs of musicians . . . So what they do around us is interesting and what we do around them is interesting." Or as Cathy Horyn, the fashion critic for the *New York Times*, ironically remarked, "[There is an] historic role that designers have played. Bill Blass endorsed the Lincoln Continental, [this] from a man who didn't know how to drive a car."

There is a reason why *US Weekly*, *People*, and other celebrity-centric magazines devote whole sections to what celebrities are wearing, how they are wearing it, and where to buy it. Jessica Simpson, a pop star and film star (most notably as Daisy Duke in the remake of the *Dukes of Hazzard*), is not a fashion editor at *Vogue*, but there are thousands of women who follow her style religiously and run to Barney's to buy the jeans she has been photographed wearing. Or, as one designer from Chaiken explained, "Women don't necessarily know how to dress so they look to the stars who look great, they read *Lucky* and *Cosmo* [*Cosmopolitan*] for direction." This designer went on to say that traditional gatekeeper magazines such as *Vogue* and *W* were not the only reviewers, but rather that the new celebrity magazines, which are not official fashion gatekeepers, have become dictators of style. Or consider when Marc Jacobs picks a particular band (for example Kasabian) for his fashion show. That band draws additional support and success because people associate Marc with "good creative and aesthetic taste," not just fantastic fashion sense. In a reciprocal sense, fashion designer John Varvatos explained to me that he chose Joe Perry of Aerosmith to model his clothing line because Perry adds a certain authenticity and cachet to the brand. I might add that behind Varvatos' office desk is a gigantic portrait of Jimi Hendrix, another example of Varvatos' affection for fusing music with his own creative work. Similarly, when the rapper Jay-Z started wearing shoes from the underground sneaker company Bathing Ape, the sneakers started selling for $400 a pair. Because of the influence of celebrities as public figures of style and creativity, many a fashion designer gives them free clothing. One fashion designer told me she had given Drew Barrymore (an actress) five T-shirts, but "it only helps if we get a Polaroid of her in one." And her insistence in actually having a photo of Drew Barrymore in her shirt makes economic sense: As Lazaro Hernandez told me, advertising is really expensive, but you can give free clothing to a celebrity and it is more effective than an ad in a magazine.

Part of this phenomenon has to do with the increasing visibility and commodification of creative individuals. As Valerie Steele noted, "The role of celebrities and performers has been incredibly important since the eighteenth century. They are on a public stage and their image is incredibly important. They get around people who want to see what they wear. A lot of people went to the theater to see what they [the actors] wore, not the play . . . With the advent of the music video there was a real upsurge in the musician [as a peer reviewer]." Indeed, across all industries, the increase in online media, television and magazines devoted to celebrities and fashion, and the ease with which one can download music, watch videos, and read about fashion trends creates a direct line between creative producers, gatekeepers, and consumers. The graffiti artists I interviewed spoke of the ability of their community to constantly share information about new graffiti work through online communities such as Writers @149 (which is a reference to the 149th Street and Grand Concourse stop on the subway where graffiti writers used to hang out and watch each other's work as the trains went by). Writers @149 or the Wooster Collective allow artists to upload photos of their work so that graffiti artists in Tokyo, Japan, can see what type of graffiti is being put up in Brooklyn, New York. Other interviewees noted that the ability to have instantaneous interaction with cultural producers around the world established a global creative community across disciplines. It has become remarkably easy to establish symbiotic relationships across creative occupations and to have those relationships shared with consumers.

Many of the fashion designers I spoke with discussed the importance of these peer relationships across industries. Interviewees emphasized constantly that what musicians, artists, and film stars wear is hardly ever arbitrary, because they are all cognizant of their influence in valorizing products. In fact, as one respondent pointed out, "If you're out as a celebrity and someone asks you what you're wearing and you don't know or say the wrong thing, that's millions of dollars worth of PR just lost . . . Think about what happened when Hilary Swank at the last minute decided not to wear Calvin Klein [to the Oscars]." During my interview with David Rabin, he mentioned that *W* magazine, a leading high-fashion publication, was going to run a whole section on his new lounge, the Double Seven. Even though *W* magazine is about clothes and fashion, it is still considered an elite tastemaker across creative industries. Those who read *W* are not just in fashion but in creative industries more generally. So the concept of peer review deviates from traditional gatekeepers because, although they are still critics, their critique is not limited to one sphere. Peer reviewers review heterarchically across creative industries.

But in these dynamics, we also must question who the peer reviewer really is. What has come across regularly in my interviews is the importance of the stylist as the influencer and the celebrity as the purveyor of the stylist's good taste. Stylist, while a broad term that includes contractors as well as employees to particular celebrities, models, musicians and so on, refers to individuals who dress high-profile individuals for their public appearances—it is the stylist who often is responsible for a celebrity's signature look. She is the one who chooses the brand, the designer, and the actual clothing the celebrity will wear. As Daniel Jackson from the fashion house Surface to Air put it, "Beyonce does and does not know what she wants. She talks to her stylist, and the stylist is who we deal with and who makes the decision." Or as another respondent said, "The celebrities are important but the celebs are driven by stylists and agents." These dynamics force us to reconsider our perception of who is the ultimate tastemaker and reviewer. While, undoubtedly, traditional gatekeepers still exist in the form of trade publications, magazines, and critics, there is clearly a more nuanced and broader framework in which creative goods are valorized—there is an informal process to creative production and there are informal reviewers who are influencing a creative good's possibilities in the marketplace.

But what do gatekeepers, tastemakers, and peer reviewers really do? While this book has focused on the importance of peer reviewers as distinct from the former two concepts, there is a broader phenomenon occurring that has implications for generating cultural value. These different types of evaluators—whether influentials or gatekeepers—can be looked at under the umbrella of creative reviewers. As Rob Walker puts it, "Marketers bicker among themselves about how these approaches differ, but to those of us on the receiving end, the distinctions might seem a little academic. They are all attempts, in one way or another, to break forth the wall that used to separate the theater of commerce, persuasion and salesmanship from our actual day-to-day life."[37]

These types of dynamics speak to three different phenomena that occur in the review process within the cultural economy. First, creative products generate value through being reviewed by people who are broadly considered reviewers of artistic and cultural production, both the formal and informal critics—and this happens across industries. But what is also a nagging question in this whole discussion is how and where the valorization occurs in the first place, which leads to a second point: The ability to actually attain success has to do with creating an ongoing credibility, which is almost always established by gatekeepers, peer reviewers, and tastemakers. Finally, and perhaps most important, valorization and credibility and thus economic opportunity have to do with having informal and social ties that are not inherently about one's work or skill set. And herein lies the central importance of place to the valorization of cultural goods.

Establishing Credibility

Some of the time credibility is established through repeat successful performance, whether through new goods and services that appeal to either a mass audience or key influentials or gatekeepers. Formal reviewers like the work, agents want to represent the producer, investors give more money, people buy the clothing line. But credibility also derives from being friends or being associated with other people who have credibility—or rather, sometimes to actually get a product evaluated by agents, investors, or consumers, a creative producer has to establish legitimacy within the creative field before he even gets out of the starting block. Drawing on the earlier discussion of "weak ties," credibility is often established by being associated with influential or credible people. Credibility also ties into the concepts of peer review and heterarchy and illuminates another way in which weak ties are at work.

JS1, a graffiti artist and DJ I interviewed, explained that he got his start because he was friends with T. LeRock, a hip-hop DJ. When JS1 was given the opportunity to meet one of his musical idols, rapper KRS-ONE, he knew that KRS and T. LeRock were friends and that KRS attributed some of his earlier success to LeRock. As JS1 explained it, he knew that any chance to do a collaboration with KRS would depend on establishing credibility, outside of his musical talents. "When I met KRS, I had no cred, once I brought up T, it was done." KRS and JS1 ended up doing a single together, which became an immediate success, and thereafter JS1 started touring globally with Rahzel, an underground hip-hop rap and beatbox sensation, and has been touring with him ever since.

Sam Wheeler of the band Soft noted that meeting and becoming friends with the influential bands Maroon 5 and Phantom Planet gave his band more credibility and also paved the way for Soft to play their first show at the well-established and prestigious Irving Plaza. "We [the band] had been together for only six months and they [Phantom Planet] had us open for five shows for them. Our first show was at Irving Plaza with them. Who can say that their first show was at Irving Plaza?!"

The significance of establishing credibility should not be taken lightly. Creative goods are inherently subjective. Credibility is established by the right people—or in this context, creative reviewers, who in some form say your product is worthy of consumption. As fashion designer Elisa Jeminez explained to me, "So no one takes you seriously and then you say, 'I dress Cameron Diaz' and they're like 'Oh you're for real.'" Q, the manager of a music group, talked to me about getting a Drum and Bass DJ to work with his band, explaining, "Roni will legitimate the project. If he thinks it is good, it's like saying 'trust me.'" The same holds true when bands sign on with particular record labels (especially those run by musicians themselves)—it sends a signal to the consumer that a respected musician thinks that the new band is worthy to listen to. Similarly, leading hip-hop and pop producer Scott Storch, who has produced albums for Lil'Kim, 50 Cent, and Paris Hilton, attributes his initial success to his affiliation with rap superstar Dr. Dre. As Storch put it in a *New York Times* interview, "Dre opened the door for me, and just having my name mentioned next to his raised my stock . . . Doors that were once closed to me were swinging wide open."[38]

GenArt, a highly respected organization that supports (financially and socially) emerging talent in fashion, music, and art exemplifies the way in which legitimacy and credibility translate into rapid career advancement. Semiannually, GenArt hand selects a series of fashion designers to showcase during Fashion Week. Funded by corporate sponsors and ticket sales, GenArt puts on an enormous fashion show. The president and founder Ian Gerard explained, "We do high production value, same caliber as Ralph Lauren or Donna Karan, not like in a basement or something." Such events have paid off big time for the chosen designers like Alexandre Plokhov, Chaiken, and Rebecca Taylor, all very successful designers today. But perhaps the most obvious example of Gen-Art's influence is Zac Posen. As Gerard told me, "When we debuted Zac Posen back when he was 20, in 2001 and Kal Ruttenstein, the fashion director of Bloomingdales was in the front row and bought the collection and bam! There was Posen in one of the top department stores in the country."

I even found the same phenomenon in my own research. To get an interview with a top-level designer, I realized that the most effective way to establish credibility was to send him or her a list of others I had interviewed. I remember when I went to interview one hip-hop group, their manager took me into a room where the rappers were hanging out and getting stoned, and paying absolutely no attention to me. In order to get them to talk to me, the manager introduced me as someone who had interviewed other hip-hop artists, and then he went down the list. As one art director said, "There is this network. It is a network. All the people I worked with before Kate Spade I met through friends. Rarely would they hire me because they recognized my work. It would be friends who would say to them 'check this out.'" In other industries, these other linkages often are a product of previously doing successful business, which adds to the credibility. In art and culture, linkages are often formed initially on social ties. This observation is not to say that an artist can base livelihood on social ties alone. Social ties open the door and then the creative producer must produce good work, often within a formal institution (a gallery, a clothing company, a record label) and continue to attain positive reviews.

Social Networks and Access to Peer Review

The social component of generating value and credibility does not detract from the importance of formal institutions and processes by which products are reviewed. Being represented by a top talent agency or record label gives clout and credibility—this component of creative valorization is obvious. How informal social dynamics impact the valorization process, and how they relate to the more formal production systems and industries present within New York City, are less clear. Chapters 4 and 5 considered the importance of social networks in the creative economy as providing community support and economic opportunity, and these types of dynamics appear straightforward. But social networks are also, in a more arbitrary and chaotic way, the paths to the gatekeepers and reviewers of the creative world. Social networks create the opportunity to meet the people who judge creative products. The social is where the value and taste for creativity are formed—but it is the particular social life of the gatekeepers, reviewers, and artistic and cultural producers that matters in creating that value. As Ian Gerard remarked, "It's very useful for talent to have other talent who are willing to promote them. Zac [Posen] is friends with Claire Danes and the Schnabels. He didn't come from Ohio, he grew up with a New York social network." As Shepard Fairey explained it, "You can say it would be better if this sort of cool factor, the vanity, the trend aspects of it weren't there but rather than be sour grapes about it, embrace it or face the consequences of not being in fashion. I'm an optimist, I believe good work will prevail [but] there is nothing wrong with putting your stuff in front of the right people at the right time as long as it has substance."

The social and geographical components of New York City provide two important components. First, they provide the nodes for collaboration, idea sharing, and new opportunities across the heterarchical field of creative production, a point I discussed in greater detail earlier. Second, the social milieu allows for gatekeepers to come into contact with creative goods and creative producers (which can lead to opening doors and giving credibility). And these interactions are geographically bound to particular places where these cultural reviewers reside and valorize the creativity that they come in contact with. As one musician said to me, "Anthony Tommasini [music critic for the *New York Times*] is not going to review outside of New York . . . already hard to get coverage, impossible if not in New York."

Similarly, social institutions from nightclubs to gallery openings to restaurants allow for influentials, gatekeepers, and reviewers to review and critique creative goods in a more informal capacity, from the music blasting out of sound systems to the style of dress women are wearing. Over and above the formal review process that the music or theater critic performs, informal reviews of trends, style, and music occur in the laboratory that is New York's social scene. Essentially, social institutions become the stage for the creative economy and its accoutrements to be reviewed, and to take note of trends. As fashion reporter Eric Wilson remarked in a *New York Times* article, "On a recent night at Bette, Amy Sacco's new restaurant in Chelsea, the fashion set was well represented: Donna Karan dined with Candy Pratts Price, the fashion director of Style.com at one table, Nicole Miller with Glenda Bailey, the editor of *Harper's Bazaar*, at another; and Roberto Cavalli was in the back mezzanine with members of the food press, who were tasting a new vodka—his."[39]

The article goes on to explain that the restaurant staff at Bette is clothed in Earnest Sewn jeans, while employees at the famed sushi restaurant Nobu wear Hugo Boss in the New York City branch, and Giorgio Armani in the Milan outpost. Calvin Klein dresses employees at the celebrity chef Jean-Georges Vongerichten's Perry St. restaurant. The jeans worn at Bette will be replicated (including the stains and damage resulting from wearing them as a part of the server uniform) and sold for between $180 and $300 at Earnest Sewn. While this points to the earlier discussion of heterarchy— the sharing and collaboration of creativity across industry—it also points to the nexus between social milieu and commerce. As the article goes on to say, "It is also an example of a designer brand vying to dress the staff of a hot restaurant, where uniforms have become as much a part of the décor as the dinner plates."[40]

As Ray Pirkle, the general manager of Bette, explained of the agglomeration of creative reviewers in particular social nodes, "They are looking for inspiration. They would love to tap into something new and fresh." *US Weekly* or *In Touch* or *Glamour* magazine editors and photographers get a huge component of their trend spotting from just trolling New York City's (and LA's) social scene. As one club owner explained, "Record labels send us music all the time to market their stuff." The reason they do is because clubs are where music editors and producers hang out and celebrities listen to music and then tout who is their favorite band during an interview. Valerie Steele commented, "If you socialize where the fashion people are . . . They [young designers] put themselves in places where they can see tastemakers and make an impact on them." Creativity is symbiotic—creative producers need, collaborate, review each other and establish nodes where their products are informally reviewed thus further emphasizing the social and economic meaningfulness of New York City's creative social scene as a nexus for the creative economy to congregate.

Flexible Career Paths

The cohesive and reflexive nature of art and culture also presents opportunities for creative producers to use their skills in a variety of different industries. The very same skill sets necessary for drawing or painting can be applied to fashion design or designing record albums. Those trained in music can also work on films, as DJs in nightclubs and sound technicians or music directors for fashion runway shows. Those producers who have established themselves in one creative industry often have enough cachet to use themselves (as a brand) in another sector (think Diddy or Gwen Stefani, both musicians with incredibly successful clothing lines). The ability to cross-fertilize creative skills across different industries is yet another example of the ability for creativity to transform itself and move into different spheres and industries of the cultural economy, in a process that I call the *flexible career path*. Many of the interviewees that I spoke with told me of their dual lives within creative industries. Many of them used their creative skills in fine arts to get jobs in advertising, art direction, and a myriad of other hybrid industries that require creative skills. What is apparent is that creative people have a lot to offer broadly across the cultural economy. The implications of this flexibility are that creative people are not forced to give up their artistic endeavors because they cannot create a viable living through their art. Instead, I found that many artists used their work in hybrid industries to pay the bills while they worked on their artistic careers on the side. This result also points to how important artists' skill sets are to the broader New York economy. As a labor pool, creative producers offer both freelance and permanent talents to corporations, advertising agencies, and marketing firms, among others, that depend on these skills and are willing to offer health benefits and a regular salary. As one young woman I interviewed explained, "I have made a life choice to do stuff I love to do. Sometimes I have jobs that aren't pleasant but [you] figure out how to do what you want to do." At the time of the interview, she was working as a freelancer on a Tylenol ad campaign. Meres, a young graffiti artist, explained his similar position, "Just did a billboard in the Lower East Side. Not graffiti but since I've mastered graffiti, I can do commercial jobs . . . It was a $5,000 job so that will hold me down for a couple of months." While economic indicators will not necessarily capture the positive externalities of having a pool of creative producers to support other "humdrum" industries, undoubtedly the presence of artistic and cultural producers is necessary for the success of other industries within the New York region—a further example of the heterarchical synchronicity of the creative economy.[41]

The occurrence of flexible career paths also points to how the economic life of a creative worker evolves and establishes longevity as an artistic and cultural producer despite the changing tides of consumer demand and artistic and cultural taste. The economic value of some creative producers, such as dancers, depreciates rapidly and their careers are short. Part of this has to do with the fleeting, youthful nature of certain types of talents, such as modeling or dancing. The other explanation for the occurrence and need for flexible career paths is that the creative spirit is capricious and constantly reinventing itself. Artists who were hot a few years ago are not necessarily so now. Yet in New York City, the ability to recreate and evolve with the changing creative scene is not just possible, it is encouraged. I found this latter point most salient in the economic lives of graffiti writers. Many of them, who were vandals and outlaws in the 1970s and glorified gallery artists in the 1980s, are now doing commissioned work for corporations and advertising firms. Some, like Jest and Claw, using the cachet of themselves as a brand or commodity, have established their own clothing lines (ALIFE and CLAWmoney, respectively), while Futura has been commissioned to do limited-edition sneakers for Nike and an ad campaign for Reebok. Lady Pink, one of New York's most prolific female graffiti artists, told me that even though she was an outlaw in the 1980s, now she paints legal murals and generates income through commissioned work for businesses. She had redesigned and painted a mural in the very restaurant where I interviewed her. In the fall of 2005, Lee Quinones painted a huge mural on Ludlow Street in the Lower East Side for Nike and streetcar company Nort-Recon— an example of how corporations' tapping into street culture for credibility has created job possibilities for creative producers. Essentially, New York offers these flexible career paths that provide opportunities to expand one's creative horizons and economic position.

This trajectory is not just associated with those who have outgrown their original creative visions. The cultural economy also offers opportunities to switch to different forms of creativity. As Bonnie Young, the senior creative director for Donna Karan International, explained to me, "I was an artist, I wasn't a fashion designer by any means and not even a sketcher." Daniel Jackson of the clothing line, Surface to Air, told me that he majored in sculpture at New York University, while his design partner, Gordon Hull, had a self-designed major at NYU's Gallatin School. Many of the other creative producers to whom I have spoken have similar stories, starting out as one type of creative worker and evolving into another, sometimes out of necessity and at other times out of opportunity. Because there is a reflexive dependence across cultural industries, creative producers can use their basic skills and fine tune them to adapt to new ventures—and in New York City there are a multitude of such possibilities because of the critical mass of creativity. The possibility to have a flexible career path lies both in the heterarchical and symbiotic nature of the cultural economy and the dense concentration of creative producers, creative industries and other hybrid industries such as publishing, advertising, and so on within New York City's geography.

The taste-driven and social nature of cultural production creates new ways of doing business, creating value, and finding a job. The evaluation of creative goods does not have to do with the speed of its microprocessor or the sturdiness of its dishwashing capabilities. It is inherently subjective. That subjectivity coupled with the malleability of creative skill sets means that for creative people, their career paths are wide and endless, especially in the density of New York. The very existence of this density is of course partly because creative industries need each other on a multitude of levels. Yet the fluidity of creativity also complicates things because not only those specifically assigned to evaluate a product do so. Other creative producers also have a say in how the latest album, spring collection, new jeans, or latest art exhibition will be valued. The unique conditions of the cultural economy make it difficult for those who can impact it, for better or for worse (the city planners, politicians, and economic developers), to use the standard economic elixirs directed toward finance, law, or manufacturing. Art and culture policymaking involves a more complicated approach. The final chapter will look at how to translate the characteristics discussed so far into new strategies for optimizing the cultural economy.

Chapter 7

THE RISE OF GLOBAL TASTEMAKERS
What It All Means for the Policymakers

On an unusually hot Thursday evening in the beginning of May, I was careening down small side streets in SoHo, ready to trip in my four-inch stilettos across a sea of cobblestones as I raced to meet my sister, Sarah, for the Jean-Michel Basquiat retrospective at Deitch Projects. When I arrived, my sister was already there on the corner of Grand and Greene Streets, her perfectly Chanel red lips pouting and her right eyebrow arched.
"You're late . . . . *comme d'habitude.*"
I was.
I had just spent the last forty-five minutes trying on Anna Sui dresses a few blocks away. The gallery owner, Jeffrey Deitch, was at the front of the door in thick-rimmed, light mint-green round glasses, with his tall, regal gallery director, Nicola Vassell, holding a clipboard. Even though my sister was already impatient, we still had to wait for Ryan McGinness, who was attending the opening with us. Ryan eventually showed up, tall and lanky with his big boyish grin that made his tardiness positively charming. Jeffrey let us in, where we were met by a compilation of Basquiat's work, from sketches on index cards to advertisements for the now closed Mudd Club to massive paintings, many of them complete with his signature symbol—the outline of a king's crown.

The crowd comprised an array of different characters, including graffiti artists like Lee Quinones and DAZE, who had been Basquiat's contemporaries, major art dealers and collectors and media gatekeepers like Carlo McCormick, senior editor for *Paper* magazine, along with directors like Charlie Ahern, in addition to a multitude of actors, artists, and scenesters. Here they were—not only those fellow graffiti artists coming to pay their respects, who had chased down subway tunnels with Basquiat and watched him transform from the graffiti outlaw SAMO to a major star on the art scene by the 1980s—but also the heavy hitter dealers and collectors

interested in his work that now sells for tens of thousands of dollars, and the new guard of artists, who see Basquiat as an inspiration, and then the others who, while not artists, ran in the same crowd and engaged in the same scene. It was a fusion of cultures, from those who were involved in the commodifying of the "Basquiat brand," to those who were his comrades when his work had no more value than an aerosol paint can, to those who never knew Basquiat but admired his work as one of the most important American artists after the Abstract Expressionists. And of course there are always those who just like to hang out with the cool kids. This blend, this confluence of creativity, is at the heart of New York City's success as a gloal cultural economy.

In the story of New York City, two observations leap out about cultural industries and where they locate. First, cultural production tends to cluster geographically[1]—from the creative flurry in the first recording of a song to the skilled workforce required to turn a sample into a hit song to the dense formal and informal review processes that give it value.[2] Second, the clustering of cultural production in particular geographies allows a particular product to brand a place—and vice versa (whether we are talking about Hollywood

The Rise of Global Tastemakers 155

films or New York art).[3] As the geographers Dominic Power and Allen Scott put it, "The association between place and product in the cultural industries is so often so strong that it constitutes a significant element of firms' success on wider markets."[4] More simply, Alexandre Plokov, the founder and chief designer for the men's clothing line Cloak, explained to me that he located in New York because "It's a New York brand . . . you're in Barney's, [you have] contacts with certain magazines and stylists." The density of all realms of production, from supplies to labor pools, not only increases the chance that more innovation and creativity will emerge in New York City but that what is produced is of a great value because it emerges from New York. It's not just the clustering of culture, but what that clustering means to the rest of the world—the mark that New York has made on the products that emerge from its cultural geography allows the city to maintain its monopoly in the global marketplace of creative goods and services.

These components—the clustering and the branding—reinforce themselves as more talented cultural producers flock to New York because of its reputation as a bastion of creativity, which results in a kind of virtuous spiral, perpetuating New York's reputation as such.[5] Quincy Jones explained the city as a "global gumbo," with New York being "enhanced by people of a like mind." More formally, geographers Powers and Scott write, "Successful cultural-products agglomerations, as well, are irresistible to talented individuals who flock in from every distant corner in pursuit of professional fulfillment."[6] The best come to New York because the best is already here and is more easily accessible (and efficient) here than anywhere else in the world—because everyone else involved in cultural production is also here and, just as important, the market for cultural goods and the channels for distributing creativity are here. When I asked the designer John Varvatos why he was located in New York, he responded, "Easy question—it's the fashion capital—all the buyers come—we're not manufacturing but sales and trading is here, and energy is here. It is the heart of fashion in the world for me. Most of the good designers will be here, [and] from a people standpoint [that's] a very big part of it." Francisco Costa, the creative director for Calvin Klein, put it this way, "I do think for designers that Seventh Avenue is great, Paris is a very creative city but there is no Seventh Avenue there, same with Milan. But New York is different. People pay attention to that difference, the garment district. I think that has an influence on us designers. Also the facility, it's so easy to move around. If you need a fabric you can go around the corner and find it. The city is so easy to move around." The designer Zac Posen had a similar response: "Travel, trade, timing . . . Because it's a marketplace—you can come to a marketplace. We're in the cultural marketplace of the United States. [You are] presenting your work in the place of exposure . . . It's geographical, it's a landing point." In other words, culture is able to translate into a marketable good in New York City. In terms of the dense social clustering (which is equally important), Ryan McGinness offhandledly commented to me one night when we were at a *Paper* magazine party, "I was really hoping Jeffrey Deitch would be here tonight so that I could talk to him about my upcoming show."

But it is not just that the product brands the place and the place brands the product. Just as important, particular places actually dictate global taste. The concentration of cultural producers, reviewers, and institutions means that New York has developed itself as the type of place where prescience regarding trends or creative production has a greater chance of occurring, and as such, leading to an inextricable link between place and generating value for cultural goods.[7] Out of these social and production agglomerations emerges New York's position as a global tastemaker, which allows it to be the geographical expert in dictating what should or should not be on the market in cultural industries.[8] Places are not just known as the global producer of a particular good, but also as the global dictators of taste and cultural movements within particular industries—and the world takes their cue.

In economic terms, the ability for a region to be a global tastemaker of cultural goods relies heavily on its ability to capture demand on all levels—which is where the *diversity* of New York City's cultural production from high-brow to subculture becomes significant. Case in point, the Lower East Side as a gritty hipster haven is also the inspiration for big fashion houses, as was the alternative modish Williamsburg, Brooklyn, club Luxx. As the Concordia University geographer Norma Rantisi has pointed out in her detailed studies of the New York fashion industry, Garment District designers have often used (or rather "exploited") the Lower East Side's edgy, street innovation in their own designs.[9]

Artistic and cultural economies are intensely important to their geographies. These industries not only provide jobs and generate profits but, more so than any other industry, their production and value is intrinsically linked to place—and this linkage is economically significant, allowing the geography, as we have seen with New York City, to benefit from being both a center of cultural production and a center of cultural taste, both of which generate extensive economic rewards. What we also know is that creative industries work horizontally together on many levels and that they are most productive within their social lives. These two key characteristics have definitive implications for both how we understand creative industries and how we facilitate their contribution to a metropolitan economy. Creative industries require a different type of policymaking that cultivates the social world in which art and culture thrive. From the beatniks to punk rock to Andy Warhol's Factory, the significance of social institutions to bohemian and creative life has long been documented. But what has not been considered, or at least not enough, is how to incorporate these very dynamics and institutions into economic development policy for arts and culture.

Why the City Should Care about Art and Culture

The cultural agglomeration of New York provides a lot of benefits, the location of various cultural actors (firms, artists and so on) in the same place, a blending of street and high culture, and the inspiration and resources they share with one another (what economists call "positive externalities"). But New York also has negative externalities, especially those that accompany density, the high cost of living that pushes artistic and cultural producers and their institutions out of the very creative spaces that they helped to form. Or as the *New York Times* put it, "Goodbye, Chelsea and Williamsburg. New York art is filing a change of address."[10] And indeed it is true, as we witness the dramatic exodus of artists to places from New Jersey to far-flung parts of Brooklyn and Queens. While, for the most part, artists remain in the collective New York region, their dispersal to farther-away geographies means that the positive spillovers of the creative agglomeration start to diminish. Quite simply, if they are not living in the same neighborhoods (as they were during Abstract Expressionism or the East Village art movement), the chances that they are hanging out in the same places, sharing ideas on a daily basis, or running into each other, lessen greatly. As Diane von Furstenberg said, "When I first came to New York in the 1970s, [it was] very cheap to live here. When cost of living is cheap it creates talent—talent drives the economy." This pushing out is not just to the outer boroughs but places like Philadelphia, which has been dubbed "the next borough." "Priced out of Brooklyn," the *New York Times* article read, "artist types head down the turnpike."[11]

Witness the closing of CBGB, arguably the birthplace of American punk rock and the venue that has supported the careers of countless musicians and artists. The music club had struggled for many months to maintain itself on the Bowery, while its landlord wanted to substantially increase the rent such that it became impossible for CBGB to remain open. In fact, many of my interviewees pointed out how the cohesive social arrangement that formed the backbone of New York City's identity as a global tastemaker is being systematically eroded by high rents and unsupportive city policy toward night life. As one nightclub owner pointed out, "[There is] active hostility toward our industry."

When the city's overall economic climate was depressed, it offered a copious number of low-rent neighborhoods where artists, designers, and musicians could live, work, and play. And here we are at a critical juncture in terms of sustaining New York's creative advantage. Increasingly high rents have displaced creative producers while public policy frequently misses the mark in terms of what cultural industries and producers really need to sustain and optimize their work. Policymakers must pursue new directions in sustaining and nurturing New York's creative advantage. New York is a center of both high art and the gritty and edgy subcultures that simultaneously inspire and draw from elite cultural production (and vice versa). It is also a place where creativity blends, high and low and across industries. Or as Andy Spade puts it, "[New York] is like orange juice concentrated. It's really dense, it's really strong. Everywhere else you pour the water in. But here it's all that stuff, every corner you turn . . . It's the capital of everything. My one friend is an accountant, my one friend is a chef. The friend who is an accountant knows more about music than anyone . . . even in conservative industries they are creative. My lawyer is so cool, she wears Alexander McQueen and goes to the Paris shows. Even the middle of New York City is more interesting than the extreme in other places . . . You've got all these people crossing over from each other's quadrant."

There is no better example of this than Andy Warhol's Factory. It was Warhol who actively invited artistic and cultural producers from all different types of creative industries to spend time in his Factory, collaborating, exchanging ideas, and socializing. The Factory was a place where he produced his own artwork, invited other artists to work there and threw parties that drew everyone from Mick Jagger to the legendary transvestite (and Warhol's muse) Candy Darling.[12] New York is also a place where the formal institutions provide training, skill sets, institutional support, along with the venue for knowledge and innovations to diffuse across the arts. Events, whether "high brow," like the Chanel exhibit at the Met or the Giorgio Armani exhibit at the Guggenheim or the 2006 Met's Costume Institute tribute to British punk, *Anglo-Mania*, or more subculture-oriented, like Deitch Projects in SoHo, CBGB, or ALIFE in the Lower East Side, offer the space in which knowledge about all types of cultural industries is diffused to the broader public. The dense clustering of the publishing and to a lesser extent TV and film industries transmits what is going on in New York's cultural sphere to the rest of the world. The combination of the formal—the universities, the museums, the galleries, the foundations—along with the quotidian street life and glamorous after-hours scene perpetuates the city's creative core. The city's collective creative community spills into its nightclubs, coffee shops, neighborhoods, and street life and these dynamics give us a rich understanding of how creativity operates within its social production system, and how we can effectively facilitate it. As go those venues and their networks, so goes creative New York.

Recently, due to the understanding that culture drives economic growth, which is partly a function of its commodification, scholars such as UCLA geographer Allen Scott and University of Minnesota economist Ann Markusen have begun focusing on how creativity within artistic and cultural production can be harnessed. In many ways, the conversation about the needs of high-technology industrial districts or the finance industry (on which policymakers and scholars have long been fixated) and the needs of artistic communities are parallel, which fundamentally is because all of these industries so inherently depend on human capital.

Creating Creative Places

Economic planners and policymakers concern themselves with how to generate and retain successful industrial clusters—whether film, fashion, or semiconductors. Successful cultivation of these clusters, however, presents difficult issues. As many scholars have noted, predicting which industries, and within each industry which firms and products, will thrive is difficult—or rather, mind-bogglingly hard.[13] As Annalee Saxenian put it with regard to Silicon Valley's high-technology industries, "National policies that direct public resources toward particular technologies or sectors are seldom effective mechanisms for industrial adaptation. It is notoriously difficult for public officials, with or without the help of business, to 'pick winners' and effectively concentrate national resources on future technologies."[14] If we knew which fads were coming and knew how to support them, then they probably wouldn't be fads.

In an economy increasingly dependent on human capital, knowledge, consumption, and services, policymakers and city government have been both a blessing and a curse in how cultural economies form and operate successfully. On the one hand, communities are less dependent on natural resources in close proximity, like waterways for ports, flat terrain for railroads, and coal for energy. Because of this, regional and urban economic fate is no longer predestined. On the other hand, the very nature of an economy driven by human capital, and the flexible way in which products and ideas are formed, requires proactive policymaking to attract the necessary factors of production (people, firms, capital). Today, natural resources alone will not guarantee success and increasingly have little impact at all in industrial development. Regions and cities have new roles in the rise of knowledge and innovation-intensive industry clusters through cultivating places and environments that are more conducive to innovation, and offer the amenity-rich and open environments that people and knowledge-intensive firms thrive in.

Complicating matters, these types of economies often operate on a large, regional level. Consider that the industrial and occupational data in this book were available in such detail at the New York City Metropolitan Statistical Area (MSA), which includes far more than just New York City—in fact, the Bureau of Labor Statistics defines the MSA as a region that consists of counties that are economically linked, so New York City's MSA concerns places like Westchester County and parts of New Jersey. Make no mistake, New York City is the core of the economic and social activity, though other neighboring cities play a role. But the United States lacks the institutional or governmental framework necessary to implement effective policy or planning at this regional level. Geographics like the Silicon Valley–San Francisco corridor do not have an overall regional government to work with this high-technology sector that spans from the venture capitalists and financial institutions located in San Francisco to Palo Alto, home to Stanford University, which churns out talented engineers and computer scientists, to the technology workers and firms in San Jose. Considerations for planning, policy, and government may require regional institutional actors or collaborative governmental entities in order to more effectively plan for sustainable urban-regional economies.[15]

As many scholars point out—and as much of this book has been devoted to showing—industries that depend on human capital very much depend on the ability to have face-to-face contact and dense networks of both collaboration and competition among a diverse network of different specialized workers and firms. Such a dynamic can be seen in how computers are made, financial transactions occur, or dresses are designed. The long-standing relationship between professional services (law, public relations) and finance has much to do with financial firms' dependence on specialists who can enable deals and acquisitions between companies, sales of capital, and the marketing of their services.

Art and culture operate under a similar framework. The idea is that the components of a successful human capital–driven economy require environments that are conducive to these dynamics—face-to-face interaction, and the ability for resources, information, labor pools, and firms to move around with flexibility. Part of this type of dynamic is dependent on the built environment—which is why New York City's dense, walking-based space has been so successful for the proliferation of art and culture. This relationship is evident in the fact that New York's creative scene revolves around a collection of particular bars, clubs, restaurants, and neighborhoods that are frequented often by foot, allowing for casual interactions both in the scene and on the street that become meaningful. Remember my meeting with Marc Jacobs' neighbor Giles, something that would be even more unlikely in a more automobile-dependent city like, say, Washington, DC, or even Los Angeles. In fact, research I conducted with my colleague James Connolly shows that artistic and cultural industries and media (arguably an extension of the creative economy) exhibit the densest clustering of all industries ranging from finance to law to management, indicating both creative firms' and workers' strong need to locate near one another.[16]

A huge component of New York's success at cultivating this type of environment is its ability to attract the human capital that drives the economy—to get the right people to show up, meet, and work. But people are capricious and diverse, how to attract and retain human capital, can be hard to figure out. George Mason professor Richard Florida has spent the last decade researching what draws highly educated and creative people—or "talent" as he calls them—to some places and not others. He has done countless studies and focus groups asking young, educated people why they live where they live. People are not wholly motivated by jobs. Instead, he has found that they go to places where they find tolerance and diversity—places where they feel they can fit in and have lifestyle options (from bike trails to gay nightclubs to 24/7 gyms). Such a place-specific characteristic is particularly important to what he calls "bohemians," artistic types who are often already on the lifestyle periphery and want a place where they (and their work) will fit in and be accepted. Unlike the traditional idea that people go to where the jobs are, Florida has found that it is increasingly the other way around: companies that need innovative people will follow suit. As Carly Fiorina, the former CEO of Hewlett-Packard, told the governors at the National Governors Association 2000 annual meeting, forget the tax incentives, we will go where the highly skilled people are.[17]

University of Chicago sociologist Terry Clark has also looked at how the amenities that draw human capital (from bike trails to Starbucks to juice bars) drive economic growth. He has found that while there are several different types of amenities (natural ones like hiking trails and constructed ones like downtown shopping centers or music venues), developing overall quality of life is necessary to draw people, wealth, and economic development to a region.[18] And this finding, like Florida's, reflects the fact that growth is driven by people, so cities must strive to be the types of places people want to live in.

Historically, New York economic development policy has been unable to pick winners, and targeting finance or big corporations to this end has been ineffectual, at best. It would behoove policymakers and economic developers to instead refocus their efforts (and funding) on more effective economic development schemes, specifically capitalizing on the potential (and competitive advantage) of the artistic and cultural community. Policies to this end would enable arts and culture to play an even more significant role in providing both jobs and revenue to the New York City region. It is in New York's best interest to invest in creative communities, arts education, and the social and physical networks that allow for cultural innovation.[19] What is clear is that art and culture are supported and sustained in nontraditional ways, and public policy toward these industries needs to be refined to address those needs.

New York's Art and Culture Policy

Historically, New York's arts and culture policy has traditionally included "artists-in-residence" permits, reserving for artists spaces in which to live and work (specifically many of these residencies are located in the SoHo/Chinatown area of New York), public art funding, and small grants. But these are problematic initiatives. The "artists-in-residence" program doesn't always do a good job of sifting out the "artists" who are actually bankers, brokers and the like.

Further, public art investments have been poorly received, misunderstood or both. As the *New York Times* has pointed out, "The phrase 'successful public art project' may sound like an oxymoron. The world is full of forlorn statues that go unnoticed . . . almost all of them below the radar of the commercial art world, which usually pays minimal attention to government-supported public art."[20] New York's "Percent for Art" program, the largest public art program in the city since the Great Depression, has been successful at times (it funds commissioned public art ranging from $50,000 to $400,000 with an artist's fee of 20 percent of the art allocation) but has supported projects that the public has met with indifference or antagonism.[21] In the same vein, the art historian Jed Perl points out that art museums have become out of touch with the city's cultural climate and increasingly removed from the contemporary art world.[22] Shepard Fairey explained, "I feel the institutions are behind the curve. The metabolism of popular culture—if you wait for the museums, the moment will pass you by . . . Case in point: Banksy's show [in an abandoned warehouse in downtown LA] got 50,000 visitors in 3 days. Rauschenberg's [at LA's Museum of Contemporary Art] got 80,000 in three months. Now the art world is freaking out—Banksy sold works for a lot of money and there were celebrities coming through. People [as in consumers of art] are following but this hasn't been acknowledged by the establishment." While the Banksy versus Rauschenberg is a Los Angeles example, the sentiment remains the same: creative producers feel that formal institutions are out of the loop when it comes to what's important in the modern cultural economy.

Mayor Bloomberg has made strides in supporting the Department of Cultural Affairs and the Mayor's Office of Film, Theater and Broadcasting, and he has been dubbed the "cultural Mayor."[23] Bloomberg's personal investments in the arts, while well-received, focus on formal organizations and institutions (for example, he has donated tens of millions of dollars of his own money to the Carnegie Corporation to benefit cultural institutions) as opposed to individuals and housing or workspace needs. In 2006, Bloomberg opened yet another office to "aggressively pitch New York City around the world as the nation's art and cultural capital." This office will help support nonprofit organizations, particularly those involved in the arts, that are unable to sustain themselves due to the increasingly high cost of living and doing business in New York City.[24] Such initiatives are timely, given the decline in corporate funding for the arts. As the *New York Times* reports, in fall 2006, Altria, formerly Phillip Morris, phased out major support for the arts. In the last 40 years, Altria has given $210 million to cultural groups, but such funding has been withdrawn. "It's the end of an era," remarked the executive director of the Alvin Ailey American Dance Theater, Sharon Gersten Luckman. "Altria and Philip Morris supported dance and Ailey for over twenty-five years. They were at the forefront. There wouldn't be an Ailey if it weren't for them."[25] Overall, corporate philanthropy for arts has declined by over 50 percent in the last ten years. The most recent data available reports that arts support was just 4 percent of total corporate philanthropy in 2004, down from 9.5 percent in 1994. Part of the problem is the disconnect between arts organizations who are focused on attracting an audience, while corporations are fixated on market results. As such, much corporate funding often entails extensive corporate influence and criteria on how the money is used.[26]

Predictably, many of my interviewees expressed frustration at grants and support, claiming that either they found the amount of money not worth applying for or that the applications took so much time that it made more sense for them to just keep working. Overall, none of them had found government support influential in the success of their careers, and most had not even considered it an option. As the artist Ryan McGinness explained, "I have never been a big fan of seeking support for my work from any of these kinds of organizations. My approach has always been to earn my own money and not ask anybody for anything. In the time it takes to write a grant proposal, I can earn more money to fund my work doing almost anything else."

Adding to this morass of misguided and generally under-funded art and culture policy, policymakers' ideas about artists and arts lack nuance. Art and culture policy needs to treat creative industries as a symbiotic whole but also to recognize the needs of individual industries. Fashion, art, music, and design need some of the same things such as supporting their social environment and finding ways to allow young creative producers to survive in an increasingly cost-prohibitive city. Yet, as Terry Clark and his colleagues have pointed out, artists and musicians often run in different scenes and have different needs that cannot always be generalized. "Though each group is engaged in artistic activity," they write, " . . . punk musicians and opera singers—all artists—move in different circles, eat at different restaurants, and attract different audiences seeking different types of experiences."[27] High-brow and low-brow cultural producers at times have different needs. For example, artists need more studio space than musicians, while musicians would benefit from subsidized recording studios. Fashion designers almost always require professional degrees, while other creative producers can sometimes fine tune their skill set with individual practice. Artistic and cultural policy must recognize the particularities—and the similarities—across creative industries to fully optimize culture's potential contribution to economic growth and vitality. Understanding the nuances, such as where creative workers infuse economic meaning into their social lives and why it happens in some places and not others, lends the necessary richness to effective policymaking and economic development. As Clark and his coauthors note, "The cultural life of a city is not defined by the aggregate number of arts organizations or amenities it contains. Cultural policy researchers can therefore usefully advise policymakers by offering insight into the ways in which different demographic profiles tend to support different clusters of amenities . . . and show where a certain type of amenity is under- or overdeveloped."[28]

Current arts and culture policy has lacked genuine insight into the real needs of artistic communities and has poorly invested money in schemes that have not been fulfilling for either the public or the artists. Economic development policy that has dumped money into public art, created tedious mechanisms for obtaining grant money, and supported a sometimes lax artists-in-residence program fails to address the issues that are really important for the direction of artistic and cultural growth in New York City. As the Center for an Urban Future (CUF) points out, the Bloomberg administration has not addressed cost-of-living issues, the scarcity of rehearsal and work space, or affordable housing for cultural workers.

Moreover, urban policy initiatives ignore the major contributions of art and culture to the New York economy. In 2001, over 150,000 jobs were generated in arts and culture, a number that has grown 52 percent from 1992 to 2001, offering more potential growth than even the much revered financial industry. In those same years, as the CUF documents, employment in TV and film and commercial theater almost doubled. In 2005, New York held 8.3 percent of the national share of cultural workers. And this number has potential to grow: Between 1998 and 2001, New York's creative workforce grew 13.1 percent, while the city's overall job total increased by 6.5 percent.[29] According to NYC & Company, the city's tourism and marketing organization, in 2004, cultural visitors pumped $9.1 billion into New York's economy, while the film industry contributes $5 billion a year and 100,000 jobs to the city economy.[30] City and state tax incentives aimed at luring the film industry back from Canada increased these figures by 6,000 jobs and $300 million in revenue in less than a year of their inception.[31]

In contrast, as discussed at length in a previous chapter, financial and high-level producer service industries, often touted as the city and region's strength, have witnessed a decline in the last several decades.[32] These industries are not as dominant as they used to be.

Two conclusions jump out from these points. First, New York's arts and cultural policy has traditionally had a one-size-fits-all approach that has been ineffective at really capitalizing on the strengths of the city's creative community. Policy has focused on fostering formal institutions. Policymakers and developers can learn from research on how creative communities work (across industries and within informal environments) and also by appreciating their nuances (for example, fashion designers and street artists do not necessarily want or need the same things, yet each requires more outside support). Second, New York's economic development schemes must include many different industries. Finance and art and culture can—and should—cohabit in public policymaking. Government officials' emphasis on how much money the financial industry generates should be balanced with how much money the financial industry is *given* by the government. Finance and professional services are undoubtedly still critical to the city's growth, revenue, and employment. That said, policymakers should look at what other industries are also playing a crucial role in the city economy—particularly the cultural sectors—and figure out how to support them as well.

And what stands in the way of such initiatives? Mostly, the simple recognition that creative producers—artists, designers, musicians—despite being messy, complicated, and ethereal, add to the financial viability of the city—of any city, really, but especially in New York. That art and culture generate real jobs and growth is not reflected in the way the city approaches them. But there are tangible ways that the city can effectively target creativity and culture, such that New York's bohemia doesn't leave for Philadelphia.

Making Art and Culture Happen

Establishing effective cultural policy requires understanding how creativity happens and how the cultural economy works, both of which this book has aimed to capture. The social networks, collective nature of creative industries, and increasing commodification of cultural skills and production can inform the ways in which governments and local organizations support artists, whether newly minted fashion designers or fledgling hip-hop musicians. Further influencing cultural policy is the increasing cost-prohibitive and institutionalized nature of creativity and the cities in which it is produced. So long to the bygone days of bohemian artists relying on their ingenuity alone—these days most successful creative workers have a degree in hand from a prestigious university before they walk in the door of their first gallery opening or fashion internship. Couple that with the exorbitant rise in cost-of-living in the world's leading cities—particularly those known as global cultural capitals. These "superstar cities," as the economists Joseph Gyourko, Christopher Mayer, and Todd Sinai have dubbed them, have become increasingly homogenized as the only influx of new human capital allowed in is that which can pay the rent—thus leaving out much of the new guard of cultural producers that further perpetuate New York's (and Los Angeles' and London's) creative economy.[33] Policy and development initiatives directed toward art and culture must take into account both how cultural economies work (redirecting carpet-bombing-style policy to something more nuanced) and the increasing economic and social constraints imposed on contemporary creative workers. The following section offers several suggestions (not exhaustive, by any means) for how to achieve this.

Accrediting Creativity

Basquiat and Miles Davis (who blew off his studies at Juilliard) notwithstanding, most successful creative producers have been formally educated. As the artist Ted Mineo puts it, "There's a career track. You get your BFA and then you get your MFA. You move to New York, you have a show, and it's like being a lawyer or something else. And that doesn't entirely square with the romantic ideal of being an artist, living in isolation and being the avant-garde hero."[34] In her study of New York's fashion industry, the geographer Norma Rantisi found that 90 percent of the designers she interviewed had attained formal education from a local institution. Many of the designers found internships in the area with fashion houses and later went on to work full-time for these companies. Almost all of my interviewees had attained formal training from an art or design school, at one of New York's premier institutions such as Parsons or FIT but also around the country at fine arts departments and design schools from Rhode Island School of Design to Carnegie Mellon in Pittsburgh (coincidentally where Andy Warhol was trained).

The university system serves three important functions. First, and most saliently, the university trains human capital, providing the skills that enable students to become productive and competitive members of the cultural economy. In particular, the ability to use various computer programs for graphic design, electronic media and the like, is a necessary prerequisite for many of the creative arts. The availability of practical artistic training allows creative people to have flexible career paths and openness in their career trajectory. Fine artists who are also trained in graphic design will be marketable and will have other job opportunities if their careers as fine artists do not pan out. Fashion designers who learn how to cut, sew, sketch, or create patterns will be able to work for fashion magazines and fashion houses, even if they are unable to successfully establish themselves as designers in their own right.

Second, attending universities and design schools creates the necessary connections and lays the groundwork for the networks that creative workers need to successfully navigate their careers. As the *New York Times* pointed out in an article on the University of Southern California's School of Cinema-Television, "Rather than a breeding ground for amateurs, film school . . . has become a path to a professional career in Hollywood, a foot in the door and a place to make connections."[35] Both FIT and Parsons have been known to invite buyers from the leading fashion stores (e.g., Barney's, Bergdorf's) to attend graduating students' final fashion shows. If buyers like the students' work, they will purchase an entire line and place it in their stores (as Barney's did with Proenza Schouler)—a surefire recipe for gaining major entry into the fashion market. Design school instructors and professors are often artists and designers themselves (or very well connected with other artists and designers) and are invaluable in internships and job placements, both of which lay the foundations for artists and designers to establish themselves individually, if they are so inclined.

Finally, New York's design schools and universities carry high prestige on a national and global scale, making them magnets for talented individuals who stay in the city. This last aspect contributes to the critical increasing returns associated with maintaining long-term influxes of talent leading to economic growth, innovation, and competitive advantage within the artistic and cultural economy. In this respect, the university, as an effective institution for both providing skilled labor and attracting talented individuals, has a similar function to the educational institutions in successful technology centers like Silicon Valley.

As self-evident as this may seem, especially after a bit of reflection, policymakers have a hard time seeing this. They ought to take an interest in the education and training of cultural producers.

Mayor Bloomberg's commissioner of cultural affairs, Kate Levin, has developed a mandated arts curriculum for public school students, the first since the dismantling of the arts education program during the 1970s fiscal crisis.[36] In higher education, particular initiatives could include funding scholarships for talented individuals, recruitment efforts to attract skilled professors, providing infrastructure, economic, and social support (new classrooms, art and studio materials from paintbrushes to fabric, supporting public-private events that allow students to engage with fashion houses, stores, opera houses, and museums), establishing cooperative relationships between New York's public schools and art and design institutes to educate younger students about careers in art and to scout for up-and-coming talent. Juilliard School and Carnegie Hall have launched programs to bring their music fellows into New York's public schools. Similar targets could be met through funding university and public school initiatives, along with sponsoring cross-university relations and providing resources that these institutions may need, whether it is a new library, more dorms or resources for students (e.g., fabric, paint, etc.). As the *New York Times* reported, free high-technology courses financed by a $3 million grant from the Department of Labor has aided in a resurgence of the city's Silicon Alley.[37] Similar initiatives could further enhance the city's creative sector. By supporting the region's artistic and cultural educational institutions, New York not only aids in optimizing the potential of these "talent factories" but also sends a broader global signal of its support for its cultural community, which is an effective lure in drawing more creative human capital.

Supporting Where Creativity Happens

In May 2006, the *New York Post*'s Page Six reported that the super exclusive Meatpacking District lounge the Double Seven was possibly going to have to shut down by the end of the year. While the owners had dumped lots of money and two years of renovations, construction, and planning into opening it, the building in which the lounge resides had been sold and the new owner had invoked a "demolition clause" that allowed him to kick out current tenants for new development. As it turns out, the speculation was accurate.

The Double Seven had to move to Gansevoort Street because the building that housed the original location of the lounge was sold for $18 million. While the owners of the Double Seven were paid to move out, they will still have to raise more money to rebuild. You know things have gotten out of control when even posh nightlife establishments are having trouble making rent. As Lotus and Double Seven owner David Rabin notes, "Rents on the south side of 14th Street *were* about $60 per square foot a few years ago, now they have skyrocketed." Similar events have surrounded Mario Batali's restaurant Del Posto, where disputes with the landlord threatened to close down the establishment. Despite the negative economic impact of these events, the city has often let the entertainment industries fend for themselves or has actively supported the real estate developers and landlords—which is ironic considering that nightlife is a $9.7 billion industry in New York City.[38]

In 2003, nightlife generated 95,000 jobs and $2.6 billion in earnings. The industry contributed an estimated $391 million in tax revenues to New York City and an additional $321 million to New York State, numbers that have undoubtedly gone up in the ensuing years.[39] My interviewees overwhelmingly pointed toward the intrinsic link between their economic success and their social life, especially the exclusive clubs, rock venues, and lounges they attend. Michael Musto, the longtime nightlife columnist for the *Village Voice*, remarked, "I've always been amazed that it [nightlife] is a place for creative expression and at the same time a place to get ahead and network." These venues offer the infrastructure where deals are made, talent is spotted, and networking is conducted. I've talked about this at length in a previous chapter, so I'll avoid details here. But the general sentiment is this: in the eyes of artistic and cultural producers, there is no overestimating the significance of nightlife to the economic well-being of their creative lives. Nightlife is also often the stage in which creative production is evaluated. This process occurs by way of creative review but also in the simple relationship between talent scouts, Artist and Repertoire (A&R) (those who come to the shows and sign musicians to big labels),[40] and the musician performing on the stage. Music venues are the systematic way in which performers are evaluated, and if evaluated well, end up with record deals.

So it's alarming, at best, that the city government has such a punitive approach toward nightlife. From the lack of support that CBGB received to the overly watchful eye that the police have on nightclubs, these very institutions that are so significant to the cultural economy are perpetually subjected to scrutiny and general acrimony. With increasing use (and impending possible expansion) of the Nuisance Abatement Law, club owners are faced with impromptu shutdowns that are based on allegations, not convictions. As David Rabin explained to me, "The manner in which enforcing and expanding the Nuisance Abatement Law (NAL) [occurs] is the problem. The NAL is the methodology by which they close down nightlife. They [the civil enforcement unit of the NYPD] do it via ex parte proceedings—meaning they go to a judge on a Tuesday or a Wednesday with a big affidavit and say, 'This club is an imminent threat to public safety, and you, judge, should close it down.' And the club is allowed to come back three days later. Generally, they wait 'til the Friday night, the start of the weekend, to close down the club during the biggest revenue nights when this could have been taken care of on a Monday or a Tuesday. And it's not just the club owners, they're hurting all the busboys, the waitresses, the attendants who depend on their weekly earnings and then they can't pay their rent . . . Philosophically we believe that nightlife is so important as an industry in terms of tourism dollars and what not and the image that NYC presents to the world as a city that never sleeps, as a center of all things exciting . . . What they should do is say, 'We've identified this problem in your nightclub, let's figure out a way to solve it.' Instead they're like 'Gotcha.' The city fails to see the importance of nightlife to the city's economy, and when you've got over 65 million nightlife entrances per year, that's a big mistake." If the city is truly interested in furthering economic development, it should adopt a more flexible and even nurturing approach to nightlife, starting with acknowledging its economic worth and the wealth it has generated for the city. Rabin notes, "When artists such as Moby, Madonna or Maxwell are discovered in New York City's clubs and go on to sell millions of records for music labels located in New York, doesn't the income generated by those record companies contribute to New York's economy? We think it does. Nightlife also helps the City and its economy when important firms like Citibank and Merrill Lynch use the City's legendary nightlife as an enticement when recruiting prospective employees to New York."[41]

What could the city government do? First, it could relax its general wariness toward New York's nightlife scene. Second, it could look toward making the process from zoning to construction to financing of new venues easier, with a support system (even a department) within the city government to help oversee their development. And it could get involved when instrumental institutions like the Double Seven or Mario Batali's restaurant are being pushed around by landlords. This is the type of approach the government uses with financial firms, the film industry, educational institutions, and myriad other industries. Three hundred art galleries crowd the West 20s between Tenth and Eleventh avenues. The city has recognized the importance (but also the needs) of Chelsea as an art district, and has developed more liberal zoning regulations for them. Such initiatives could serve as a model for more relaxed nightlife zoning. These same policies must establish a balance between supporting nightlife and containing it such that it does not interfere with quality of life for residents living near clubs, bars, and lounges. As the *New York Times* reports, the city has been unresponsive to local residents "forced to regularly confront the city's nightlife mayhem."[42] Part of the problem has been the expansion of residential zoning into all parts of Manhattan, thus areas that were once zoned for industry or entertainment venues have become residential enclaves as well, which means an influx of people who don't want to be awoken at 2 a.m. by club-goers. And, even those who do want to live in hip neighborhoods bring a set of unanticipated concerns. As Rabin explains, "As is typical of New York, areas that were 'dead' because the existing businesses left—like the Flatiron District, once a printing center, or SoHo, historically the center of manufacturing—are pioneered by galleries and restaurants and clubs. Usually what follows is residential use mixed in, which is what causes so many problems—When people think it would be 'cool' to live in the 'hot' area and then realize how noisy that area can really be . . . whatever that area is." Tensions can also occur as the demographic changes. Rabin notes, "People when they are younger want to live in a 'hot' area, but then a few years later, when they are married with a kid, they don't want to hear any noise anymore." One tack could be restricting the number of clubs or bars that can locate in close proximity to residential areas, thus preventing disruption to community residents, or, alternatively, zoning areas for nightlife and entertainment. Another would be to actually create nightlife districts with no residential use.

In the spirit of encouraging these cultural nodes, policymakers should look to the success of associations and clubs in the development of Silicon Valley as an example of how to foster creativity. Indeed, New York's semiannual Fashion Week (responsible for dictating the trends and styles for the next season) and the Council of Fashion Designers of America (the leading trade association for fashion, touting almost 300 designers as members) are two great examples of associations that are publicly supported and that generate an exciting dialogue regarding ideas and creativity, along with promoting future endeavors within the industry. Starting with these as fine examples, the city should find other ways of encouraging public discourse about culture. By way of example, "South by Southwest," the Austin, Texas, annual four-day music festival, which has become a celebration for artists and politicians alike, includes over 10,000 diverse musicians from rappers to folk singers.

While New York City certainly has its share of music festivals and art fairs, the city itself could become more involved in these efforts. The lack of support and the subsequent removal of the International Freedom Center, a cultural center that was to be built at Ground Zero, has proved divisive, causing Agnes Gund, a leading arts patron, to resign from the World Trade Center Memorial Foundation Board. Further, many cultural organizations feel that the city has been unsupportive of the arts since 9/11. Particularly, arts groups feel that the Lower Manhattan Development Corporation has been less than ambitious in accomplishing the goal of relocating cultural institutions downtown—the $45 million in funding for cultural groups has still not been distributed.[43] The lackluster approach that some of New York's arts policies have taken has led to strained relationships across the cultural economy and has certainly diluted the faith that cultural organizations have in the administration and each other. As artists have indicated, the social network and associations that they have are intrinsic to their success, and economic development policy should address and capitalize on these relationships, not hinder them. Undoubtedly, targeting the social production system is an ambiguous task at best. I do not have the final word on how to facilitate these dynamics other than to allow it to exist and in that sense avoid overregulation and ignoring its importance.

Tax Initiatives and Public Funding

Other possibilities include supporting creative industries through tax breaks and incentives. Already, the city offers a 10 percent tax credit or refund on film projects' spending in New York, along with an additional 5 percent if the film is produced in New York City. Other regions, such as California and even more so Louisiana, offer significant resources and breaks to the film industry. In 2005, some Californian politicians promoted a bill that would offer $50 million a year or more to the industry, twice what is available from the New York State film office (the bill, AB 777, failed to go through in May 2006).[44] While the city has walked a slippery (and unrewarding) slope in its tax incentive strategies directed toward the financial industry, it would be useful to see if artistic and cultural industries responded more positively (or actually kept their word) to such schemes, and if they are more effectively directed toward creative industries than the financial sector. To that end, I am not advocating directing billions of dollars toward art and culture strategy, but instead, more economically cautious but possibly effective steps in encouraging art and culture industries to remain and encourage the creative agglomeration that the region possesses.

Right now, through New York City's Department of Cultural Affairs (DCLA), the nation's largest cultural funding agency (with a 2006 capital budget of $803 million distributed over the next four years and a 2006 expense budget of $131 million), the government funds specific cultural organizations, gives direct subsidies to thirty-four cultural institutions residing on city-owned land (e.g., museums, performing arts centers, theaters), and offers capital spending for construction and renovation at selected institutions. Recently, Mayor Bloomberg has changed the city's arts financing for the better. While the thirty-four organizations known as the Cultural Institutions Group will continue to receive funding (increased from a base of $102 million to $119.7 million for fiscal year 2008), the new funding process will distribute additional cultural funds through peer-review panels. Now, art organizations big and small will compete for the Department of Cultural Affairs' Cultural Development Fund of $30 million, a dramatic increase from the $3.8 million annual allotment established in 2003. Further, cultural organizations will now be given money based on merit (as opposed to effective lobbying or political ties), which will be monitored through CultureStat, a measuring tool borrowed from the police department's performance-evaluation process. These changes in government financing of the arts may cause larger organizations like the Metropolitan Museum of Art or Carnegie Hall to take a hit, but will significantly give smaller organizations more of a shot at funding.[45] The Department of Cultural Affairs also runs the Materials for the Arts program, which provides physical resources to institutions with arts-related agendas or programs. The DCLA is responsible for the aforementioned Percent for Art program. Despite the recent increases in budget and funding capabilities, the DCLA is still working with limited resources, and the government's economic support directed toward art and culture is a mere fraction of the support that the financial industry receives in tax incentives and the like.

Rethinking Artists-in-Residence

In the spring of 2005, on a date with my then boyfriend, I had the opportunity to attend a party in a SoHo "artists" loft. The "artists" were actually a professor at Columbia University's Business School and a finance whiz for Goldman Sachs. Their apartment was very nice (completely remodeled with a marble and steel bathroom, giant deck, and hardwood floors) but certainly did not conjure up visions of starving artists needing a work/live space. The city's "artists-in-residence" program seems a bit problematic in its ability to sort out who's really an artist and who's an investment banker with a knitting hobby. As rents for apartments and workspaces skyrocket in New York, cultural producers need real caps on how much they have to pay for where they live and work, to prevent what my former professor Elliot Sclar has called the *SoHo Effect—*

artists move to a blighted neighborhood, make it interesting, and then, with rents rising because of the neighborhood's new creative cachet, wealthier residents come in, push up the rents, and push out the very artists out that made the place special and interesting in the first place. As Lorraine Gordon of the Village Vanguard put it, "Look, there are a lot of art galleries that started in SoHo moved to Chelsea, there was an out flux of galleries to Chelsea [because] SoHo was being turned into a shopping mall."

The city could also consider subsidizing rent for artists or purchasing apartment buildings for artists to live (and cluster) together, as was done with the Westbeth artists' residence on the West side of Manhattan. For those in arts who are eligible for Section 8 housing, such clustering would encourage a denser art community, while also providing subsidized housing. Another option would be to provide subsidies or redevelopment support for artists who redevelop old buildings—which would encourage home ownership. In an attempt to avoid $2,000-a-month rents, artists have renovated an old schoolhouse communal work-live space in Bushwick, a neighborhood in Brooklyn. These artists have redeveloped the space in their own right and allow new artists to live there when space is made available.[46] The city should look at how it can support more of these types of communities, by providing loans and grants for the redevelopment of old buildings. Because there is a certain revolving door to these communal work-live spaces, they allow for new artists to come to New York and find affordable housing.

Another alternative is to provide free or highly subsidized workspace for writers, musicians, artists, and designers. For on average $100 a month, writers can join places like Paragraph, off Union Square, and The Village Quill in Tribeca, which offer writing space (complete with a desk, a lamp, and a power strip) and sometimes gallery space for artists, open twenty-four hours a day.[47] Part of the problem for artists in New York is that even if they can afford rent, they do not have the space to work (where does an easel or piano go in a 400-square-foot studio?). A way to alleviate this problem would be to create free or subsidized workspace for artists in older or abandoned buildings. It has long been noted that artists often revitalize areas just by living or working in a particular neighborhood. Placing these work-live spaces in economically depressed areas of the city such as the Bronx and parts of Brooklyn and Queens may actually aid in overall revitalizing of these neighborhoods while also providing inexpensive spaces for cultural production.

Another difficult but essential task for those creating policy for art and culture is determining how to handle the social nature of cultural production and valorization, and the fact that so much of its value is subjective and so much of attaining value is by virtue of which social networks a creative producer is running in and which gatekeepers an artist has access to.

Policymakers do have opportunities to create better environments for art and culture. As the sociologist Howard Becker points out in his seminal book *Art Worlds*, "States, and the governmental apparatus through which they operate, participate in the production and distribution of art within their borders. Legislatures and executives make laws, courts interpret them and bureaucrats administer them. Artists, audiences, suppliers, distributors—all the varied personnel who cooperate in the production and consumption of works of art—act within the framework provided by those laws . . . Failing to exercise forms of control available to it through that monopoly, of course, constitutes an important form of state action."

While Becker is focused on contracts, nuisance, censorship, and counterfeits, his point applies here too. Policymakers may not be able to regulate which designers become friends with which editors, but they can monitor whether money is being exchanged for photo shoots, radio play (payola), and editorials (advertorials). Or what sort of illegal contracts gallery owners have with buyers or if artists' demand is being rigged, as Attorney General Spitzer has done in attempting to control payola practices in the music industry.

Further, by supporting industry associations, institution building, academic fellowships, rent control, and support for "real" artists, and knowledge exchange, the social networks that only the wealthy and highly privileged have access to could be more reachable for those with fewer social skills but lots of talent. Policymakers may not be able to build the types of nightclubs and restaurants where creative producers will want to fraternize until 4 a.m., but they can encourage dialogue and access for more artists through the support of the Council of Fashion Designers of America, Fashion Week, and the various music and art fairs that New York holds several times a year. Creativity and the arts are an integral part of New York City. If the city and its denizens want to take advantage of culture—and they clearly seem to want to—then they must be prepared to support the venues where it happens.

Lessons from New York

New York is not the only great center of cultural production, but understanding New York's art and culture system sheds light on how creativity works more broadly and gives us some avenues to apply these findings to other cities and places. Aspen, Colorado, has fantastic skiing and yet people still ski in Canada and Vermont. Santa Fe, New Mexico, has amazing art; Atlanta, Georgia, produces fabulous rap music; and San Francisco and Chicago publish great books. But before I make some recommendations to other cities based on the evidence here, I will point out that places must build on their own strengths. Not everyone can produce and support a thriving creative scene to bolster the region's economy. Just as there is no point in trying to create a high-tech cluster or develop the steel industry if your region does not possess computer scientists and venture capitalists or iron ore and Andrew Carnegie money, regions should not jump on the bandwagon to create a cultural Mecca if they do not have at least the beginnings in place. This would be a recipe for disaster and a lot of wasted time and money that could go to targeting a city's real strength. Locales should look to build on their advantages, not try to create ones that do not at least partly exist already.

That said, many places have a cultural core or niche, whether it be in rap music, folk music, Southwestern painting, or fashion. Some places, like New York, Los Angeles, San Francisco, and Chicago, have concentrations of a variety of different cultural industries from publishing to music to graphic design. Part of understanding a city's economic advantage is to actually do a systematic analysis of the region or city's industrial and occupational distribution. Often such research unearths surprising results. For example, while art and culture have always been associated with New York City, it was surprising to find that creative industries are far more concentrated in the city than even finance, advertising, and CEO positions, for which New York has perhaps an even greater reputation.

So how does what we have found in New York City tell us something about art and culture more broadly, and how can we apply these insights to other places? There are four important and discreet observations that this book intended to convey, and I believe these points apply to art and culture anywhere that it can be observed as a part of an urban or regional economy.

Art and culture matter to economic growth. Dismissive assumptions that label cultural production as frivolous, extraneous, or as a mere amenity for other important industries like finance, do art and culture a disservice. More pertinently, such stereotypes are remarkably myopic when it comes to economic growth. Art and culture certainly do provide entertainment and serve as a tourist attraction—but this entertainment and tourism generates millions and millions of dollars. Places that have a cultural center that draws visitors should aim to make it a focal point of their policy and economic development ventures, because culture truly draws economic vitality and creates strong positive associations with place. Above attracting tourists, art and culture attract educated, productive, wealth-generating people who want to live in cultural hubs. Wealthy people like to be in places with strong quality-of-place and diverse lifestyle options to consume (whether high-end fashion or the opera or live theater). Places always want educated people who are productive and innovative and contribute to the overall growth of the economy. In this respect understanding the importance of the arts to urban and regional economies is a no-brainer. Educated people have more options about where they want to go (they are in high demand and have the opportunity to work in many different places and firms), and given these options they will go to places that have things they like to do, scenes they want to be a part of, and often this means having a strong and diverse cultural scene. It is not just that they like to spend money on culture; it is that they want to feel like they are a part of a culturally alive, edgy, progressive, modern, or refined place. A city's art and culture scene is responsible for cultivating this reputation—and this will attract or repel depending on how supportive local policymaking is in supporting the arts and making sure it remains vibrant. But art and culture, as this book has shown, create lots of jobs and lots of wealth in their own right. In other words, they stand on their own. Art and culture are not the little sisters to finance or management, they are just as good and should be treated as such. To put it simply, regional and urban economies should not underestimate the economic contribution that art and culture makes to their economy and they should do everything in their power to utilize culture as a tourist attraction, an amenity and as a job and wealth generator.

Art and culture are at their most efficient within their social life. While we know the importance of the art and culture scene, we have not always been sure of how it works. Most fundamentally, what this book has conveyed is that art and culture, by their nature, are inherently social. In terms of how products are diffused, creativity is valued, careers are developed, jobs are offered, the social environment is a very important backdrop to the creative production process. In that vein, it is important that cities with an artistic and cultural core work toward supporting (as opposed to shutting down) the places in which art and culture "happen." Part of this is less punitive approaches toward nightlife, and part of this is supporting nontraditional institutions, from small galleries to music venues, not just dumping money into big museums and public art. If art and culture are primarily happening after-hours, then does it not make the most sense to support these industries and organizations the most?

Art and culture work best when they are most dense. It is the concentrated environment of work-live-play that makes art and culture work in New York City. The neighborhoods that are most creatively dense are also those that have a diversity of galleries, nightlife, coffee shops, and residences that allows a constant, to use Jane Jacobs' poignant phrase, "intricate sidewalk ballet."[48] In that sense, cities should look to ways to facilitate this, both in zoning to allow for mixed-use work-live spaces, and by making it affordable for artists to live collectively in the same neighborhoods. Pricing out artists inherently prices out creativity and its density, and that of course destroys the fabric of how art and culture work.

Art and culture work as a unified whole. In terms of the intangible inspiration that different industries give one another and also with regard to developing careers, valuing each other's products and diffusing ideas, trends and artistic movements, art and culture operate across a broad creative economy. As this is the case, cities should create initiatives (from public events to institution-building) and policy that target art and culture as a whole. Sure, the film industry will still need its own tax breaks and fashion will always have Fashion Week. But artistic and cultural producers do not see themselves as completely separate entities; they see themselves as a cohesive and synchronistic community. The establishment of policies to further creative production should include ways to facilitate more interaction, collaboration, and exchange of creativity. For example, the establishment of a mayoral office that deals with finding housing, university fellowships, or funding should include lots of different creative workers, from painters to musicians. Further, housing for artists, especially collective residences, should invite applications from not just painters or sculptors but also struggling fashion designers and musicians. We know that these different occupational groups have often collaborated and produced important and economically rewarding products, events, and artworks.

Consider GenArt, the cultural organization that funds and launches all types of creative producers from film to fashion. GenArt has been responsible for the initial success of Zac Posen, Rebecca Taylor, and Alexandre Plokhov, to name a few fashion designers that have been supported by the organization. GenArt actually puts together high-caliber fashion shows during Fashion Week for a select group of promising designers. Who's to say city government can't have a fund to help out designers, artists, and musicians? Other countries such as Canada, Australia, and New Zealand all have state, federal, and public-private funds that support musicians. Factor, a Canadian public-private agency that offers musicians funding, has a budget of $12.4 million and in 2005 handed out awards to over 30 percent of applicants, with grants of up to $140,000. In Australia, federal funding offers up to 50 percent support for a music band's traveling expenses (past recipients include the endlessly popular Wiggles).[49]

Fundamentally, arts and culture policy should aim to encourage and sustain the creative agglomeration that attracts thousands of artistic and cultural producers to the New York region—and cities like Los Angeles, Chicago, New Orleans, Santa Fe, and countless other places, year after year. Instead of shutting down nightclubs and supporting inarticulate public art, policymaking should look to ways in which this artistic and cultural environment is reinforced and should establish public policy to address the needs of the vibrant creative economy. Policymakers must appreciate art and culture as a collective strength and understand that its production does not always happen within the formal walls of institutions but instead in a very free-flowing synergy across all types of creative production and in all types of nontraditional places—and in that vein develop policy and an environment that nurtures and optimizes these dynamics.

Artistic creativity happens in New York because it is a city that allows for the production of culture, not just in galleries and music venues but in bars and nightlife and on the street. Creating culture is only possible by creating the places that not only permit but encourage creativity to happen. New York is such a place.

Epilogue

It was the usual state of affairs before an important interview. I was dead late, racing to get there in inappropriate shoes that were dangerously tempting my downfall. Only this time, I was in Los Angeles, having just moved here from New York City, and the journey first required that I drive, making my trip far more taxing (and perilous—I have no idea how to drive). In New York, I would have efficiently multitasked, applying mascara and lip gloss as a cab bombed me downtown.

As I slammed on my brakes at the junction of Sunset and Hollywood Boulevards, I realized there was no chance I would be on time. I was in Los Feliz and still needed to get into Hollywood, and the traffic lights were not on my side. I was scrambling to meet Lee Sargent, one of the guitar players and keyboardists for the indie band Clap Your Hands Say Yeah, which had made a splash in 2006 with their independently produced and released eponymous debut. My dress, a very tiny Diane von Furstenberg number unconducive to driving, was moving around in an unseemly fashion while my stiletto heels threatened to rip through the carpet each time I slammed on the brakes.

Racing into the smoggy sunset past the palm trees and fluorescent neon signs advertising girls, liquor, and celebrity, I arrived at the Henry Fonda Theater and found parking on Vine Street off Sunset. I parked exactly on time, which meant that by the time I hobbled over to the theater, passing an enormous Hummer/limousine monstrosity and a line of hipster kids waiting to go inside for that night's show, I found myself less than ten minutes late. I walked up to one of the too-cool-for-school bouncers clad in an impeccable black suit. "Um, I'm here to interview the band. I tried Lee Sargent's cell, it went straight to voicemail but I'm supposed to be here. . . . Can I just come in?" The bouncer naturally looked at me with complete disdain. "No, you can't 'just come in here.' Go around the back, maybe they can help you."

That sure went well. I stomped into an alleyway behind the theater. It had rained for the first time since I had moved out here and the alley was covered in puddles that I nimbly tried to avoid. I met another two security personnel, this time more casually dressed in hooded sweatshirts, guarding the theater's back entrance. The same conversation ensued, except that this bouncer simply told me to stand outside and wait. "But he might be inside, and I'm supposed to interview him at 7 p.m.," I whined. The bouncer remained adamant, as ten minutes late turned quickly into fifteen and then twenty minutes. I tapped my foot impatiently in the cold floodlights and directed mean glares at him, but he was impervious. Even in Los Angeles it gets a bit chilly for bare legs in October.

A few more minutes went by and a black-clad, stylishly scruffy character came swaggering around the corner. I don't know if it was my shivering and looking pathetic or perhaps my self-righteous outthrust hip on which I rested my hand, but he stopped and asked, "You looking for someone?" just as a car turned into the alley and splashed water from a big muddy puddle all over my legs. I started the same conversation with him as I had with bouncers number one and two, but this time the guy (manager, part of stage crew, who knows?) said he'd find Lee for me and went inside. A little bit later he emerged to inform me that Lee was out to dinner and would be back in an hour or two. (I've done enough of these interviews to know this is the standard artist/musician time warp I'm dealing with here, so I'm not offended.) Simultaneously, a tall lanky guy with strawberry blond hair strolled into the alleyway carrying a big cardboard box of T-shirts. Robbie Guertin: one of the other guitar players and keyboardists for the band.

"So are your questions 'Lee specific'?" he asked, laughing, "because I can talk to you, too." I am relieved and grateful as I follow Robbie in (while giving a few final mean looks to the bouncers). We head into the main theater lobby and I help him fold T-shirts as he checks off inventory (being an indie band, Clap Your Hands takes care of a lot of their own stuff). Afterward we go backstage to start the interview in his dressing room. Robbie says, "You know, I'm really hungry, can we go get sushi?" Into the night we went, passing by the long line of fans waiting to get into the theater, who oddly don't notice one of the stars of the show casually strolling by. We headed east on Sunset Boulevard looking for a sushi restaurant Robbie had spotted earlier that turns out to be closed. So we kept walking until we came to a Thai restaurant with Elvis music echoing through the doorway. We're greeted with bright fluorescent lighting and a cafeteria-esque layout of tables and booths, and naturally, because we are in Los Angeles, an Asian Elvis impersonator in a red velvet blazer belting out "I Can't Help Falling In Love With You."

While Robbie downed his green curry, I peppered him with questions about New York, the band's speed-of-light success, and all those questions I've asked dozens and dozens of times. After talking about New York, my move to LA to work at University of Southern California, his impending trip to Tokyo, we realize that he probably should get back to the theater. The show is starting in an hour and Robbie's still eating sticky rice.

When we get outside the sky has cleared up and it has become that typical Los Angeles night—warm, dry, and filled with palm trees. Robbie and I parted ways and I found my friends who were also coming to the show. As I stood in line at the ATM in the lobby, Robbie appeared again. "Hey, do you have one of these?" he asked as he handed me a green paper bracelet. "It's a backstage pass if you want to come after the show." Robbie, in a faded T-shirt and corduroys with naturally tousled hair (no gel involved here), encapsulated the appeal of Clap Your Hands: unassuming, unpretentious, and just plain nice.

After two opening acts, Clap Your Hands came on around midnight. The show had sold out and the crowd was packed. It was the last show of the band's U.S. tour, so maybe that's why they seemed particularly rambunctious. Much to the crowd's delight the band played tracks from their album that would be out in January 2007 (which as it turns out also received impressive reviews). The songs were as good as the quirky, emotional songs off their first album that had made them stars. And, despite all their recent success, they were still a bunch of Brooklyn kids in grungy clothes who acted more like they were playing music for their friends in a small venue on the Lower East Side, not a big sold-out theater in Los Angeles.

Members of Clap Your Hands Say Yeah with members of their opening acts, Architecture in Helsinki and Taka Taka, in Los Angeles at the end of the final show of their 2006 U.S. tour. Photographer: Rachael Porter. © Rachael Porter. Used by permission.

But it was because Clap Your Hands had bothered to play in the gritty LES bars for friends and then friends of friends and then music critics and then David Bowie and David Byrne that they were here in Los Angeles and then off to Tokyo in a week for another string of shows. Because of New York, they were here in Los Angeles. Even 3,000 miles away, they are still creating New York, just as New York helped create them.

Appendix

Interviews

Fashion Designers

Francisco Costa
Lazaro Hernandez of Proenza Schouler
Gordan Hull, Surface to Air
Daniel Jackson, Surface to Air
Elisa Jimenez
Matthew Jurecic
Donna Kang
Jean Claude Mastroianni
Alexandre Plokhov of Cloak
Zac Posen
Cynthia Rowley
Gillian Schwartz, former art director for Kate Spade
Andy Spade
John Varvatos
Jennifer Vendetti, fashion casting, Jennifer Vendetti
Diane von Furstenberg
Bonnie Young, senior creative director, Donna Karan
Min Young, Chaiken

Artists/Graphic Designers

Claw
Colt45
Will Cotton
DAZE
Wendy Dembo
Shepard Fairey
Futura
Ari Joseph
Ryan McGinness
Bill McMullen

Kenzo Minami
Anja Mohn
Morgan Phillips
Lady Pink
Ricky Powell
Steve Powers
Lee Quinones
Semz
Reuban Sinha
Tobias Wong

Musicians

Aesop Rock
Beans
Coleman
Ben Dietz
Robbie Guertin, bass player/keyboardist, Clap Your Hands
    Say Yeah
Jerry Harrison, guitarist, Talking Heads
Quincy Jones
JS1
Richard Lloyd, guitarist, Television
Marshall Law
Kevin McHugh
Soheil Nassari
Lee Sargent, guitarist/keyboardist, Clap Your Hands Say Yeah
Larry Tee
Sam Wheeler, guitarist, Soft
The Xecutioners

Club Owners and PR

Jo Addy, Soho House
Saidah Blount, APT
Lorraine Gordon, owner, Village Vanguard
Jared Hoffman, president, Knitting Factory
KPlus, PR, 105.1

Hilly Kristal, founder/owner CBGB
Ray Pirkle, APT/Bette
David Rabin, owner, Lotus

Cultural Institutions

Paola Antonelli, curator, MoMA
Jeffrey Deitch, art dealer and gallery owner, Deitch Projects
Ian Gerard, president, GenArt
Vardit Gross, Creative Time
Robin Keegan, Center for an Urban Future
Alan Klotz, gallery owner, Klotz Gallery
Maureen McKnighton, Upper Manhattan Empowerment
 Zone
Meres, Five Points
Voza Rivers, director, Harlem Arts Alliance
Tom Sokolowski, the Andy Warhol Museum
Valerie Steele, curator, the Museum at the Fashion Institute
 of Technology

Media

Stephen Blackwell, editor, *Death + Taxes* magazine
Lisa Gabor, editor (formerly), InStyle.com (magazine)
Cathy Horyn, fashion critic, the *New York Times*
Faran Krentcil, writer, the *Daily Mini* and *Nylon* magazine
Carlo McCormick, editor, *Paper* magazine
Michael Musto, columnist, *Village Voice*
Tony Silver, director, *StyleWars*
Sally Singer, fashion news and features director, *Vogue*
 magazine
Ingrid Sischy, editor, *Interview* magazine

Table 1 [a]

2004 Occupational Location Quotients for Major MSAs: Management and Finance

Occupation	New York	Austin	Boston	Charleston	Chicago	Los Angeles	Miami	Minneapolis-St. Paul	Raleigh-Durham	San Diego	San Francisco	Washington, DC
Command and Control/Management												
Administrative services managers	1.46	0.00	1.54	1.82	1.16	0.91	0.63	0.86	0.66	0.82	1.14	2.16
Chief executives	1.02	0.69	2.45	1.64	1.64	0.91	1.00	0.59	0.27	1.03	1.39	1.03
Food service managers	0.63	1.60	1.26	1.18	0.84	1.28	0.86	1.00	1.10	1.24	1.15	0.72
Advertising and promotions managers	2.17	1.13	1.61	1.03	1.46	1.39	0.75	0.50	0.84	1.19	2.37	1.54
General and operations managers	0.74	1.28	1.30	1.37	1.08	1.05	0.62	0.89	1.10	1.04	1.33	1.39
Human resources managers	1.83	0.76	1.52	0.58	1.06	0.92	0.46	2.14	1.28	1.14	1.74	1.70
Industrial production managers	0.43	1.16	1.02	1.13	0.96	0.94	0.40	1.34	1.03	1.02	0.55	0.28
Legislators	0.27	0.00	0.00	1.80	1.61	0.43	0.52	1.43	0.00	0.75	1.34	0.45
Marketing managers	1.44	1.19	2.14	0.65	1.30	1.14	0.70	1.44	1.58	1.35	2.34	1.10
Managers, all other	1.09	0.56	1.36	0.51	2.17	0.86	0.78	1.48	1.32	1.15	1.68	2.23
Purchasing managers	0.77	0.87	1.32	1.10	1.36	1.25	0.60	1.32	1.26	1.27	0.98	1.37
Sales managers	0.73	0.94	1.50	0.91	1.32	1.16	0.70	1.24	1.15	1.08	1.58	0.90
Management Overall	1.05	0.85	1.42	1.14	1.33	1.02	0.67	1.18	0.97	1.09	1.47	1.24
Finance												
Accountants and auditors	1.68	1.76	1.16	0.79	1.17	0.95	1.16	1.13	0.86	0.86	1.20	1.29
Actuaries	2.54	2.00	3.05	0.00	3.16	0.79	0.00	2.17	0.00	0.00	2.38	0.93
Budget analysts	0.94	0.00	1.66	0.78	0.88	0.99	0.59	0.29	0.70	1.50	1.42	4.14
Credit analysts	1.31	0.51	1.19	0.30	1.48	1.09	0.96	1.68	0.89	0.91	1.27	0.78
Financial analysts	3.16	1.21	2.16	0.26	1.47	0.86	0.75	1.66	1.75	0.63	2.25	1.34
Financial examiners	2.58	0.00	2.19	0.00	2.10	0.73	0.99	1.48	1.41	0.31	3.73	1.38
Financial managers	1.93	0.97	1.74	0.95	1.08	0.95	0.68	1.14	1.24	1.02	1.64	1.15
Financial specialists, all others	1.89	0.93	0.00	0.59	2.18	1.03	0.93	2.19	2.09	0.00	0.00	1.87
Personal financial advisors	5.23	0.98	1.76	0.76	0.97	1.25	1.75	0.69	0.75	0.79	2.01	0.81
Securities, commodities, and financial service sales agents	3.83	0.61	1.22	0.39	1.57	0.79	1.54	1.69	0.75	1.05	3.81	0.66
Taxpreparers	1.38	0.74	1.00	0.00	1.31	1.97	4.12	1.05	2.91	1.06	1.59	1.75
Finance Overall	2.41	0.88	1.56	0.44	1.58	1.04	1.23	1.38	1.21	0.74	1.94	1.47

Source: Bureau of Labor Statistics, Occupational Employment Statistics.

[a] The data reporting location quotients originally appeared in an earlier article in *Economic Development Quarterly* (Currid 2006a).

Table 2
2004 Occupational Location Quotients for Major MSAs: Professional Services

Occupation	New York	Austin	Boston	Charleston	Chicago	Los Angeles	Miami	Minneapolis-St. Paul	Raleigh-Durham	San Diego	San Francisco	Washington, DC
Law												
Judges, magistrate judges, and magistrate	1.30	0.00	0.00	2.99	1.76	0.00	0.00	1.56	0.00	0.00	0.00	0.00
Lawclerks	3.22	0.00	0.51	0.00	1.26	1.29	1.14	1.12	0.41	0.73	1.97	2.65
Lawyers	2.44	1.30	1.34	0.79	1.24	1.06	1.64	1.09	0.89	0.84	2.07	2.72
Paralegals and legal assistants	1.76	1.36	1.26	1.27	0.61	0.95	1.59	1.29	1.47	1.04	1.97	1.99
Arbitrators, mediators, and conciliators	2.08	0.00	2.50	0.00	1.17	1.97	0.00	4.98	0.00	0.00	0.00	3.89
Administrative law judges, and Court reporters	0.00	0.00	0.00	0.00	0.99	1.37	1.92	0.93	2.96	1.93	3.20	3.64
Court reporters	3.48	0.00	1.89	0.00	0.57	5.98	0.00	0.00	0.00	0.00	0.00	3.02
Law Overall	2.04	0.38	1.07	0.72	1.09	1.80	0.90	1.57	0.82	0.65	1.31	2.56
Education												
Adult literacy, remedial education	1.41	2.45	1.57	2.01	0.99	0.00	1.06	1.88	1.96	1.39	1.10	1.23
Graduate teaching assistants	4.61	0.00	9.92	0.00	0.00	0.00	0.00	0.00	0.00	0.00	0.00	1.19
Self-enrichment education teachers	1.79	0.90	1.25	1.12	0.59	1.01	1.23	0.93	1.74	2.07	1.99	0.99
Education Overall	2.60	1.12	4.25	1.04	0.52	0.34	0.76	0.93	1.23	1.15	1.03	1.14
Medicine												
Medical scientists, except epidemiologist	1.37	2.60	4.66	0.00	0.47	1.18	0.41	1.59	5.19	3.15	8.15	1.46
Internists, general	3.40	0.00	1.33	0.52	1.03	0.52	0.00	2.08	1.56	0.00	0.00	1.28
Podiatrists	6.13	0.00	1.12	0.00	1.34	0.00	1.31	2.43	0.00	0.00	1.31	1.60
Psychiatrists	5.98	1.09	3.36	0.00	0.72	0.00	0.85	1.35	0.00	1.46	1.45	2.13
Medicine Overall	4.22	0.92	2.62	0.13	0.89	0.42	0.64	1.86	1.69	1.15	2.73	1.62
Professional Services Overall	2.95	0.81	2.64	0.63	0.83	0.85	0.77	1.45	1.24	0.98	1.69	1.77

Source: Bureau of Labor Statistics, Occupational Employment Statistics.

Table 3

2004 Occupational Location Quotients for Major MSAs: Engineering and High Technology

Occupation	New York	Austin	Boston	Charleston	Chicago	Los Angeles	Miami	Minneapolis-St. Paul	Raleigh-Durham	San Diego	San Francisco	Washington, DC
Biomedical engineers	0.34	0.00	6.54	0.00	1.99	1.25	0.00	6.37	1.67	6.20	0.00	1.91
Chemical engineers	0.36	0.00	1.85	2.67	0.55	1.34	0.15	1.07	1.72	0.80	0.40	1.36
Civil engineers	0.78	1.49	1.23	1.19	0.62	1.00	1.23	0.62	1.58	1.27	1.81	0.96
Computer and information scientists	0.95	0.00	4.87	3.99	0.67	0.73	0.00	0.00	1.27	3.98	0.00	9.04
Computer and information systems managers	1.25	1.16	1.97	0.72	1.23	0.82	0.52	1.61	1.84	1.00	2.20	2.11
Computer hardware engineers	0.49	8.49	3.95	0.90	0.24	0.92	0.46	0.53	2.37	2.68	2.30	2.75
Computer programmers	1.61	2.18	1.22	0.49	1.04	0.74	0.66	0.84	1.75	0.96	1.53	2.15
Computer software engineers, applications	0.96	1.66	2.41	0.22	0.80	1.10	0.42	2.08	1.58	1.67	2.88	2.45
Computer software engineers, systems software	0.82	3.52	2.75	0.73	1.10	0.83	0.61	1.00	0.00	1.31	2.33	3.62
Computer specialists, all others	0.64	1.03	1.37	0.13	0.00	1.08	0.52	4.20	1.85	2.03	3.23	2.81
Computer support specialists	1.01	1.64	1.48	0.59	0.91	0.86	0.97	1.11	2.55	0.88	1.13	1.84
Computer systems analysts	0.82	2.75	1.53	0.70	1.23	0.71	0.87	1.05	2.00	0.92	1.47	3.36
Electrical engineers	0.57	3.12	2.02	1.05	0.86	1.16	0.35	1.21	0.93	1.32	0.68	1.24
Electro-mechanical technicians	0.00	2.43	7.54	0.00	1.40	1.30	0.00	0.00	0.00	2.69	1.62	0.00
Engineering managers	0.49	1.53	1.51	0.89	0.89	0.95	0.41	1.20	1.62	1.57	1.31	1.39
Environmental engineers	0.59	2.95	1.80	2.39	0.78	0.74	0.38	0.47	0.00	1.07	1.93	4.19
Industrial engineering technicians	0.14	6.88	1.02	1.81	1.08	0.59	0.81	2.61	0.00	0.97	0.00	0.33
Industrial engineers	0.29	1.61	1.41	1.22	0.81	0.81	0.52	1.83	1.07	1.27	0.67	0.48
Materials engineers	0.00	0.00	2.37	0.00	1.72	0.68	0.57	0.96	0.54	2.01	0.67	1.02
Mechanical engineering technicians	0.28	1.45	1.94	0.00	1.05	1.31	0.27	3.39	0.76	1.90	0.57	0.52
Mechanical engineers	0.43	0.70	1.60	0.68	0.94	0.96	0.25	1.74	0.62	1.04	0.59	0.92
Network systems and data communication analysts	1.14	2.16	1.56	0.00	0.98	0.69	0.97	1.27	3.15	1.03	2.23	2.61
Operations research analysts	0.71	4.48	2.28	0.67	0.67	0.67	1.55	1.74	1.12	0.98	2.39	3.90
Engineering and High Technology Overall	0.64	2.23	2.44	0.91	0.94	0.92	0.54	1.60	1.30	1.72	1.39	2.22

Source: Bureau of Labor Statistics, Occupational Employment Statistics.

Table 4

2004 Occupational Location Quotients for Major MSAs: Art and Culture

Occupation	New York	Austin	Boston	Charleston	Chicago	Los Angeles	Miami	Minneapolis-St. Paul	Raleigh-Durham	San Diego	San Francisco	Washington, DC
Artistic and Cultural Occupations												
Architects, except landscape	2.35	1.60	1.80	1.42	1.34	1.06	2.37	1.03	1.07	0.80	3.22	1.54
Art directors	4.90	1.31	1.98	0.00	1.70	1.83	1.11	2.13	0.83	0.69	2.96	1.06
Art, drama, and music teachers	1.19	0.00	2.85	0.00	1.88	1.49	1.54	1.50	1.47	1.02	1.77	1.51
Artists and related workers, all others	4.30	0.00	2.29	0.00	3.76	0.68	0.00	4.06	0.00	2.66	0.00	2.49
Choreographers	1.72	0.00	0.30	0.00	1.81	0.84	0.00	0.39	0.00	0.00	1.59	1.63
Commercial and industrial designers	1.96	0.00	3.92	0.00	0.76	1.19	0.36	1.27	0.00	0.77	1.33	0.46
Craft artists	4.72	0.00	0.00	0.00	0.00	0.00	0.00	7.91	0.00	7.86	0.00	0.00
Curators	3.31	1.23	5.57	0.00	0.81	2.20	1.63	0.58	5.03	0.00	0.00	2.30
Dancers	2.82	0.00	0.00	0.00	0.61	3.98	1.89	4.36	0.00	0.00	7.28	1.45
Designers, all other	2.65	0.00	1.13	0.00	1.95	1.71	1.45	2.08	0.00	0.87	0.00	4.44
Fashion designers	15.98	0.00	0.00	0.00	0.43	4.78	0.88	0.47	0.00	0.57	2.01	0.00
Fine artists, including painters, sculptors	4.98	0.00	3.39	0.00	1.59	1.47	2.58	1.90	3.11	0.75	1.39	1.36
Floral designers	0.84	0.75	0.69	1.97	1.12	0.52	1.07	1.06	0.00	1.37	0.77	0.70
Graphic designers	2.10	1.35	1.21	0.65	0.99	1.25	0.93	1.35	1.04	1.04	1.71	1.15
Interior designers	1.38	2.43	1.03	1.16	1.17	0.75	3.59	1.27	0.91	1.43	1.37	1.41
Multimedia artists and animators	2.61	0.85	2.23	0.00	1.52	6.43	0.00	1.25	0.54	1.88	6.22	1.01
Music directors and composers	0.00	0.00	0.44	0.00	0.75	7.97	3.00	2.07	0.00	1.13	6.62	0.98
Musicians and singers	6.79	0.00	0.97	0.00	1.18	3.41	0.00	0.78	0.00	1.53	3.19	0.90
Film and video editors	6.09	0.00	1.44	0.00	0.57	8.79	2.12	0.73	0.79	0.55	1.75	0.84
Makeup artists, theatrical and performance	19.28	0.00	0.00	0.00	0.00	0.00	0.00	0.00	0.00	0.00	0.00	0.00
Producers and directors	4.15	0.94	0.69	1.14	0.69	6.21	1.38	0.93	1.04	0.70	2.46	1.51
Set and exhibit designers	3.71	1.58	0.00	0.00	2.52	2.66	1.31	0.97	0.00	1.98	3.94	2.99
Writers and authors	2.89	1.81	1.48	0.50	0.00	2.98	1.10	2.46	1.09	0.88	2.10	3.10
Art and Culture Overall	4.38	0.60	1.42	0.30	1.18	2.70	1.23	1.76	0.73	1.24	2.25	1.43

Source: Bureau of Labor Statistics, Occupational Employment Statistics.

Table 5
2004 Occupational Location Quotients for Major MSAs: Media and Broadcasting

Occupation	New York	Austin	Boston	Charleston	Chicago	Los Angeles	Miami	Minneapolis-St. Paul	Raleigh-Durham	San Diego	San Francisco	Washington, DC
Media												
Public Relations/Advertising												
Advertising sales agents	2.83	0.79	0.99	0.68	0.89	1.19	1.12	0.74	0.81	0.89	2.17	0.89
Agents and business managers	3.57	0.00	0.98	0.00	0.89	7.04	1.08	0.36	0.00	1.01	2.02	7.36
Market research analysts	2.15	2.27	0.00	0.34	1.52	0.95	0.71	2.21	1.42	0.77	1.73	1.92
Management analysts	1.11	0.00	1.66	0.83	1.17	0.86	1.04	1.22	0.84	0.90	1.71	4.41
Public relations managers	2.92	1.35	2.00	0.87	1.01	0.95	0.98	1.16	1.72	0.87	2.39	2.14
Public relations specialists	2.06	1.50	0.00	0.53	0.60	0.92	1.48	0.93	1.37	1.06	2.16	2.42
PR/Advertising Overall	2.44	0.99	0.94	0.54	1.01	1.99	1.07	1.10	1.02	0.92	2.03	3.19
Broadcasting, Television etc.												
Audio and video equipment technicians	2.59	0.00	1.21	1.01	0.92	4.12	1.15	1.32	1.31	1.33	1.34	1.83
Broadcast technicians	2.04	1.14	1.32	2.09	0.56	2.68	3.42	0.69	1.29	0.38	1.41	1.33
Camera operators, television, video, and motion picture	3.25	0.55	1.69	0.00	0.69	6.35	1.99	1.17	0.73	0.89	2.21	1.44
Editors	3.82	0.00	2.18	0.00	1.05	1.46	1.21	1.40	0.94	0.87	2.65	2.67
Sound engineering technicians	6.21	0.00	0.00	0.00	0.93	7.25	1.58	0.70	0.00	0.40	1.19	0.90
Media and communication workers	2.89	0.00	1.67	1.07	2.09	2.17	1.93	1.54	0.00	0.60	1.99	4.11
Broadcasting,TV, etc. Overall	3.47	0.28	1.35	0.70	1.04	4.01	1.88	1.14	0.71	0.74	1.80	2.05
Media Overall	2.95	0.63	1.14	0.62	1.03	3.00	1.47	1.12	0.87	0.83	1.91	2.62

Source: Bureau of Labor Statistics, Occupational Employment Statistics.

Charts

All charts for New York City capture the Metropolitan Statistical Area (MSA), which includes the following counties: Bronx, Kings, New York, Putnam, Queens, Richmond, Rockland, and Westchester.

I have also collected and analyzed data for New York City only (Bronx, New York, Kings, Queens, and Richmond counties). The results for NYC proper are virtually identical to those for the MSA, indicating that most economic activity going on within the MSA is occurring in NYC. Thus, the region reflects the economic dynamics of the city. As the MSA has become the standard methodological approach for analyzing urban economies, I have chosen to use this geographical unit in my analysis. In the charts and discussion, this research uses the terms region, city, New York City, and MSA interchangeably because much of the economic activity in the region (MSA) occurs in New York City.

High-skilled occupations (also labeled "advanced" in charts) are defined as human capital–intensive industries (including finance, art and culture, professional services and so on), while service is defined as basic services (food, hotel, retail and wholesale trade, clerical, etc.); working includes labor-intensive industries (construction, manufacturing, transportation); professional services includes highly skilled services (medicine, law, education). When the service industry is discussed more generally, it does not include professional services (which fall into the high-skilled category). NEC represents those industries not easily classified and captures all industries and occupations that could not be clearly placed in any of the former categories.

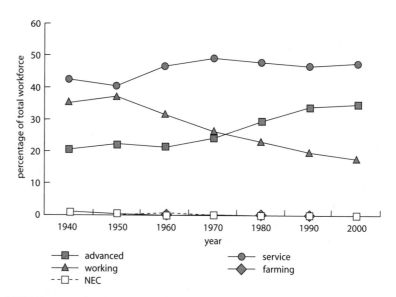

NYC Economy by Occupational classification, 1940–2000. Source: *U.S. Census of Population, PUMS data 1940–2000.*

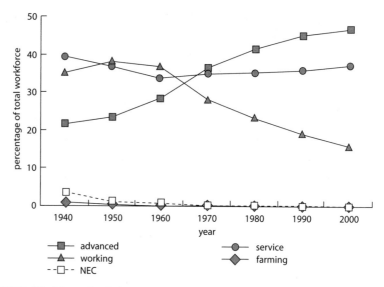

NYC Workforce by Industry, 1940–2000 (industrial classification). Source: *U.S. Census of Population, PUMS data 1940–2000.*

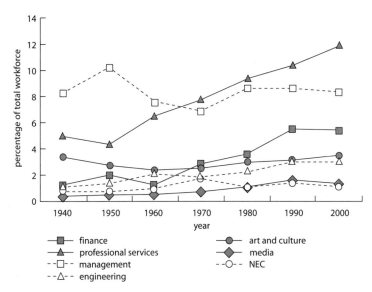

High-skilled Industries in NYC, 1940–2000 (by occupation). Source: *U.S. Census of Population, PUMS data 1940–2000.*

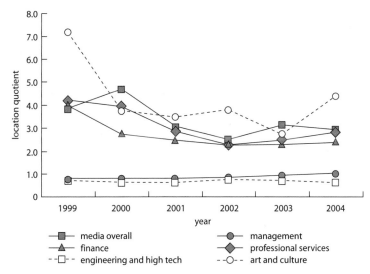

High-skilled Occupational Clusters in NYC, 1999–2004 (by location quotient). Source: *Bureau of Labor Statistics, Occupational Employment Statistics 1999–2004.*

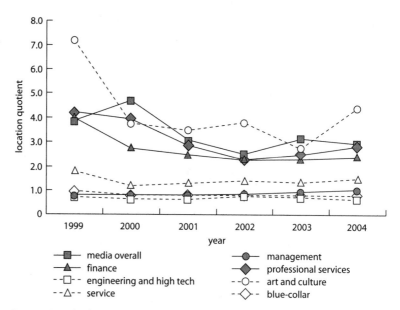

Occupational Clusters in NYC, 1999–2004 (by location quotient). Source: *Bureau of Labor Statistics, Occupational Employment Statistics 1999–2004.*

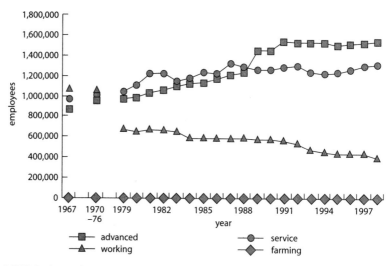

NYC Industrial Growth, 1967–1997 (by employment). Source: *Bureau of Labor Statistics, County Business Patterns 1967–1996.*

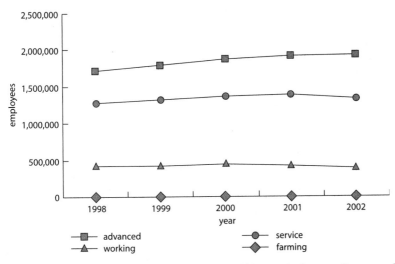

NYC Industrial Growth, 1998–2002 (by employment). Source: *Bureau of Labor Statistics, County Business Patterns 1997–2002.*

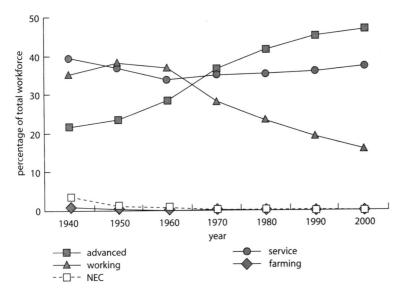

NYC Workforce by Industry, 1940–2000 (industrial classification). Source: *U.S. Census of Population, PUMS data 1940–2000.*

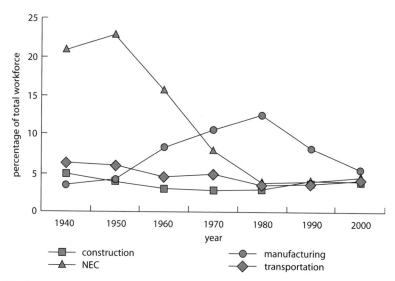

Working Class Industries in NYC, 1940–2000 (by occupation). Source: *U.S. Census of Population, PUMS data, 1940–2000.*

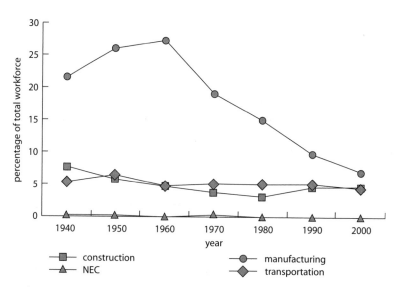

Working-Class Industries, 1940–2000 (by industrial classification). Source: *U.S. Census of Population, PUMS data, 1940–2000.*

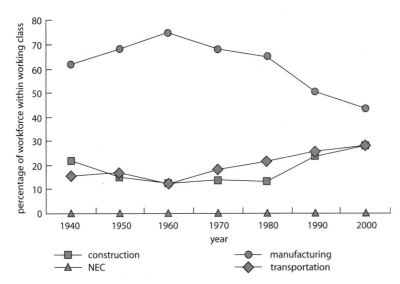

Working Class in NYC, 1940–2000 (by industry). Source: *U.S. Census of Population, PUMS data, 1940–2000.*

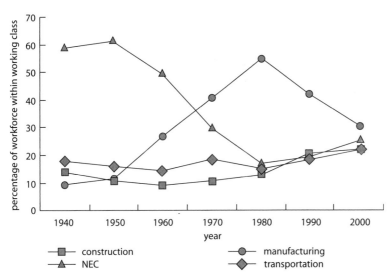

Working Class Occupations in NYC, 1940–2000 (by occupation). Source: U.S. *Census of Population, PUMS data, 1940–2000.*

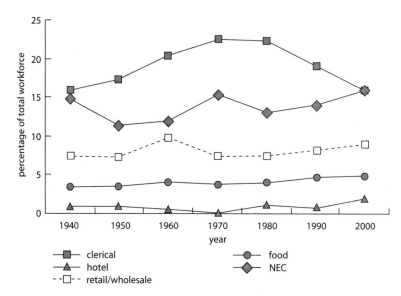

The Service Industry, 1940–2000 (by occupation). Source: *U.S. Census of Population, PUMS data, 1940–2000.*

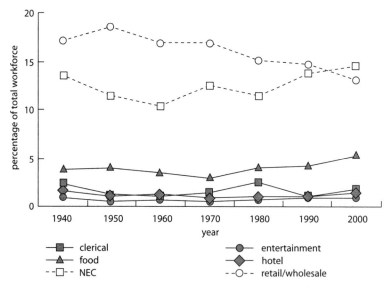

Service Industry, 1940–2000 (by industry). Source: *U.S. Census of Population, PUMS data, 1940–2000.*

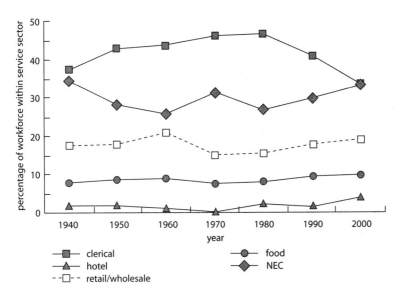

Service industries in NYC, 1940–2000 (by occupation). Source: *U.S. Census of Population, PUMS data, 1940–2000.*

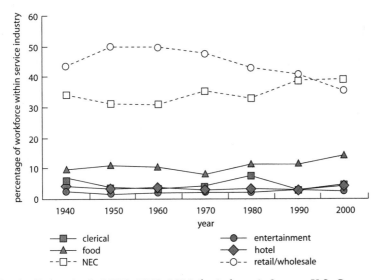

Service Industries in NYC, 1940–2000 (by industry). Source: *U.S. Census of Population, PUMS data, 1940–2000.*

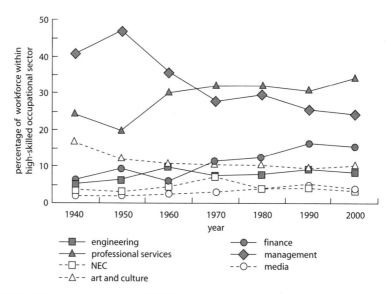

High-skilled Occupations in NYC, 1940–2000 (by occupation). Source: *U.S. Census of Population, PUMS data, 1940–2000.*

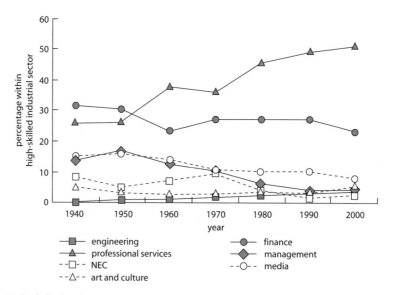

High-skilled Industries in NYC, 1940–2000 (by industry). Source: *U.S. Census of Population, PUMS data, 1940–2000.*

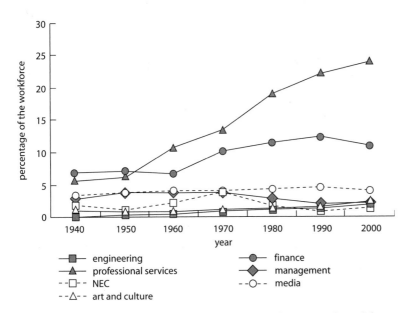

High-skilled Industries in NYC, 1940–2000 (by industry, total workforce).
Source: *U.S. Census of Population, PUMS data, 1940–2000*.

Notes

PREFACE

1. O'Hara 1957.

CHAPTER 1. ART, CULTURE, AND NEW YORK CITY

1. See Richard Marshall 1992. *Jean-Michel Basquiat*. New York: Whitney Museum of American Art. Distributed by Harry N. Abrams, Inc; *Basquiat* (1996). Directed by Julian Schnabel. Mirimax Studio; Taylor 2006.
2. Collins 2006, p. 332.
3. Becker 1982.

CHAPTER 2. HOW IT ALL BEGAN: FROM THE RISE OF THE FACTORY TO THE RISE OF BLING

1. This chapter is an account of the history of creativity in New York, and many of the topics are of common knowledge (e.g., beatniks, Andy Warhol, etc.). That said, to get historical detail I consulted a wide variety of encyclopedic databases, newspaper articles, and so forth. The use of these sources is different from using books or academic journal articles in that I used them to confirm or provide greater details to events I was already aware of.
2. Please see Stansell 2000; Bender 1988, for in-depth histories of early New York's art and culture. Much of my account of this time period draws from their work, unless otherwise noted.
3. Stansell 2000.
4. Ibid.
5. Ibid.
6. For more on the Dada art movement, please see Richter 1997; Elderfield 1996; Huelsenbeck 1991.
7. Unless otherwise noted, the sources which were most useful in my discussion of the fashion industry are Green 1997, Rantisi 2004.
8. See Rantisi 2004 for a complete discussion on the history of New York fashion.
9. See Huggins 1973; Watson 1995; Lewis 1995, 1997; and Hutchinson 1997 for a thorough history and analysis of the Harlem Renaissance.
10. Rantis 2004.
11. Ibid.
12. Ibid.
13. http://www.fineartstrader.com/wpa.htm.

14. Lynton 1980.
15. Ibid.
16. Perl 2005.
17. For a very detailed and interesting account of the Abstract Expressionists, see Perl 2005. Much of this chapter's discussion on Abstract Expressionists is derived from Perl's book unless otherwise noted. Also see Crane 1989 for an historical account of the places and people responsible for shaping and influencing New York's art world.
18. Perl 2005.
19. Ibid.
20. Ibid.
21. Ibid.
22. Ibid.
23. Ibid.
24. Taken from Wikipedia: http://en.wikipedia.org/wiki/The_factory.
25. For more information on the Beats, please see Charters 1992; Campbell 2001; Watson 1998; Threads 2003.
26. Rantisi 2004.
27. Ibid.
28. Ibid.
29. Ibid.
30. See Taylor 2006 for a complete discussion of New York City's 1970s–1980s downtown art scene.
31. Currid 2006a.
32. See Hager 1986; Taylor 2006.
33. Goldberg 2006.
34. Taylor 2006.
35. Alteveer 2006.
36. See Hager 1986; Musto 1986; Goldberg 2006; McCormick 2006 for excellent discussions on the intersection of nightlife and cultural production.
37. Goldberg 2006.
38. Ibid.
39. Taylor 2006, Interview with Richard Lloyd.
40. Taylor 2006.
41. Gendron 2006.
42. Rantisi 2004.
43. McCormick 2006.
44. Bourdieu 1993; Taylor 2006.
45. Taken from the New Museum exhibition *East Village USA*: http://www.newmuseum.org/now_cur_evusa.php.
46. While not about New York City, Richard Lloyd's 2006 *Neo-Bohemia*, an ethnography of the Chicago Wicker Park neighborhood, provides an excellent account of the way in which artists with little resources used the neighborhood and its institutions and social networks to establish community, performance venues, exchanges of ideas and jobs.

47. See Robinson and McCormick 1984, along with Taylor 2006.

48. Alteveer 2006; New Museum 2004.

49. See Frank 1998; Hickey 1997; Lloyd and Clark 2001; Glaeser 2000; Scott 2000; Rantisi 2004; Clark 2004 for detailed discussions on the commodification of culture.

50. Alteveer 2006.

51. Rantisi 2004.

52. See Bboys 2005 for a chronology of hip-hop.

53. Musto 2006.

54. Ibid.

55. Thomas 2005.

56. Currid 2006a.

57. Seabrook 2001.

58. Thomas 2005.

CHAPTER 3. BECOMING CREATIVE

1. Glaeser 2005.

2. For a historical account of New York's economy and history please see Hoover and Vernon 1962; Vernon 1960; Burrows and Wallace 1999; Glaeser 2005. Much of the narrative in this chapter has been compiled using these sources.

3. Vernon 1960.

4. The data I collected to analyze New York's metropolitan economy come from several different sources and have been collected in different manners as well. The two main sources of data are the U.S. Census of Population and the Bureau of Labor Statistics (BLS). I have gathered data from the Census from 1790 to 2000. However, data from this source are fuzzy and incomplete until about 1940, when Public Use Microdata Sample (PUMS) data became available. The BLS data come in two forms—County Business Patterns (CBP) (available almost yearly from 1967 to 2002) and Occupational Employment Statistics (OES) (available from 1999 to 2004). OES data collect occupational data as opposed to industrial data, which allows us to see what people *do*, not just what industry they work for, providing a richer picture of the metropolitan area's aggregate skill sets. Further, OES data are industry-reported, meaning that they capture only those workers gainfully employed in that particular occupation within an industry, which is demonstrative of actual economic output. All BLS data are industry reported; however, the CBP shows data for broader industries (e.g., finance), while OES shows data for a particular occupation (e.g., photographer). However, as both OES and CBP data are industry collected, they only report those individuals working for a firm (as opposed to being self-employed).

With some occupations (particularly artistic ones), this collection method means that there can be significant undercounting of an occupation's presence within the metropolitan area if there is a tendency for that occupation to be more self-employed than affiliated with a firm. This is where Census PUMS data are particularly useful, as they capture which occupations individuals identify themselves with. The caveat is that these data are only made available decennially as opposed to yearly. Pre-1940 Census data are far less detailed, but do offer some insights into the general industrial mix. This book focuses primarily on data at the occupational level, but for those interested in comparisons between industrial and occupational level data collected, a detailed discussion of industrial data (including both PUMS and CBP) can be found in the appendix.

I look at the New York metropolitan economy both through occupations and industries. In terms of industry, I look at it through specific sectors (e.g., manufacturing, clerical, finance) and also broader categories: service, working or labor, and skilled. The terms labor, blue-collar, and working are interchangeable in this discussion. Skilled occupations are mostly those requiring a higher level of education, but that is not the rule. Some occupations, particularly artists and actors, may not be formally educated but are required to be innovative in their daily work—a definition similar to Florida's 2002 "creative class." I chose to collect data similar to the creative class data collection approach (as opposed to traditional human capital measures) because I feel that it is a better way of measuring a metropolitan area's skill set as it shows what people are doing with their skills as opposed to just baseline educational measures.

Percentage of workforce is an accurate measure of the actual position an industry or occupational cluster has within the metropolitan area, but it does not measure how an area's industrial makeup compares to other metropolitan areas. Therefore, in looking at the industries and occupations powering New York's economy in the present day, I use three methods for this analysis. First, employing self-reported earlier Census data and from 1940 onward, Census PUMS data, I look at the percentage of the total New York regional workforce that these different industrial and occupational sectors represent. Using BLS CBP data, I look at actual number of employees and establishments. Then, using BLS OES data (which is industry reported and annual from 1999 onward), I run a location quotient looking at New York City's PMSA as compared to all other metropolitan statistical areas, both within occupational clusters and also looking at a sampling of occupations within each sector. The location quotient, explained further in the following footnotes, is the best proxy for analyzing the region's competitive advantage and distinction as compared to other metropolitan areas. The location quotient allows us to see how much more or less an occupation or industry is concentrated within one metropolitan area as compared to a broader geography. In the vein of Markusen's 2004d discussion of the "distinctive" city, I argue that the results of this occupational analysis tell us in which occupations New York is more concentrated than other metropolitan areas, giving us insight into where New York might further optimize its competitive advantage over other regions and cities.

Unless otherwise noted, all data from 1790 to 1940 were obtained through the Inter-university Consortium for Political and Social Research. HISTORICAL, DEMOGRAPHIC, ECONOMIC, AND SOCIAL DATA: THE UNITED STATES, 1790–2000 [Computer file]. ICPSR02896-v2. Hamilton, NY: Colgate University/Ann Arbor: MI: Inter-university Consortium for Political and Social Research [producers], 2004. Ann Arbor, MI: Inter-university Consortium for Political and Social Research [distributor], 2005-04-29.

5. Kevin Stolarick of Carnegie Mellon University was invaluable in his assistance in data collection for this project.

6. The most accurate and accessible data available are the U.S. Census of population (which is reported by people, like me and you) and the Bureau of Labor Statistics (reported by industries and firms). These different approaches paint different pictures of the economy. An actor whose primary job is waiting on tables will be reported as a waitress by the BLS but as an actor by the Census (the waitress is likely to report herself as an actor, despite the reality of her full-time job). There are also different ways to assess the dynamics of an economy. One is the percentage of a workforce employed by a particular industry, another is by actual employment numbers, and a third is the concentration of a particular industry within New York City as compared to other cities. These different methodological approaches illuminate how the New York economy has changed since the 1950s and 1960s, the last time a major study of the New York economy occurred.

7. With reference to data results: More than any other industry, the link between industry and occupation is most seamless within art and culture. Undoubtedly this is a result of the fact that if you are working in art and culture, you are more than likely actually doing something artistic or cultural. These firms are, in the aggregate, less financially secure, so they simply cannot afford to have a web of different types of services employed directly by them. Harkening back to Jacobs 1969 and Vernon 1960, arts and culture firms often contract out the services they need, from tax returns to legal advice. That said, the art and culture industry has steadily increased by industrial classification, despite a decrease from 1950 to 1960, peaking in 2000 at 2.54 percent. As an industry, it is fourth, ranked behind finance and professional services, and close behind media.

8. Competitive advantage can be measured through an analysis called a location quotient (LQ), which allows us to see how New York competes with other metropolitan areas by measuring New York's concentration in a particular occupation (say, designers) compared to that occupation's concentration in other metropolitan areas. This is a method for measuring the concentration of a particular occupation in a region in comparison to its concentration in the aggregate U.S. metropolitan areas. $LQ = (O_R/TE_R)/(O_N/TE_N)$ where O_R = regional occupational employment; TE_R = total regional employment; O_N = national occupational employment; TE_N = total national employment.

This research classifies LQs with the following strata: Occupations with an LQ of 0.00–0.99 have below average representation in the region, those with an LQ of 1.00 have an average representation, while those occupations with an LQ greater than 1.00 have above average representation within the region. Using 1999–2004 OES data, which are taken from the Bureau of Labor Statistics (BLS), the location quotient was used to measure the concentration of occupations in the New York Primary Metropolitan Statistical Area (PMSA).

In other words, an LQ over 1.00 means that New York is more concentrated than other cities, less than 1 means it is less concentrated, while an LQ of 1 means that it's on par with the national average. An LQ of 1.95 for say, dancers, means that New York has almost twice as many as other cities, while an LQ of 0.65 for CEOs means that New York has significantly fewer chief executives, relative to the size of its overall workforce.

9. Markusen 2004a provides a detailed and relevant discussion of the importance of urban and regional "distinctiveness" in order to remain competitive in the global economy.

10. New York City's art and culture sector possesses a 4.38 LQ. While this result is a decrease from its peak in 1999 of 7.16 LQ, it appears that this sector is on the upswing again, making up for any losses in concentration over the past several years.

11. Please see appendix for detailed LQ data on select U.S. cities.

12. There are several overall findings worth mentioning before going into each sector. First, the significance of NEC employment in the high-skilled sector both in terms of the industry and occupational categorization is minimal (often less than 1 percent and at most 2 percent of total workforce; see appendix). This result is very different from the categorization problems that were found within the service and labor-intensive industrial sectors. One might say that as skilled human capital occupations became more important, the classification system simultaneously got better. We can see, however, that NEC has never been dominant within the skilled sector. This result indicates that within human capital–driven sectors, what people do is more closely aligned with particular industries. Or rather, as a general rule, participating directly in a skilled industry (as opposed to being a support industry) requires one's occupation to be human capital–intensive as well. It also indicates that within a human capital–driven industry, occupations are more clearly linked to particular industries (for example, a fashion designer is art and culture, a financial analyst is a part of the finance industry, and an industrial engineer is part of engineering and high technology). Even though at times there is a discrepancy between occupation and industry, the difference is far less than what we observed in the other industrial groups. In other words, there is less of a difference between what you do and what industry you work for. We can see this link also when we compare percentage of the workforce and overall ranking of sectors through industry versus occupational categories—generally speaking, each sector maintains its position and relative percentage of workforce through both classification systems. The exception to this general trend is management, which dominates the workforce in terms of occupation but we see a significant decline in its industrial position. This indicates that a significant portion of

jobs within skilled industries are management-related, a finding that corroborates with Sassen 1991 and Castells' 2000 contention that world cities are those that have a dominant management workforce.

13. Friedmann, 1986; Knox and Taylor 1995; Sassen 1991; Beaverstock et al. 1999; Castells 2000.

14. Other high human capital industries also have been instrumental economic drivers in the present period. As early as 1973, Bell posited the rise of a post-industrial service economy which would be characterized by high-skilled human capital. Piore and Sabel 1984 and Castells and Hall 1994 have argued for the increasing significance of high-technology industrial districts in the post-industrial economy. An emerging framework explaining New York City's dominant position argues for the importance of art and culture in economic development (Molotch 1996; Florida 2002; Markusen and King 2003; Markusen, Schrock, and Cameron 2004; Scott 2000, 2005). This line of thinking considers the importance of innovation and artistic and cultural production in the generation of growth and competitive advantage. In the main, these different approaches have attempted to explain more broadly how economic growth happens and why it happens in particular places in the wake of deindustrialization and the rise of a world system of cities and economies. The theories presented argue that a metropolitan area's competitive advantage in the world economy is a result of its concentration and advantage in particular industries.

15. This distinction between industry versus occupational classification is as follows: those who have job titles that are media-related, as opposed to those who work for media as an industry (though are not necessarily doing media jobs). Industries often hire people who are not doing work directly related to the industry but are often part of the broader support that the industry needs to function. We see the same results with regard to finance, and the converse results with regard to management (in other words, management is important to all industries, thus it is a large occupational group, but as an industry, management is less pervasive).

16. While media is less dominant as an occupation (1.34 percent in 2000), it has a strong position as an industry (3.90 percent in 2000).

17. A point that Markusen and King 2003 and Markusen 2004 have also made.

18. The media sector possesses a 2.95 LQ.

19. Los Angeles media has a 3.00 LQ.

20. New York possesses a 3.47 LQ and Los Angeles a 4.01 LQ in TV and broadcasting.

21. Please see Sassen 1991; Castells 2000.

22. Management is 8.44 percent of the workforce.

23. New York's CEO location quotient at 1.02, ranks below, most notably, Boston (2.45), Charleston, SC (1.37), Chicago (1.08), Raleigh-Durham, NC (1.10), San Diego (1.04), San Francisco (1.33), and Washington, DC (1.39). See appendix for tables with occupational LQs for major MSAs.

24. A CMSA is a combined geography of two or more contiguous MSAs. New York City's CMSA includes Bergen–Passaic, NJ PMSA; Bridgeport, CT PMSA; Danbury, CT PMSA; Dutchess County, NY PMSA; Jersey City, NJ PMSA; Middlesex–Somerset–Hunterdon, NJ PMSA; Monmouth–Ocean, NJ PMSA; Nassau–Suffolk, NY PMSA; New Haven–Meriden, CT PMSA; New York, NY PMSA; Newark, NJ PMSA; Newburgh, NY–PA PMSA; Stamford–Norwalk, CT PMSA; Trenton, NJ PMSA; Waterbury, CT PMSA.

25. Center for an Urban Future 2003.

26. Please see appendix for more detailed data on finance as an industry.

27. While the LQ is reasonably high at 2.41 in 2004, this concentration has declined substantially over the last several years. All location quotients were computed using BLS OES data from 1999 to 2004.

28. *Crain's*, 2006.

29. Center for an Urban Future 2003.

30. Sassen 1991.

31. The concentration of the financial sector and "command and control" or management occupations has been linked to a broader argument of cities as post-industrial production sites Sassen 1991, 126, Bell 1973, Beaverstock et al. 1999, Glaeser 2005 among others have noted the tight linkages between finance, management and the high-level producer and business services that these industries require. Beaverstock et al. 1999 characterize world cities as centers of "innovations in corporate services and finance [that] have been integral to the recent restructuring of the world-economy now widely known as globalization" (5).

32. Professional services are 24.9 percent of the workforce by industrial categorization and 11.89 percent occupationally. Within the industrial classification, professional services witnessed their greatest increase from the years 1960 to 1980, increasing 23 percent from 1960 to 1970 and 43 percent from 1970 to 1980.

33. Within professional services, the most important sectors have been the medical industry and educational occupations. In 2000, health (as an industry) accounted for 11.49 percent of the total workforce, while education was at 8.5 percent. Education grew over 111 percent between 1950 and 1960. When we look at professional services by occupation, education is the most dominant with 5.38 percent of the total workforce by occupation in 2000, and medicine at 4.69 percent.

34. Both education and medicine have exhibited a steady increase in their presence in the city's economy over the past sixty years. The medical sector's dominance in industry represents the all-encompassing nature of medicine from doctors to nurses to recordkeepers—meaning that the industry as a whole employs a variety of occupations, while education as an industrial category is narrower in scope.

35. Contrary to images of New York City as a great law center, legal occupations surprisingly are not strongly represented within the region's workforce, possessing just 1.81 percent by occupation in 2000.

36. New York's professional services possess a 2.83 LQ. Within professional services, the region has a particular advantage in medicine (a 4.22 LQ), but also fares well both in law (2.04) and education (2.60).

37. While my research looks at the PMSA; region, and city as the same economic unit, the Center for an Urban Future's data do a comparison between New York City proper (that is Queens, Richmond, Manhattan, and Bronx counties) and the New York MSA as a whole. Unless otherwise indicated, use of the terms region, city, and MSA are interchangeable in this chapter.

38. To note, George Washington is included in these records.

39. 10.4 percent were skilled, high human capital; 22.5 percent working, 2.4 percent farming, 37 percent service, and 28 percent not easily classified (NEC), or rather the occupation did not fit clearly into a particular sector. These results are cautiously thought-provoking. On the one hand, the data are limited in scope—it is a composite of landowners in Manhattan but not of those who lived there but did not own property. On the other hand, the data reveal some interesting results, particularly the surprisingly strong presence of the service economy.

40. As previous tales have told, manufacturing began to take hold in the region as early as 1820 with 14,673 employees and continued to grow. From 1870 to 1890, manufacturing increased its employment within the city by over three times, capturing almost 60 percent of the state's employment within the industry. While its peak was in 1920, with 621,386 people employed in manufacturing, actual establishments were declining by this point across both the city and the state (particularly rapidly in the state as a whole). Even in 1940, when New York City had lost manufacturing employees, it was at its peak with regard to its proportion of manufacturing firms within the state, capturing 78 percent of the state's manufacturing firms, even though the city had been losing firms since at least 1920. This incongruence between the absolute decline in firms (and employees to a much lesser extent) but greater proportional representation indicates both the state's more rapid decline in the industry relative to the city and also the possible merging of manufacturing firms within the city and the state, thus decreasing the overall firm numbers but not really impacting overall employment (yet). Agriculture, which never became a prominent part of New York's economy, had approximately the same number of employees as manufacturing in 1820 (representing 5.77 percent of the state's employment in agriculture), but New York City's share of the state's agriculture never got higher than its peak of 5.91 percent in 1840. While agriculture remained a large industry throughout New York State, its production was not located within the city's economy.

41. Unfortunately, before 1940, when the Census created a systematic approach to data collection with the establishment of the Public Use Microdata Sample (PUMS), data collection was somewhat disorganized and slapdash. As such, from about 1840 onward, occupational data for New York can only be found on the state level, as opposed to the county or city level. Perhaps such

data can be found in dusty books somewhere, but the electronic data used for this research was missing great chunks of data till 1940.

42. While I primarily use Census PUMS data, I would like to point out that County Business Patterns shows similar results in terms of the evolution of each industrial sector I analyze in this chapter. These charts can be seen in the appendix.

43. It is important at this point to elaborate more on the data collection methods. PUMS uses the same data and classifies them twice—once as an occupation and once as part of a particular industry. Therefore, a manager in a steel plant will be classified as part of management (occupation) and then as a part of manufacturing (industry). While this seems straightforward, it actually produces a world of difficulties as we get more detailed in our analysis and start breaking down these broader categories—and this situation is particularly problematic with regard to manufacturing. Earlier economic analysis focused on industry as the most telling indicator of a region's employment makeup. Recent scholars, especially Markusen 2004a, 2004b; Markusen, Schrock, and Cameron 2004; and Florida 2002, have begun to do occupational analysis, arguing that what people do is more important than what industry they work for. As industries have become more and more complex, occupations, such as a computer programmer or photographer, are affiliated with many different industries from finance to public relations to media. And in order to break down the production process in space—where does design versus manufacturing occur, occupational analysis is necessary. However, earlier on, this type of focus was not considered particularly significant, as industry was indicative of what people did. Over the years, occupational classification has become more nuanced. Many of the occupational categories were vague as the main mode of analysis was the industry. In the labor-intensive industries, occupations like "laborer" become very difficult to unearth because they could be affiliated with any number of industries, and thus, in this research, "laborer" and other similarly vague occupations were categorized as not easily classified (NEC) within their industry. By way of example, with regard to occupational analysis within labor intensive or working-class industries, you will see a large number of NEC occupations and low manufacturing (which does not add up given our understanding of the New York economy). However, when we look at the same data through the lens of industry, the NEC category declines and manufacturing increases significantly, indicating that many of the NEC occupations are actually part of the manufacturing sector. I look at both occupational and industrial categorizations in my analysis of New York City's economy but keep the explanations for these different approaches in mind when looking at the charts and data presented.

44. Please see the appendix for a detailed look at New York's economy from an industrial perspective, and also for a look at County Business Pattern data on the region's economy from 1967 to 2002.

45. This chapter focuses on those industries that are dominant in New York City's economy in present day. There are, however, a multitude of data on the

manufacturing industry, along with engineering and high technology—both of which are not dominant in New York's economy so are not discussed in great detail. However, information on these industries can be found in the appendix of this book.

46. Of all the industries, clerical work dominates, primarily because it is an important support service for the other industries in the city from finance to law to public relations.

47. That NEC service jobs represent such a high percentage of total work-force is indicative of both the highly ambiguous classification system and the multitude of industries that the service sector supports in their production of goods and services, historically trade and manufacturing, and today, finance and professional industries.

48. See Glaeser 2000; Lloyd and Clark 2001; Clark 2004 for a discussion on the relationship between amenities/consumption and economic growth.

49. Vernon 1960.

50. See Jacobs' 1969. This point is also made by Quigley 1998 and Desrochers 2001.

51. Center for an Urban Future 2002.

CHAPTER 4. THE SOCIAL LIFE OF CREATIVITY

1. I had the same experience at a boutique in the Silver Lake neighborhood of Los Angeles. While I was looking at handbags, I complimented a woman on her skirt and asked her if it was designed by Cynthia Rowley. Just as Giles did not directly answer me with a simple yes or no (as he easily could have), this woman too went the extra distance, saying, "Yes, she dresses me and is a good friend of mine." As it turns out, I interviewed Cynthia Rowley, but despite Giles' help and my best efforts, I was never able to sit down with Marc Jacobs for this book. These stories exemplify the paradoxical meaningfulness and arbitrariness of random social interactions. That these interactions take place at all, and that they have the potential to translate into an interview, a job and so forth, is exponentially more likely in a place where like-minded people congregate. Being in the right place still remains important in transforming prosaic, quotidian behavior into something far more significant.

2. His empirical findings confirm what Daniel Bell had theorized nearly three decades before: Bell's stories were part of a larger systematic model for predicting economic vitality findings; the cities that were most productive (as defined by income) also possessed the highest levels of human capital, controlling for wealth, population, density among other independent variables. Glaeser 2000, 2003, 2005 provides a remarkable and detailed analysis of the impact of high-skilled human capital on urban economic growth.

3. See Florida 2002b and 2005.

4. See, for example, Baumol 2002.

5. See Nalebuff and Ayres 2006 for a discussion of these types of relationships.

6. For an in-depth discussion of these relationships, see Marshall 1961; Storper 1997; Castells and Hall 1994; Scott 1993, 2000; and Saxenian 1994.

7. See Romer 1986 and 1990 for his most seminal papers on "increasing returns" to knowledge and New Growth Theory. Also see Warsh 2006.

8. Please see Freiberger and Swain 1999 for a fascinating account of the Homebrew Computer Club and the bohemian culture of early Silicon Valley.

9. Saxenian 1994.

10. Strumsky et al. 2005.

11. Marshall 1890.

12. The article I speak of is Granovetter 1972.

13. Granovetter 1972.

14. Ibid.

15. Granovetter 1985.

16. For a very complete discussion of the economic geography of the Hollywood movie industry, see Scott 2005.

17. I am certainly not the first to note the significance of social structure in the production of culture and the cultivation of cultural taste. Please see Lloyd 2006; DiMaggio 1987; Wolff 1993; Crane 1989.

18. See Joe Donnelly, "Citizen Beck," *LA Weekly*, September 27, 2006, for full interview.

CHAPTER 5. THE ECONOMICS OF A DANCE FLOOR

1. See, for example, Jacobs 1969; Granovetter 1985; Piore and Sabel 1984; Saxenian 1994; Audretsch and Feldman 1996 for discussions regarding the importance of the social in innovation.

2. For some useful discussion on the importance of place and cultural production, see for example, Perl 2005, Dylan 2004, Stansell 2000; Musto 1986; Jacobs 1961.

3. See Storper 1997, Saxenian 1994; Castells and Hall 1994 for a more complete discussion of agglomeration, spillovers, and innovation.

4. See White 2002 and Massey 1984 for a detailed discussion regarding the relationship between the social and the marketplace.

5. See Glaeser 2000 and Clark 2004 for discussion on the importance of amenities and entertainment as consumption.

6. Marshall 1890.

7. Kennedy 2006.

8. Sisario, 2006.

9. Bourdieu 1993.

10. Rollins, 2006.

11. See Jacobs 1961, 1969; Glaeser 1998; Porter 1998; Thompson 1965 for discussions on the role of agglomeration economies and economic growth.

CHAPTER 6. CREATING BUZZ, SELLING COOL

1. The term used for graffiti done on streets as opposed to trains.

2. Please see Kawamura 2005 for an in-depth analysis of the role of gate-keepers in valuing and legitimating fashion.

3. Fairey 2006: 16.

4. For more information on Shepard Fairey's artwork, Andre the Giant, and OBEY, please see Fairey 2006; Lemons 2000; the official OBEY Giant Web site: http://www.obeygiant.com/.

5. Fairey 2006 Introduction: i.

6. Hebdige 1979.

7. See Lachmann 1988; Frank 1998 and Scott 2000.

8. For a discussion of culture, commodification, and consumption, please see Hickey 1997; Lloyd and Clark 2001; Glaeser 2000; Scott 2000; Rantisi 2004; Clark 2004; Leland 2004. In his book, *Hip: A History*, John Leland deconstructs the significance of what it means to be "hip" and how such an intangible quality emerges with regard to particular cultures, from beatniks to jazz musicians. Part of the ability to be hip is rooted in cultural borrowing, particularly the white population's tireless incorporation of black culture in its effort to become "hip." More broadly, it is the ability for subculture, while subversive, to still be attractive (and envied by) dominant society.

9. See Frank 1998. The commodification of culture has created an economic boon for the creative producers who produce the culture in the first place and the marketers and corporations which can repackage it and sell it on a grand scale. This commodification captures demand on several levels. First, there are those consumers within a particular culture who recognize the product for its cultural value (a graffiti writer's tag name on a sweatshirt, a particular design-er's dress) and purchase their goods as a type of endorsement. There are also those who buy these products as a way to attain identity, those who want to be a part of this mythology, even if they are removed from the culture in their daily lives. (Consider upper middle-class teenagers in the suburbs wearing hip-hop gear and singing along to 50 Cent's lyrics about the ghetto, or Tom Frank's consumer hippies.) Finally, there are those who purchase these types of goods from a strictly aesthetic perspective, or rather, they just like the way they look or sound.

10. Walker 2004a.

11. See White and Fernando 2002 and Dyson 2006 for excellent biographies of the life of Tupac Shakur.

12. Throwback jerseys are sports uniforms (e.g., hockey, basketball, baseball, football) with the name of the sports team and the number (usually retired) of a famous sports figure (e.g., Magic Johnson, Michael Jordan). They have been increasingly worn by hip-hop artists (e.g., Jay-Z, Nelly) and their followers.

13. Rozhon 2005, B6.

14. Ibid.

15. Ibid.

16. Klosterman 2006.

17. Ibid.

18. Jacobs 1969.

19. Schumpeter 1942.

20. See Stark 2000. The German geographer Gernot Grabher (2001) expanded this framework to look at how London and New York's advertising industries operated within the same capacity. Michael Porter, a Harvard Business School professor, has made great headway in his exploration of the interconnectedness within industrial clusters. While Porter deals with one industry at a time, what makes his work interesting is his look at the different industries and subsidiaries that produce a product, whether it is wine, Italian shoes, or automobiles. For example, in Porter's detailed analysis of the wine industry in California, he outlines an intricate web of industries necessary to producing a bottle of wine—from grape farms to bottle producers to wine label designers. In looking at both the wine industry and Silicon Valley, Porter and also Annalee Saxenian found that firms who were working on the same problems, innovations, and so on often engaged in tightly knit communities that offered both competition and collaboration. In other words, the small firm networks (that I talked about in depth in the previous chapters) offer ease in production (sharing resources, ideas and so on) but also, because many of them are producing the same products, they are working in a densely competitive environment (and can take the shared information and ideas and turn them into the next big thing).

But these relationships remain inside of their respective industries, whether high technology or wine making. Each entity is linked through the common theme of supporting and sustaining a particular industry. And what I have found with regard to cultural industries is that these relationships of collaboration and competition span across creative production at large. Creative industry innovation is not a product of hierarchical supplier-core industry or collaboration and competition relationships within one industry; rather, it results from a heterarchical peer review process across the cultural economy.

21. Field theory, which originated in the biological and physical sciences, explains how seemingly different variables that are not related to one another are able to affect each other. Or as the University of Wisconsin, Madison sociologist John Levi Martin explains, it is the "transfer of energy to an element that is not necessarily in contact with any other element." For example, Einstein's theory of general relativity, or Isaac Newton's understanding of gravity. If we think about the moving of different particles—a positive one moves one way and a negative charge the other way—the way they move is dependent on where the other moves. More generally, as Martin puts it, scientific field theory looks at the relationship between different variables and their ability to "impel" change on other variables. But this type of dynamic has been considered with regard to fields not just within science but other disciplines and categories, particularly sociology. "Field theory is a more or less coherent approach

in the social sciences whose essence is the explanation of regularities in individual action by recourse to position vis-à-vis others." In other words, people's behavior is a part of the social context they are embedded in and the people they interact with. Pierre Bourdieu made famous the term, "the field of cultural production" and is one of the leading scholars in the study of field theory. He writes about this most notably in his famous books *Distinction* (2002) and *The Field of Cultural Production* (1993). The field, Bourdieu argues, is a constantly changing set of roles and relationships, where status, money, and information are exchanged and at stake. Bourdieu's discussion of cultural production begins with understanding the social conditions under which it operates—primarily cultural production's symbolic capital, which had to do with honor or prestige or status rather than economic value—think of a starving artist's work as opposed to a financial analyst's quarterly report. The artist's work only becomes economically valuable when its aesthetics are determined to be worth money. Cultural production in this sense operates under "restricted production"—or, produced as "art for art's sake" rather than for money or a product being sold on a market. The introduction of commodification, however, transformed much cultural production into "large-scale" production sold as commodities.

Within the field of cultural production, values for artwork change from being symbolic and restrictive to large-scale (Andy Warhol's paintings being made into silk-screened T-shirts). The field consists of many different actors or "variables" and "elements," to put it in a scientific way. There are the art dealers, the curators, the artists themselves, the media and so forth. All of these different people play roles and react and act based on each other's moves, compounding the effect of one initial move. So, for example, let's go back to the graffiti-turned-gallery-artist, Jean-Michel Basquiat. When Basquiat was working at nightclubs, painting subway trains, and living in the economically poor but culturally rich East Village, he was still, for all intents and purposes, a starving artist. But when famous gallery owner Mary Boone gave him his own show, it automatically sent a signal to the broader marketplace that Basquiat should be taken seriously—and he was. Shortly after his showing at the Boone gallery, the auction house Christie's sold a painting of his for over $20,000. Between the gallery exhibition and Christie's auction, there were undoubtedly other variables that elevated Basquiat's success—good write-ups in magazines, important art collectors who bought his work, and so on. But the point here is that Boone, Christie's, and Basquiat did not act independently—their actions, and the way in which Basquiat's status as an artist rose, was dependent on these variables interacting and affecting one another.

But Bourdieu's conception of the field of cultural production does not explore how fields collide. In other words, art or music or fashion would be considered their own separate fields, with their own rules, norms, and variables that impact the rise and fall of particular cultural producers, whether Mick Jagger or Jeff Koons. But, how do these distinct fields actually affect one another? Or, rather, are music, fashion, art, or design really separate from one another? We know that those in music are inspired, affected, evaluated and so forth by those in fashion—and the relationship is reciprocal. The "field" is actually across all of these industries, even though such a category is outside of how a field is traditionally defined. Fashion and music, while both cultural and artistic, would not usually be considered in the same field, even though there is a strong innovational and creative link, and, as I will discuss later, a review process exists between these two industries. There is a reciprocal force through which each of these industries affects one another outside of traditional conceptions of the "field." What I have found is that creative and cultural industries operate within a large field and they exert forces upon one another, partly as a result of the networks and agglomerations across suppliers and producers of cultural products.

22. Romer 1986, 1990.

23. Simmel 1904.

24. Blumer 1969.

25. DiMaggio 1987.

26. Hirsch 1972.

27. Ibid.

28. Walker 2004b.

29. David Carr, 2006, The Hard Edge of a Fluff Machine. *New York Times*, April 17.

30. Walker 2004b.

31. Gladwell 2000.

32. Caves 2000.

33. Ibid.

34. Hirsch 1972.

35. Or, as the cultural sociologist Howard Becker describes it in his book *Art Worlds*: "Aestheticians study the premises and arguments people use to justify classifying things and activities as 'beautiful' . . . 'bad art' . . . They construct systems with which to make and justify both the classifications and specific instances of their application. Critics apply aesthetic systems to specific artworks and arrive at judgments of their worth and explications of what gives them that worth. Those judgments produce reputations for works and artists. Distributors and audience members take reputations into account when they decide what to support emotionally and financially, and that affects the resources available to artists to continue their work" (Becker 1982: 131).

36. Walker 2004b.

37. Ibid.

38. Ogunnaike 2006.

39. Wilson 2005.

40. Ibid.

41. See, for example, Markusen and King 2003.

CHAPTER 7. THE RISE OF GLOBAL TASTEMAKERS: WHAT IT ALL MEANS
FOR THE POLICYMAKERS

1. Increasingly, with the emphasis on the "commodification of culture" and the importance of place-specific products, a number of scholars have started unearthing the how, why, and where of cultural agglomeration. Scholars have found that place matters in cultural production and that these places exhibit a cumulative advantage, or rather, an initial advantage in producing a particular good often predicts future success in maintaining that advantage. Indeed, part of how this occurs is what economists call "first mover advantage"—or simply, if a particular place establishes an innovation or an advantage in a particular industry, they can often capture the whole market leading to a "lock-in," whereby other cities and regions cannot outperform or catch up. This happened with Pittsburgh's steel industry and Detroit's automobile industry—and New York's fashion industry. And as things like this go, there is a certain path dependency (a city's future depends on its past), that is, it's cumulative. Because a region gets an increasing advantage in a particular industry or innovation (and this initial advantage may be due to luck of discovering a new technology, new design or so forth), and they continue to dominate in that area because the initial discovery or innovation brings more wealth, more investors and more inventors who want to get involved. Often their future is dependent on the accumulation of advantages (and in some cases disadvantages) and over time the attraction of more people, firms, resources reaffirms these dynamics and advantages over and over again (similar to the concept of increasing returns).

2. For a more in-depth look at the cultural geography literature, please see, most notably, recent explorations of the film industry (Christopherson and Storper 1986; Scott 2000, 2005; Coe and Johns 2004; Molotch 1996, 2002, 2003); fashion (Rantisi 2004; Santagata 2004); and the general exploration of culture in space (Bourdieu 1993; Blau 1989), all of which have considered how place intersects with creative production. Particularly, the new regionalists argue that vertical disintegration, agglomeration, and "neo-artisanal forms of production" allow for successful flexible and diverse production, and keeping up with fickle consumer tastes and trends (Christopherson and Storper 1986; Scott 2000, 2005). Coe and Johns 2004 argue that there is too much emphasis on the production and not enough on the distribution and financing of cultural goods, which happens on a global but not necessarily local level. Across the board, scholars looking at the production of culture have explored how the local networks of suppliers, adjunct industries, and talented labor pools allow for a dense agglomeration that translates into producing successful place-based products with a global following. While first-mover advantage and subsequent path dependency have arguably played a role in the success of geographic leaders in particular types of cultural production (e.g., New York fashion, Hollywood films, LA's music scene), scholars have also pointed to the critical nexus

where policy and general public support have been the determining factors in cementing the competitive advantage that one region has over another (Scott 2005; Rantisi 2004)—a topic to which I will return later in discussing policy implications for the artistic and cultural economy.

3. Harvey Molotch's 2003 book *Where Stuff Comes From* is an excellent and witty account of the relationship between place and product.

4. Power and Scott 2004.

5. These findings are in line with what urban economists and geographers have suggested for decades—agglomerations reinforce themselves by creating and recreating dense networks of supply and demand, laborers and firms, and the necessary reviewers who evaluate and also transmit the knowledge and ideas emerging from a regional cluster.

6. Ibid.

7. Or as the New York University sociologist, Harvey Molotch, remarks in his famous article, "LA as Design Product," "While they are choosy and fickle, L.A.'s indigenous immigrants from everywhere act as a proxy for world taste as well as sources of creativity" (1996). They are creating both the products and the taste by which to evaluate those products.

8. This general observation is one that has been discussed by, most influentially, Piore and Sabel 1984 but also Molotch 1996; Glaeser 1998 and Scott 2000, 2005. These dense agglomerations create a certain lock-in that, as Blau 1989 has rightly pointed out, means "particular regions are able to control cultural production and maintain hegemony and are thereby able to shape national tastes and standards" (13). Molotch 1996 most succinctly sees the relationship between place and the production of culture in his careful look at Los Angeles "as design product." Or more specifically, he points out that "Designers are sensors of emerging needs, tastes and cultural patterns" (265).

9. Rantisi 2002b.

10. Cotter 2005.

11. Ibid.

12. This type of environment is similar in nature to the vertical disintegration found in the Third Italy or Silicon Valley, as documented by Storper 1997; and Saxenian 1994.

13. Piore and Sabel 1984; Scott 1993; and Saxenian 1994 have noted, it is often hard to identify which industries will actually succeed.

14. Saxenian 1994.

15. The rise in flexible specialization has allowed for a new type of industrial community that is often thought of in terms of the region rather than the city. Such regional agglomerations appear to sustain themselves not only due to physical resources but also the success of informational and institutional spillovers that allow firms and people to share relevant knowledge and inputs that can be applied in different ways (Piore and Sabel 1984; Saxenian 1994; Castells and Hall 1994; Scott 1993, 2000; Storper 1997). The Marshall-Arrow-Romer (MAR) framework (Mathur 1999) argues that knowledge-intensive industries, in particular, rely on the informal economies of face-to-face

interaction, tacit knowledge, and information spillovers that are constantly used and permutated by different actors. In this web of people and firms, the contradictory notions of complements and competition spur a strange brew of constant innovation that is fueled by networks of knowledge and ideas. (See Romer 1990 for a discussion of knowledge spillovers and Saxenian 1994 for a look at rivalry and collaboration.) The rise of "technopoles" as planned centers for the catalyzing of high-technology industry is an example of such efforts (see Castells and Hall 1994). Vogel 1985 recounts how active planning in North Carolina created a high technology-university agglomeration in the establishment of the Research Triangle. A path to success appears to lie in establishing the networks and collaborative competition that generate new innovations. Saxenian's explanation for the success of Silicon Valley can be applied to other regions as well: "Technological advance in Silicon Valley depends on shifting patterns of collaboration and competition among networks of specialist producers. The dynamism of the region's industrial system lies not in any single technology or product but in the competence of each of its constituent parts and their multiple interconnections" (Saxenian 1994, 166).

16. We measured the statistical significance of industrial clustering across U.S. metropolitan areas using two geo-spatial statistical methods: the Moran's I and the Getis Ord General G statistic. The Moran's I gauges spatial autocorrelation among zip codes of different industries for each city and region examined. This measure indicates the general tendency of an industry to agglomerate through its level of clustering on a scale of −1 to 1, where 1 indicates a clustered pattern, −1 indicates a scattered pattern, and 0 indicates randomness. In other words, it allows us to see whether or not an industry exhibits statistically robust clustering patterns. This scaled result allows the industries to be compared across different geographies, but does not tell us the nature of the observed clusters.

In order to discern what types of values (high or low) cluster together, we also utilize a second level of spatial analysis, the G-statistic. The G-statistic identifies spatial clusters of statistically significant high ("hot spot") or low ("cold spot") attribute values, and allows for the identification of which type of value is clustering together. In other words, the G-statistic measures to what extent these variables are clustering (e.g., Are there a lot of firms or only a few within the specified geography?).

17. Florida 2002b.

18. Clark 2004.

19. This policy direction builds off of a general consensus in regional studies on the importance of promoting strengths and establishing networks of support, a strategy initiative that Markusen 2004a has succinctly called the "distinctive city." Scott 1993, 2000; Piore and Sabel 1984; and Castells and Hall 1994 argue that in efforts to sustain innovative industries, regions should avoid attempts to establish industries that are not already present in their geography; instead they should seek to maximize the networks and resources they already possess.

The state can play an active and effective role in these efforts. Scott's 2000 discussion of the cultural economy indicates how policy can foster creativity. The nature of an economy so dependent on agglomeration of diverse firms, people, and resources means that regions must not just nurture a particular industry but all of the necessary externalities that are associated with its success. Although Scott notes that policy directed toward creativity can be difficult due to its unpredictability, he points to the ways government can stimulate it by investing in the R&D, skilled workforce, small diverse firms, and institutional networks that facilitate the free flow of information and ideas that generate creativity. Castells and Hall 1994 argue that innovation can begin by creating solutions for local problems that can transcend into products of a national or global market. Again, like Scott 2000, they argue for collaborative networks of research and education by creating public-private relationships. Markusen and King 2003 and Markusen 2004, focusing specifically on the arts, promotes the development of institutional actors to provide "collective care" for artists (such as health care and retirement plans) and of artistic networks that enable entrepreneurship. She has found that artists are not tied to industry or firms but instead to a neighborhood or city. Factors such as social networks, as well as public and private contributions to the artistic community, create desirable environments, not just jobs, which attract creative workers.

From an industrial perspective, creativity can be encouraged by establishing networks of cultural and noncultural industries, which can inform production processes of the vital elements of creative urban life (ESRC 2000a, 2000b). Mathur argues from a human capital perspective and stresses the importance of a regional human capital strategy. "The productivity of human capital in knowledge growth rises with the accumulation of knowledge stock" (1999, 213). Mathur argues that regions must look to establishing networks and environments that encourage exchange of information and ideas without compromising competitiveness. He notes that a "subsidy to capital is shortsighted" (214). Instead, the state should play a role in upgrading worker skills and training and subsidizing R&D because on a micro level such investments may not pay off for the firm (for example, training a worker who may leave shortly thereafter would not be considered a good investment). By encouraging and fostering knowledge spillovers and knowledge accumulation from a state level, firms will be far more receptive to exchanging knowledge without the risks of losing out to their competitor and thus enabling the exchange of ideas that leads to new creative thoughts and innovation.

20. Kimmelman 2005b.
21. Ibid.
22. Perl 2006.
23. Steinhauer 2005.
24. Ibid.
25. Pogrebin 2007a.
26. Ibid.
27. Silver, Clark, and Rothfield 2005.

28. Ibid.

29. Center for an Urban Future 2005.

30. Morgan 2005.

31. Ibid.

32. Center for an Urban Future 2003.

33. Please see Gyourko et al. 2006 for a complete discussion and analysis of the superstar cities concept in United States metropolitan areas.

34. Rollins 2006.

35. Waxman 2006.

36. Steinhauer 2005.

37. Fried 2006.

38. Rabin and Rasiej 2004.

39. Ibid.

40. A&R refers to the department within a music record label that is responsible for scouting, creating, and developing new artists and music groups.

41. Rabin and Rasiej 2004.

42. Mindlin 2006. Please see Kurutz 2005 and Steinhauer 2005 for current New York arts and culture policy.

43. Pogrebin 2005b.

44. Halbfinger 2005.

45. For more details on these changes and their implications, please see Pogrebin 2007b; Pogrebin 2007c; and Department of Cultural Affairs updates on cultural organizations funding: http://www.nyc.gov/html/dcla/downloads/pdf/CulturalFundingReform.pdf.

46. McAninch 2005.

47. Please see Schillinger 2005 for a more detailed reporting of this artists' space.

48. Jacobs 1961.

49. Leeds 2005.

References

Alteveer, Ian. (2006). "Chronology." In *The Downtown Book: The New York Art Scene 1974–1984*, edited by Marvin Taylor, 176–91. Princeton: Princeton University Press.

Audretsch, David B., and Maryann P. Feldman. (1996). Knowledge Spillovers and the Geography of Innovation and Production. *American Economic Review* 86: 630–40.

Baumol, William J. (2002). *The Free-Market Innovation Machine: Analyzing the Growth Miracle of Capitalism*. Princeton: Princeton University Press.

Bboys. (2005). www.bboys.com.

Beaverstock, J. V., R. G. Smith, and P. J. Taylor. (1999). "A Roster of World Cities." *Cities 16*, 6: 445–58.

Becker, Gary. (1975). *Human Capital*. New York: Columbia University Press.

Becker, Howard. (1982). *Art Worlds*. Berkeley/ Los Angeles: University of California Press.

Bell, Daniel. (1973). *The Coming of Post-Industrial Society: A Venture in Social Forecasting*. New York: Basic Books.

———. (1976). *The Cultural Contradictions of Capitalism*. New York: Basic Books.

Bender, Thomas. (1988). *New York Intellect: A History of Intellectual Life in New York City from 1750 to the Beginnings of Our Own Time*. Baltimore: Johns Hopkins University Press.

Berman, Marshall. (1997). "Justice/Just Us: Rap and Social Justice in America." In *The Urbanization of Injustice*, edited by Andy Merrifield and Erik Swyngedouw, 161–79. New York: New York University Press.

Blau, Judith. (1989). *The Shape of Culture: A Study of Contemporary Cultural Patterns in the United States*. American Sociological Association Rose Monograph Series. New York: Cambridge University Press.

Blumer, Herbert. (1969). Fashion: From Class Differentiation to Collective Selection. *Sociological Quarterly*. 10: 275–91.

Bourdieu, Pierre. (1993). *The Field of Cultural Production*. New York: Columbia University Press.

———. (2002). *Distinction: A Social Critique of the Judgment of Taste*. Cambridge: Harvard University Press.

Burrows, Edwin G., and Mike Wallace. (1999). *Gotham: A History of New York City to 1898*. New York: Oxford University Press.

Campbell, James. (2001). *This Is the Beat Generation: New York-San Francisco-Paris*. Berkeley: University of California Press.

Castells, Manuel. (2000). *The Rise of the Network Society*. New York: Blackwell.

Castells, Manuel, and Peter Hall. (1994). *Technopoles of the World: The Making of 21ˢᵗ Century Industrial Complexes*. London: Routledge.

Caves, Richard. (2000). *Creative Industries: Contracts Between Art and Commerce*. Cambridge, MA: Harvard University Press.

Center for an Urban Future. (2002). *The Creative Engine: How Arts and Culture Is Fueling Economic Growth in New York City Neighborhoods*. New York: Center for an Urban Future.

———. (2003). "Engine Failure." September.

———. (2005). "Creative New York." December.

Charters, Ann, ed. (1992). *The Portable Beat Reader*. New York: Penguin Books.

Christopherson, Susan, and Michael Storper. (1986). The City as Studio: The World as Back Lot: The Impact of Vertical Disintegration on the Location of the Motion Picture Industry. *Environment and Planning D: Society and Space* 4, 3: 305–20.

Clark, Terry N. (2004). *The City as an Entertainment Machine*. Oxford: Elsevier.

Coe, Neil, and Jennifer Johns. (2004). "Beyond Production Clusters: Towards a Critical Political Economy of Networks in the Film Industry and Television Industries." In *Cultural Industries and the Production of Culture*, edited by Dominic Power and Allen J. Scott, 188–206. London and New York: Routledge.

Collins, Amy. (2006). Best Dressed List. *Vanity Fair*, September.

Cotter, Holland. (2005). The New Bridge and Tunnel Crowd. *New York Times*, March 13.

Crain's New York Business. (2006). NYC's Wall Street Economy. Viewpoint, January 16.

Crane, Diana. (1989). *The Transformation of the Avant-Garde: The New York Art World, 1940–1985*. Chicago: University of Chicago Press.

Currid, Elizabeth. (2002). "The Urban Elixer: Immigrants and the Growth of Cities." Prepared for Grantmakers of Western Pennsylvania, June.

———. (2006a). The Kids Are Still Alright. *Death and Taxes* 100: 55–6.

———. (2006b). New York as a Global Creative Hub: A Comparative Analysis of Four Theories on World Cities. *Economic Development Quarterly* 20, 4.

Currid, Elizabeth, and Espino, Leah. (2003). "Building a Creative Hub: A Competitive Analysis of New York City's Creative Occupational Clusters." Prepared for Heinz School of Public Policy and Management, Carnegie Mellon University, December.

Department of Cultural Affairs updates on cultural organizations funding: http://www.nyc.gov/html/dcla/downloads/pdf/CulturalFundingReform.pdf.

Desrochers, Pierre. (2001). Local Diversity, Human Creativity, and Technological Innovation. *Growth and Change* 32: 369–94.

DiMaggio, Paul. (1987). Classification in Art. *American Sociological Review* 52, 4: 440–55.

Dylan, Bob. (2004). *Chronicles: Vol. I*. New York: Simon & Schuster.

Dyson, Michael Eric. (2006). *Holler If You Hear Me: Searching for Tupac Shakur*. New York: Basic Civitas Books.

East Village USA. (2004). The New Museum. New York. www.newmuseum.org/now_cur_evusa.php.

Economist. (2000). The Geography of Cool. April 15: 91.

Elderfield, John. (1996). *Flight Out of Time: A Dada Diary*. Berkeley: University of California Press.

ESRC Cities. (2000a). "Urban Networks, the Knowledge Economy and Planning for Growth." Cities Summary. Liverpool: Liverpool John Moores University, March.

———. (2000b). "Cultural Industries and the City." Cities Summary. Liverpool: Liverpool John Moores University, March.

Fairey, Shepard. (2006). *Obey: Supply and Demand: The Art of Shepard Fairey*. Corte Madera: Gingko Press.

Florida, Richard. (2000a). "The Economic Geography of Talent." H. John Heinz School of Public Policy and Management. Carnegie Mellon University, September.

———. (2000b). Pittsburgh Let's Wake Up and Play. *Pittsburgh Post-Gazette*. June 11.

———. (2000c). Competing in the Age of Talent: Quality of Place and the New Economy. A report prepared for R. K. Mellon Foundation, Heinz Endowments and Sustainable Pittsburgh. January.

———. (2002a). Bohemia and Economic Geography. *Journal of Economic Geography* 2, 1:55–71.

———. (2002b). *The Rise of the Creative Class: And How It's Transforming Work, Leisure, Community and Everyday Life*, New York: Basic Books.

———. (2004a). Email correspondence with Edward Glaeser. May 26.

———. (2004b). Revenge of the Squelchers. *The Next American City*. 5 (Spring).

———. (2005). *The Flight of the Creative Class*. New York: Harper Collins.

Florida, Richard, and Gary Gates. (2001). "Technology and Tolerance: The Importance of Diversity to High-Tech Growth," Brookings Institution, Center for Urban and Metropolitan Policy, June.

Florida, Richard, and Sam Youl Lee. (2001). "Innovation, Human Capital and Diversity." Carnegie Mellon University. November.

Frank, Thomas. (1998). *The Conquest of Cool: Business Culture, Counter Culture and the Rise of Hip Consumerism*. Chicago: University of Chicago Press.

Freiberger, Paul, and Michael Swaine. (1999, originally 1984). *Fire in the Valley: The Making of the Personal Computer*. New York: McGraw-Hill.

Fried, Joseph. (2006). Retraining for Silicon Alley. *New York Times*, January 22.

Friedmann, John. (1986). The World City Hypothesis. In *Development and Change* 17: 69–83.

Gendron, Bernard. (2006). "The Downtown Music Scene." In *The Downtown Book: The New York Art Scene 1974–1984*, edited by Marvin Taylor. 41–5. Princeton: Princeton University Press.

Gladwell, Malcom. (2000). *The Tipping Point: How Little Things Can Make a Big Difference*. New York: Back Bay Books.

Glaeser, Edward. (1998). Are Cities Dying? *Journal of Economic Perspectives*, 12, 2: 139–60.

———. (2000). Consumer City. Discussion Paper 1906. Harvard Institute of Economic Research.

———. (2003a). The Rise of the Skilled City. Discussion Paper 2025. Harvard Institute of Economic Research.

——— coauthored by Jesse M. Shapiro. (2003b). Urban Growth in the 1990s: Is City Living Back? *Journal of Regional Science* 43, 1: 139–65.

———. (2004). "Review of Richard Florida's The Rise of the Creative Class." http://post.economics.harvard.edu/faculty/glaeser/Review_Florida .pdf, May.

———. (2005). Urban Colossus: Why Is New York America's Largest City? HIER Working Paper, June.

Goldberg, Roselee. (2006). "Art After Hours: Downtown Performance." In *The Downtown Book: The New York Art Scene 1974–1984*, edited by Marvin Taylor. Princeton: Princeton University Press, pp. 97–116.

Grabher, Gernot. (2001). Ecologies of Creativity: the Village, the Group and the Heterarchic Organisation of the British Advertising Industry. *Environmental Planning A*, 33: 351–74.

———. (2006). Trading Routes, Bypasses and Risky Intersections: Mapping the Travels of "Networks" Between Economic Sociology and Economic Geography. *Progress in Human Geography* 30, 2:1–27.

Granovetter, Mark S. (1972). The Strength of Weak Ties. Chicago: *American Journal of Sociology* 78, 6:1360–1380.

———. (1985). Economic Action and Social Structure: The Problem of Embeddedness. *American Journal of Sociology* 81, 3: 481–510.

Green, Nancy. (1997). *Ready-to-Wear, Ready-to-Work: A Century of Industry and Immigrants in Paris and New York*. Durham: Duke University Press.

Gyourko Joseph, Christopher Mayer, and Todd Sinai. (2006). Superstar Cities. National Bureau of Economic Research Working Paper.

Hager, Steven. (1986). *Art After Midnight: The East Village Scene*. New York: St. Martin's Press.

Halbfinger, David. (2005). California Considers Tax Breaks for Filming. *New York Times*, August 18

Hall, Peter. (1985). "The Geography of the Fifth Kondratieff." *Silicon Landscapes*, edited by Peter Hall and Ann Markusen, 1–19. Allen & Unwin.

Hall, Peter, and Ann Markusen. (1985). *Silicon Landscapes*. Boston, London, and Sidney: Allen & Unwin.

Hebdige, Dick. (1979). *Subculture: The Meaning of Style*. London: Methuen.

Hickey, Dave. (1997). *Air Guitar: Essays on Art and Democracy*. Los Angeles: The Foundation for the Advanced Critical Studies.

Hirsch, Paul M. (1972). Processing Fads and Fashions: An Organization-Set Analysis of Cultural Industry Systems. *American Journal of Sociology* 77, 4: 639–59.

Hoover, Edgar M. and Raymond Vernon. (1962). *Anatomy of a Metropolis: The Changing Distribution of People and Jobs Within the New York Metropolitan Region*. New York: Anchor Books, Doubleday.

Huelsenbeck, Richard. (1991). *Memoirs of a Dada Drummer (The Documents of Twentieth Century Art)*. Berkeley: University of California Press.

Huggins, Nathan. (1973). *Harlem Renaissance*. New York: Oxford University Press.

Hutchinson, George. (1997). *The Harlem Renaissance in Black and White*. New York: Belknap Press.

Jacobs, Jane. (1961). *The Death and Life of Great American Cites*. New York: Random House.

———. (1969). *The Economy of Cities*. New York: Random House.

Kawamaura, Yuniya. (2005). *Fashion-ology*. Oxford, UK and Gordonsville, VA: Berg Publisher.

Kennedy, Randy. (2006). Chelsea: The Art and Commerce of One Hot Block. *The New York Times*. November 3.

Kimmelman, Michael. (2005a) Art, Money and Power. *New York Times*, May 11.

———. (2005b). Risks and Rewards of Art in the Open. *New York Times*, August 19.

Klosterman, Chuck. (2006). The DJ Auteur. *New York Times Magazine*, June 18.

Knox, Paul L. (1995). "World Cities in a World System." In *World Cities in a World System*, edited by Paul L. Knox and Peter J. Taylor. Cambridge: Cambridge University Press, 3–20.

Knox, Paul L., and Peter J. Taylor. (1995). *World Cities in a World System*. Cambridge: Cambridge University Press.

Kurutz, Steven. (2005). As Their Walls Fill Up, Galleries March Farther West. *New York Times*, October 23.

Lachmann, Richard. (1988). Graffiti as Career and Ideology. *American Journal of Sociology* 94, 2: 229–50.

Leeds, Jeff. (2005). The New Ambassadors. *New York Times*, November 12.

Leland, John. (2004). *Hip: A History*. New York: Ecco.

Lemons, Stephen. (2000). Andre the Giant Bombs the World! Salon.com, June 22.

Lewis, David Levering, ed. (1995). *The Portable Harlem Renaissance Reader*. New York: Viking Penguin.

———. (1997). *When Harlem Was in Vogue*. New York: Penguin.

Lloyd, Richard and Terry N. Clark. (2001). "The City as Entertainment Machine." In *Research in Urban Sociology, Vol. 6, Critical Perspectives on*

Urban Redevelopment, edited by Kevin Fox Gatham, 357–78. Oxford: JAI/ Elsevier.

———. (2006). *Neo-Bohemia: Art and Commerce in the Postindustrial City.* New York: Routledge.

Lucas, Robert. (1988). On the Mechanics of Economic Development, *Journal of Monetary Economics*, 22: 1–42.

Lynton, Norbert. (1980). *The Story of Modern Art.* New York: Phaidon.

Markusen, Ann. (1985). "High-tech Jobs, Markets and Economic Development Prospects: Evidence from California." In *Silicon Landscapes*, edited by Peter Hall and Ann Markusen, 35–48. Boston, London, and Sidney: Allen & Unwin.

———. (2004a). "The Distinctive City: Evidence from Artists and Occupational Profiles" Project on Regional and Industrial Economies. Humphrey Institute of Public Affairs: University of Minnesota.

———. (2004b) Longer View: Targeting Occupations in Regional and Community Economic Development. *Journal of the American Planning Association* 70, 3: 253–68.

Markusen, Ann, and David King. (2003). "The Artistic Dividend: The Arts' Hidden Contributions to Regional Development." Project on Regional and Industrial Economics, July.

Markusen, Ann, Greg Schrock, and Martina Cameron. (2004). "The Artistic Dividend Revisited." Humphrey Institute of Public Affairs: University of Minnesota, March.

Marshall, Alfred. (1961; originally 1890). *Principles of Economics.* London and New York: Macmillan for the Royal Economic Society.

Martin, John Levi. (2003). What is Field Theory? *American Journal of Sociology* 109, 1: 1–49.

Mason, Christopher. (2005). She Can't Be Bought. *New York Magazine*, March 7.

Massey, Doreen. (1984). *Spatial Divisions of Labor.* New York: Metheun.

Mathur, Vijay. (1999). Human Capital-Based Strategy for Regional Economic Development. *Economic Development Quarterly* 13, 3: 203–16.

McAninch, David. (2005). The 21st Century Garret. *New York Times*, November 27.

McCormick, Carlo. (2006). "A Crack in Time." In *The Downtown Book: The New York Art Scene 1974–1984*, edited by Marvin Taylor, 67–96. Princeton: Princeton University Press.

Mindlin, Alex. (2006). In Party Central, Clamor to Keep Tabs on the Tap. *New York Times*, February 12.

Molotch, Harvey. (1996). "L.A. as Design Product: How Art Works in a Regional Economy." In *The City: Los Angeles and Urban Theory at the End of the Twentieth Century*, edited by Allen J. Scott and Edward W. Soja. Los Angeles: University of California Press.

———. (2002). Place in Product. *International Journal of Urban and Regional Research*, 665–88.

————. (2003). *Where Stuff Comes From*. New York: Routledge.

Morgan, Richard. (2005). New York Incognito. *New York Times*, July 24.

Musto, Michael. (1986). *Downtown*. New York: Vintage.

————. (2006). "Chronology: The Orwellian Year of Disaster." In *The Downtown Book: The New York Art Scene 1974–1984*, edited by Marvin Taylor, 192. Princeton: Princeton University Press.

Nalebuff, Barry J., and Ian Ayres. (2006). *Why Not?: How to Use Everyday Ingenuity to Solve Problems Big and Small*. Cambridge: Harvard Business School Press.

New Museum for Contemporary Art. (2004). "East Village USA" Exhibition, December 3–March 19.

North, Douglass C. (1956). Exports and Regional Economic Growth: A Reply. *Journal of Political Economy* 64, 2: 165–68.

Ogunnaike, Lola. (2006). A Producer of Hip Hop Gets Behind an Heiress. *New York Times*, January 16.

O'Hara, Frank. (1957). "Meditations in an Emergency." In *Meditations in an Emergency*. New York: Grove Press.

Ouroussoff, Nicolai. (2006). Art and Architecture, Together Again. *New York Times*, January 19.

Perl, Jed. (2005). *New Art City: Manhattan at Mid-Century*. New York. Alfred A. Knopf.

————. (2006). On Art: Arrivederci MoMA. *The New Republic*. www.tnr.com/pdf-archive.mhtml, February 2.

Piore, Michael J., and Charles F. Sabel. (1984). *The Second Industrial Divide: Possibilities for Prosperity*. New York: Basic Books.

Pogrebin, Robin. (2005a). Arts Patron Resigns Over Move By Pataki. *New York Times*, October 1.

————. (2005b). Arts Groups Pessimistic Over Prospects for Culture Downtown. *New York Times*, October 31.

————. (2007a). Arts Organizations Adjust to Decline in Funding. *New York Times*, February 21.

————. (2007b). Arts Groups Seek Plums in a New Budget Pie. *New York Times*, February 1.

————. (2007c). Bloomberg and Council Change Arts Financing. *New York Times*, January 25.

Porter, Michael. (1998). Clusters and the New Economics of Competition. *Harvard Business Review* (November–December): 77–90.

Power, Dominic, and Allen J. Scott. (2004). "A Prelude to Cultural Industries and the Production of Culture." In *Cultural Industries and the Production of Culture*, edited by Dominic Power and Allen J. Scott. London and New York: Routledge.

Pressler, Jessica. (2005). Philadelphia Story: The Next Borough. *New York Times*, August 14.

Quigley, John. (1998). Urban Diversity and Economic Growth. *Journal of Economic Perspectives* 12, 2: 127–38.

Rabin, David, and Andrew Rasiej. (2004). The $9 Billion Dollar Economic Impact of the Nightlife Industry on New York City. Prepared by the New York Nightlife Association and Audience Research Analysis.

Rantisi, Norma. (2002a). The Local Innovation System as a Source of "Variety": Openness and Adaptability in New York City's Garment District. *Regional Studies* 36, 6: 587–602.

———. (2002b). The Competitive Foundations of Localized Learning and Innovation: The Case of Women's Garment Production in New York City. *Economic Geography.* (October): 441–62.

———. (2004). The Ascendance of New York Fashion. *International Journal of Urban and Regional Research* 28, 1: 86–107.

Richter, Hans. (1997). *Art and Anti-Art (World of Art).* London: Thames and Hudson.

Ridgeway, Sally. (1989). "Artists Groups: Patrons and Gate-keepers." In *Art and Society: Readings in the Sociology of the Arts*, edited by Arnold W. Foster and Judith R. Blau, 205–20. Albany: State University of New York Press.

Robinson, Dwight E. 1961. The Economics of Fashion Demand. *Quarterly Journal of Economics* 75, 3: 376–98.

Robinson, Walter and Carlo McCormick. (1984). Slouching Towards Avenue D. *Art in America*, 72 (Summer): 134–61.

Rollins, Meredith Kahn. (2006). The Debutante's Ball. *New York Times*, Arts & Leisure, December 3.

Romer, Paul. (1986). Increasing Returns and Long-Run Growth. *Journal of Political Economy* (October): 1002–37.

———. (1990). Endogenous Technological Change. *Journal of Political Economy* 98, 5: S71–S102.

———. (1994). The Origins of Endogenous Growth. *Journal of Economic Perspectives* 8, 1: 3–22.

Rosenberg, David. (2002). *Cloning Silicon Valley: The Next Generation High-Tech Hotspots*. London: Reuters.

Rozhon, Tracie. (2005). The Rap on Puffy's Empire. *New York Times*, July 24.

Santagata, Walter. (2004). "Creativity, Fashion and Market Behavior." In *Cultural Industries and the Production of Culture*. Edited by Dominic Power and Allen J. Scott, 75–90. London and New York: Routledge.

Sassen, Saskia. (1991). *The Global City: New York, London, Tokyo*. Princeton: Princeton University Press.

———. (2001). "A New Geography of Centers and Margins: Summary and Implications." In *The City Reader*, edited by Richard T. LeGates and Frederic Stout, 208–12. London, New York: Routledge.

Savage, Mike, and Alan Warde. (2001). "Cities and Uneven Economic Development." In *The City Reader*, edited by Richard T. LeGates and Frederic Stout, 264–77. London, New York: Routledge.

Saxenian, Annalee. (1985). "The Genesis of Silicon Valley." In *Silicon Landscapes*, edited by Peter Hall and Ann Markusen, 20–34. Boston: Allen & Unwin.

———. (1994). *Regional Advantage: Culture and Competition in Silicon Valley and Route 128*. Cambridge, MA: Harvard University Press.

Schillinger, Liesl. (2005). A Cubicle for You and Your Muse. *New York Times*, October 9.

Schumpeter, Joseph. (1942). "The Process of Creative Destruction." In *Capitalism, Socialism and Democracy*, 81–86. New York: Harper & Brothers.

Scott, Allen. (1993). *Technopolis*. Berkeley: University of California Press.

———. (2000). *The Cultural Economy of Cities*. London: Sage Publications.

———. (2005). *On Hollywood: The Place, The Industry*. Princeton: Princeton University Press.

———. (2006). "Creative Cities: Conceptual Issues and Policy Questions." *Journal of Urban Affairs* 28, 1: 1–17.

Seabrook, John. (2001). *Nobrow: The Culture of Marketing, The Marketing of Culture*. New York: Vintage.

Shakur, Tupac. (1994). Cradle to the Grave. In A Thug's Life: Vol. 1. Jive Records.

Silver, Daniel, Terry N. Clark, and Lawrence Rothfield. (2005). "A Theory of Scenes." Working Paper, University of Chicago.

Simmel, Georg. (1957; originally 1904). Fashion. *American Journal of Sociology* 62, 6: 541–58.

Sisario, Ben. (2006). Where the Beat Goes On. *New York Times*, October 27.

Solow, Robert M. (1956). A Contribution to the Theory of Economic Growth. *Quarterly Journal of Economics* 70, 1: 65–94.

Stansell, Christine. (2000). *American Moderns: Bohemian New York and the Creation of a New Century*. New York: Metropolitan Books, Henry Holt.

Stark, David. (2000). "For a Sociology of Worth." Center on Organizational Innovation. Columbia University, October.

Steinhauer, Jennifer. (2005). The Arts Administration. *New York Times*, October 23.

Storper, Michael. (1997). *The Regional World: Territorial Development in a Global Economy*. New York: Guilford Press.

Strumsky, Deborah, Jose Lobo, and Lee Fleming. (2005). "Metropolitan Patenting: Inventor Agglomeration and Social Networks: A Tale of Two Effects." Working Paper. Harvard Business School, January.

Taylor, Marvin. (2006). "Playing the Field: The Downtown Scene and Cultural Production, An Introduction." In *The Downtown Book: The New York Art Scene 1974–1984*, edited by Marvin Taylor. Princeton: Princeton University Press.

Theado, Matt. (2003). *The Beats: A Literary Reference*. New York: Carroll and Graf Publishers.

Thomas, Kelly Devine. (2005). The Selling of Jeff Koons. *ArtNews*. (May): 17–40.

Thompson, Wilbur R. (1965) *A Preface to Urban Economics*. Prepared for Resources for the Future, Inc. Baltimore: Johns Hopkins Press.

Vernon, Raymond. (1960). *Metropolis 1985: An Interpretation of the Findings of the New York Metropolitan Region Study*. Cambridge, MA: Harvard University Press.

Vogel, Ezra (1985). "North Carolina's Research Triangle: State Modernization." In *Comeback*. New York: Simon and Schuster.

Walker, Rob. (2004a). The Buzz Guru. *Inc. Magazine*. March.

———. (2004b). The Corporate Manufacture of Word of Mouth. *New York Times Magazine*, December 5.

Warsh, David. (2006). *Knowledge and the Wealth of Nations*. New York: Norton.

Watson, Steven. (1995). *The Harlem Renaissance: Hub of African-American Culture, 1920–1930*. New York: Pantheon.

———. (1998). *The Birth of the Beat Generation: Visionaries, Rebels and Hipsters (1944–1960)*. New York: Pantheon.

Waxman, Sharon. (2006). At U.S.C., a Practical Emphasis on Film. *New York Times*, January 31.

White, Armond, and S. H. Fernando. (2002). *Rebel for the Hell of It: The Life of Tupac Shakur*. New York: Thunder's Mouth Press.

White, Harrison. (2002). *Markets as Networks*. Princeton: Princeton University Press.

Wilson, Eric. (2005). A Little Calvin Klein On the Side, Please. *New York Times*, August 4.

Wolff, Janet. (1993). *The Social Production of Art*. New York: New York University Press.

Index

human capital (*cont'd*)
89–90, 164; spillover and, 89; subsidized work and, 178–79; superstar cities and, 169–70; urban policy and, 164–69; weak ties and, 75–86
hypersocialization, 79

indie music, 91–92, 137–39
Industrial Revolution, 95
innovation: flexible specialization and, 70–72; Granovetter on, 75–76; high-technology and, 71–72; Homebrew Computer Club and, 72–73, 88; Jacobs on, 73–75; networking and, 71–73, 87–93; Saxenian on, 71–74; Silicon Valley and, 71–72; untraded interdependencies and, 71; vertical disintegration and, 70–71; weak ties and, 75–86
institutions: cultural economy and, 99–101, 112; policy and, 164–69; tax initiatives and, 177–78
Insurgent Mexico (Reed), 20
Interview magazine, 3, 34, 110
In Touch magazine, 149
IRAK, 123
Iraq, 41
Irving Plaza, 146

Jabberjaw, 82
Jackson, Daniel, 81, 93, 96, 105, 144
Jackson, Janet, 124
Jacobs, Jane, xvi, 73–74, 94, 127, 183
Jacobs, Marc, 163, 221n1; creative culture and, 2, 15, 36, 38, 40, 45, 66; interview of, 66–67; marketing and, 116, 142; weak ties and, 78–79
Jagger, Mick, 26, 160, 224n21
Japan, 52, 69
Jay-Z, 2, 11, 16, 102, 116, 126, 142
jazz, 11, 20, 44; Harlem Renaissance and, 22; loft jazz movement and, 33; post–World War II era and, 27–28; weak ties and, 80
Jeminez, Elisa, 146
Jobs, Steve, 73
Johansson, Scarlett, 140
Johns, Jasper, 26
Johnson, Betsey, 128–29
Johnson, Richard, 109, 133

Jones, Grace, 17
Jones, Nas R, 97, 137
Jones, Quincy, x, 2, 15, 80, 95, 156
Jordache, 17
Joyce, James, 19
JPMorgan Chase, 11, 54
JS1, 145
Juilliard School, 170, 172

Karan, Donna, ix, 84, 146, 149, 152
Kasabian, 142
Kelly, R., 137
Kennedy School of Government, 69
Kerouac, Jack, 27
"Kids Are Alright, The" (McGinley), 123
King, David, 217n14, 229n19
Kitchen, 32–33
Klein, Calvin, 140, 143, 149, 156
Kline, Franz, 26
Klosterman, Chuck, 126
Klotz, Alan, 92, 108
Knight, Suge, 124
Knitting Factory, 94
Knopf, Alfred, 20
Kolm, Ron, 29
Koons, Jeffrey, 29, 31, 40, 43, 224n21
Kristal, Hilly, 29, 33, 98
KRS-ONE, 145
Kubrick, Stanley, 128

labor movement, 20
LaChappelle, David, 102
Lady Pink, xvi, 15, 151–52
Laroche, Guy, 140
Law & Order (TV show), 57
LA Weekly, 82
lawyers, 57–58
Lee, Spike, 116
Lee Jeans, 139
legal sector, 57–58
LeRock, T., 145
Let It Rock, 129
Levin, Kate, 172
Levis, 99
Liberal Club, 20
Lichtenstein, Roy, 26
"Like a Virgin" (Madonna), 17
Lil'Kim, 146
Lincoln Center, 109

Lincoln Continental, 141
Linkin Park, 102
literature, 18; Abstract Expressionist era
    and, 26; Beat writers and, 27, 30–31;
    Greenwich Village and, 20; labor
    strikes and, 20; poetry and, 20–21, 32,
    46, 98, 102; politics and, 19–20;
    post–World War II era and, 27
Little Review, 19
LL Cool J, 121
Lloyd, Richard, 32, 80, 125, 129
location quotient (LQ), 50–51, 55,
    63–64, 194–98, 215n8
lock-in, 18
lofts, 9, 15, 33, 59, 105, 178
Lohan, Lindsay, 140
London, 2, 52, 170
Lopez, Jennifer, 40
Lord & Taylor, 21, 28
Los Angeles, x, 187, 190; creative culture
    and, 2, 9–10, 51–52; media sector and,
    53–54; tastemakers and, 163, 165,
    170, 181, 185
"Loser" (Beck), 82–83
Lotus, 87–88, 95–96, 109, 139–40, 173
Louisiana, 177
Lower East Side, 59; garment industry
    and, 21; marketing and, 114, 138,
    152; networking and, 104, 106; reces-
    sion and, 51; tastemakers and, 157–58
Lower Manhattan Development Corpora-
    tion, 176
Lucas, Robert, 3
Luckman, Sharon Gersten, 166
Lucky, 142
Lucky Strike, 102
Ludlow, 105, 152
Luxx, 128, 157
Lynton, Norbert, 24

Mackie, 136
MacPherson, Elle, 116
Macy's, 21, 125
Madison Avenue, 53
Madonna, 1, 17, 38, 88, 174
Manhattan, 25, 54, 59, 96, 175, 179
Man Ray, 20–21
manufacturing sector, 59–60, 219n40;
    autarky and, 70–71; flexible specializa-

tion and, 70–72; high-technology and,
    69–70; Homebrew Computer Club
    and, 72–73; innovation and, 68–69;
    networking and, 71–73; recession and,
    67–68; reputation and, 77–78; re-
    stricted production and, 73; Saxenian
    on, 71–74; untraded interdependencies
    and, 71; vertical disintegration and,
    70–71
Marie Claire magazine, 136
Maripol, 17
Maripolarama, 17
Maritime Hotel, 117
marketing: Bloomberg and, 165–66;
    branding and, 156–57; buzz and, 130–
    32, 139; career path flexibility and,
    150–53; clustering and, 156–57,
    229n16; commodification and, 115–
    26; credibility and, 124–26, 145–47;
    cultural producers and, 115–17; gate-
    keepers and, 130–37; gossip column in-
    fluence and, 132–34; interdependency
    of, 114; international firms and, 122–
    23; peer review and, 115–16, 140–45,
    147–50; product blending and, 126–
    29; word-of-mouth, 137–40
Markusen, Ann, 161, 217n14, 220n43,
    229n19
Maroon 5, 146
Marquee, 96, 99
Marshallian industial districts, 95
Martin, John Levi, 224n21
Mason, George, 163
Masses, 19
Materials for the Arts program, 178
Max Fish, 41, 96, 105, 107
Max's Kansas City, 29, 32–33
Maxwell, 174
Mayer, Christopher, 169
Mayor's Office of Film, Theater and
    Broadcasting, 165
McCollough, Jack, 79
McCormick, Carlo, 31–37, 154
McGee, Barry, 43
McGinley, Ryan, 41, 123
McGinness, Ryan, xvi, 41–42, 44, 90,
    100–101, 154, 157, 166
McHugh, Kevin, 81–82
McLaren, Malcolm, 129

McMullan, Patrick, 109
McMullen, Bill, 83–85, 128
McQueen, Alexander, 81, 160
McSwain, Frederick, xiv
Me Against the World (Shakur), 124
Meatpacking District, 59, 87, 93, 96, 172
media sector, 53–54, 91, 116, 124, 136
medical sector, 57–58
Mercer Arts Center, 32–33
Mercury Lounge, 41–42
Meres, 123, 151
Merrill Lynch, 175
Metropolis 1985 (Vernon), 47
Metropolitan Museum of Art, 7
Michael Jackson and Bubbles (Koons), 40
Microsoft, 73
Milan, 2, 71, 149, 157
Miller, Nicole, 149
Minton's Playhouse, 97
Misshapes, ix, 109–10
Mitchell, Joni, 27
Mizrahi, Isaac, 41
Moby, 174
modernism, 30
Molotch, Harvey, xiii, 217n14, 227n2, 228nn3, 7
Mondrian, 24
Moss, Kate, 131, 141
Mos Def, 97
MTV Music Awards, 1–2
Mudd Club, 31–33, 37–38, 154
Mullican, Matt, 32
Museum of Contemporary Art, 165
Museum of Modern Art (MoMA), 23, 25–26, 30, 45, 84, 111, 160, 178
music, 2; after-parties and, 95; blending and, 126–29; Bowery and, 106; commodification of, 36–42; Downtown Collection and, 29; festivals and, 176–77; Harlem Renaissance and, 22; interdependency of, 27–28; Juilliard and, 170, 172; marketing and, 124–25 (*see also* marketing); networking and, 81–83, 91–92, 97–98, 109; nightlife and, 31–34; payola and, 180; peer review and, 142; postmodernism and, 30–32; post–World War II era and, 27–28;

public policy and, 176; record labels and, 7–9, 37, 81, 121, 124, 131, 137, 146–47, 149; weak ties and, 80–83. *See also specific genres*
Musto, Michael, 38–39, 173
Myers, Dowell, xv

Naked Lunch (Burroughs), 27
Nassari, Soheil, 109
National Governors Association 2000, 164
Nautica, 125
Nazis, 23
Neo-Bohemia (Lloyd), 80
neo-Dada, 18, 26, 31
Neo-expressionism, 1
networking, 160, 183–84, 229n19; creativity and, 89–93; education and, 81; environment for, 161–64; hypersocialization and, 79; innovation and, 87–89; music and, 81–83; nightlife and, 87–89, 128; peer review and, 147–50; reputation and, 77–78; scene importance and, 102–10; social production system for, 110–11; weak ties and, 75–86, 91. *See also* social issues
New Art City (Perl), 88
New Deal, 23–24
New Jersey, 28, 55–56, 158, 162
New Mexico, 181
New Museum, 35
New Orleans, 185
New Republic, 25
Newton, Isaac, 224n21
new wave music, 3, 33–34, 128–29
New York City, ix–xv; "Andre the Giant Has a Posse" campaign and, 118; Bloomberg and, 165–68, 172, 177–78; bohemians and, 18–22; CEOs of, 54–55; creativity in, 1–3, 15–16 (*see also* creativity); Department of Cultural Affairs (DCLA) and, 165, 177–78; diversity of, 157–58; economic environment of, 11–12, 168; employment growth in, 168; as entertainment machine, 95; as financial center, 3, 10; geographical influences in, 4, 7–10, 155–56; as global center of creativity, 1–3, 15; historical perspective on, 28–44, 58–59;